Managing Kubernetes Resources Using Helm

Second Edition

Simplifying how to build, package, and distribute applications for Kubernetes

Andrew Block

Austin Dewey

BIRMINGHAM—MUMBAI

Managing Kubernetes Resources Using Helm
Second Edition

Copyright © 2022 Packt Publishing

All rights reserved. No part of this book may be reproduced, stored in a retrieval system, or transmitted in any form or by any means, without the prior written permission of the publisher, except in the case of brief quotations embedded in critical articles or reviews.

Every effort has been made in the preparation of this book to ensure the accuracy of the information presented. However, the information contained in this book is sold without warranty, either express or implied. Neither the authors, nor Packt Publishing or its dealers and distributors, will be held liable for any damages caused or alleged to have been caused directly or indirectly by this book.

Packt Publishing has endeavored to provide trademark information about all of the companies and products mentioned in this book by the appropriate use of capitals. However, Packt Publishing cannot guarantee the accuracy of this information.

Group Product Manager: Rahul Nair

Publishing Product Manager: Niranjan Naikwadi

Senior Editor: Arun Nadar

Content Development Editor: Adrija Mitra

Technical Editor: Arjun Varma

Copy Editor: Safis Editing

Book Project Manager: Aishwarya Mohan

Proofreader: Safis Editing

Indexer: Tejal Daruwale Soni

Production Designer: Shankar Kalbhor

Marketing Coordinator: Nimisha Dua

First published: June 2020

Second Edition: September 2022

Production reference: 1070922

Published by Packt Publishing Ltd.
Livery Place
35 Livery Street
Birmingham
B3 2PB, UK.

978-1-80324-289-7

www.packt.com

To the open source community for their ongoing support and collaboration.

– Andrew Block

To my wife, Lindsey, for her unwavering love and support.

– Austin Dewey

Foreword

This is an enjoyable and informative book about Helm, the Kubernetes Package Manager, from *Andrew Block* and *Austin Block*. I do not know the authors personally, but can tell that they have a wealth of knowledge and experience in the subject. Andrew Block recently became the core maintainer of the Helm project, so to him I say: nice to have to you there!

This book is for all levels, from basic to advanced, and everyone will find useful information and tips within it.

This book has three parts, starting with introduction to Kubernetes, and finishing with advanced deployment patterns for Helm.

Part 1 will explain Kubernetes at a high level, alongside the basics of Kubernetes app installation with kubectl. You will then learn what Helm is, and learn about its bases. This part of the book covers how to decompose monolithic apps into smaller applications. You will learn how to setup a local Kubernetes environment, install kubectl and Helm cli, and install, upgrade, and rollback your first application with Helm.

If you are an advanced user, you can skip this part and move straight to Part 2.

Part 2 will take you through Helm charts development, dependency management, and a thorough explanation of all chart templates. This part also covers Helm lifecycle hooks, which allow you to extend helm charts to another level of usefulness. You'll also learn how to publish charts to the Helm repository and OCI registry. Finally, you'll learn how to validate charts using helm lint locally and against a live cluster.

I really recommend learning to use the chart testing tool. Making it part of your local and CI process will save you a lot of time, as you won't be looking for chart bugs at the end of your process.

Of course you aren't going to write all the Helm charts you need during your normal working life, as there are many Helm charts that have been written by the community or by existing companies. However, understanding how to develop Helm charts will also allow you to use third party charts, modify their values, and even enhance them too. It will also aid you in learning how to provide PRs (pull requests) to the charts' git repositories.

This section of the book is extremely valuable if you want to learn how to develop Helm charts, and therefore should not be skipped.

In Part 3, you will learn how to automate Helm releases with CD and GitOps. There is a very detailed explanation of how to do that with Argo CD (which happens to be my favourite GitOps Kubernetes operator as well)

You will also learn about the Operator Framework, which is an advanced topic. This section covers Kubernetes operator bases, how to create Helm operators, and how to manage them with Custom Resources Definitions (CRDs) and Custom Recourses (CRs).

This part of the book also covers Helm security best practices, which is a very important topic. You'll also learn how to verify Helm binaries, how to sign and verify Helm charts, use secure images, and, of course, how to set up charts resources requests and limits. Finally, you'll also learn how to handle secrets in Helm charts which is an important feature to know, as at the end Helm releases should be deployed in the most secure way.

Rimantas Mocevicius "rimusz"

Helm Co-Founder

Author of kubectl: Command-Line Kubernetes in a Nutshell Book

Senior DevOps Engineer at JFrog Ltd (Nasdaq: FROG)

Contributors

About the authors

Andrew Block is a core maintainer on the Helm project and a Distinguished Architect at Red Hat. He specializes in the use of continuous integration and continuous delivery methodologies to streamline the delivery process and incorporate security at each stage. He works with organizations to adopt and implement these technologies and concepts within their organization. As an open source enthusiast, Andrew not only has authored several publications, but he is also a contributor to several open source communities and a lead within the sigstore project, which aims at simplifying how software is signed and verified.

Austin Dewey is a DevOps engineer focused on delivering a streamlined developer experience on cloud and container technologies. Austin started his career with Red Hat's consulting organization, where he helped drive success at Fortune 500 companies by automating deployments on Red Hat's Kubernetes-based PaaS, OpenShift Container Platform. Currently, Austin works at fintech start-up Prime Trust, where he builds automation to scale financial infrastructure and supports developers on Kubernetes and AWS.

About the reviewers

Shashikant Bangera is a DevOps architect with 22 years of IT experience. His technical expertise spans across digital transformation, DevOps, the cloud, and containerization. He has helped a wide range of customers, from small, medium, and large businesses, with digital adoption for domains such as banking, e-commerce, and retail. He has architected and implemented enterprise DevOps at a large scale and also contributes to many open source platforms. He has authored and reviewed a number of books on DevOps with Packt. Shashikant has also contributed to lots of blogs on DevOps. He has designed an automated on-demand environment with a set of open source tools that is available on GitHub. You can reach him on Twitter @shzshi.

Suraj S. Pujari is an accomplished customer engineer working with Microsoft India Corp. Ltd and has more than 11 years of experience in the IT industry. He has extensive experience in working with Azure app and infrastructure technologies. From his work as a systems engineer with one of the largest Indian multi-national corporations, his career has evolved through constant learning and applying his inquisitive side.

> *I would like to express my gratitude to my mom, Vidya, and wife, Pooja, who had to look after my 20-month-old son, Likhit, while I was busy reviewing this book. A big shoutout to all my friends and colleagues who have encouraged me to review books.*

Table of Contents

Preface   xiii

Part 1: Introduction and Setup

1

Understanding Kubernetes and Helm   3

From monoliths to modern microservices	4
What is Kubernetes?	**5**
Container orchestration	6
HA	7
Scalability	7
Active community	7
Deploying a Kubernetes application	**8**
Approaches to resource management	**9**
Imperative and declarative configurations	9
Resource configuration challenges	**13**

The many types of Kubernetes resources	13
Keeping live and local states in sync	14
Application life cycles are hard to manage	14
Resource files are static	14
Helm to the rescue!	**15**
Understanding package managers	16
The Kubernetes package manager	17
The benefits of Helm	18
Summary	**21**
Further reading	**21**
Questions	**21**

2

Preparing a Kubernetes and Helm Environment   23

Technical requirements	**23**
Preparing a local Kubernetes environment with minikube	**24**
Installing minikube	24
Installing VirtualBox	26

Configuring VirtualBox as the default driver	27
Configuring minikube resource allocation	28
Exploring the basic usage of minikube	28
Setting up kubectl	**29**
Installing kubectl	30

Setting up Helm	33	Tab completion	38
Installing Helm	33	Authentication	39
Configuring Helm	34	Authorization/RBAC	41
Adding upstream repositories	34	**Summary**	42
Adding plugins	36	**Further reading**	42
Environment variables	37	**Questions**	43

3

Installing Your First App with Helm 45

Technical requirements	46	Choosing between --set and --values	65
Understanding the WordPress		**Accessing the WordPress application**	66
application	46	**Upgrading the WordPress release**	70
Finding a WordPress chart	47	Modifying the Helm values	70
Searching for WordPress charts from the		Running the upgrade	71
command line	48	Reusing and resetting values during an upgrade	73
Viewing the WordPress chart in a browser	49	**Rolling back the WordPress release**	74
Bitnami repository chart retention policy	50	Inspecting the WordPress history	74
Adding the full Bitnami repository	51	Running the rollback	76
Showing the WordPress chart information from the command line	52	**Uninstalling the WordPress release**	78
Creating a Kubernetes environment	54	**Shutting down your environment**	79
Installing a WordPress chart	55	**Summary**	79
Creating a values file for configuration	55	**Further reading**	79
Running the installation	58	**Questions**	80
Inspecting your release	60		

Part 2: Helm Chart Development

4

Scaffolding a New Helm Chart 83

Technical requirements	83	**Understanding the YAML format**	85
Understanding the Guestbook		Defining key-value pairs	85
application	84	Value types	86

The JSON format	87	Updating the Guestbook Chart.yaml file	99
Scaffolding the Guestbook Helm chart	88	Summary	99
Deploying the scaffolded Guestbook chart	91	Further reading	100
Understanding the Chart.yaml file	94	Questions	100

5

Helm Dependency Management   101

Technical requirements	102	Altering dependency names and values	112
Declaring chart dependencies	102	Updating the guestbook Helm chart	117
The dependencies map	103	Cleaning up	119
Downloading chart dependencies	104	Summary	119
Creating conditionals	108	Further reading	119
		Questions	120

6

Understanding Helm Templates   121

Technical requirements	122	Helm template validation	148
Helm template basics	122	The fail function	148
Template values	124	The required function	150
Built-in objects	125	The values.schema.json file	151
The .Release object	127	Enabling code reuse with named templates and library charts	153
The .Chart object	128		
The .Template object	130	Creating CRDs	155
The .Capabilities object	130	Post rendering	156
The .Files object	131	Updating and deploying the Guestbook chart	158
Helm template functions	133		
Helm template control structures	140	Updating Redis values	158
Generating release notes	145	Updating Guestbook's deployment template and values.yaml file	158
Helm template variables	146		
		Deploying the Guestbook chart	160

Summary	161	Questions	162
Further reading	161		

7

Helm Lifecycle Hooks — 163

Technical requirements	164	Creating the pre-rollback hook to restore the database	174
The basics of a Helm hook	164	Executing the life cycle hooks	178
Helm hook life cycle	167	Cleaning up	180
Helm hook cleanup	169	Summary	180
Writing hooks in the Guestbook Helm chart	170	Further reading	181
Creating the pre-upgrade hook to take a data snapshot	171	Questions	181

8

Publishing to a Helm Chart Repository — 183

Technical requirements	183	Publishing to an OCI registry	190
Understanding Helm chart repositories	184	Pulling the OCI Guestbook chart	193
Publishing to an HTTP repository	184	Summary	194
Creating a GitHub Pages repository	185	Further reading	194
Publishing the Guestbook chart	187	Questions	194

9

Testing Helm Charts — 195

Technical requirements	195	Adding server-side validation to chart rendering	198
Setting up your environment	196	Linting Helm charts and templates	199
Verifying Helm templating	196	Testing in a live cluster	202
Validating template generation locally with helm template	196	Running the chart test	203

Improving chart tests with the Chart Testing tool	205	Cleaning up	214
Summary	214
Introducing the Chart Testing project	206	Further reading	215
Installing the Chart Testing tools	208	Questions	215
Running the lint-and-install command	211		

Part 3: Advanced Deployment Patterns

10

Automating Helm with CD and GitOps   219

Technical requirements	220	Deploying an application from a remote Helm chart repository	229
Understanding CI/CD and GitOps	220
CI/CD	220	Deploying a Helm chart to multiple environments	230
Taking CI/CD to the next level using GitOps	221
Setting up your environment	222	Cleaning up	234
Installing Argo CD	222	Summary	234
Deploying a Helm chart from a Git repository	225	Questions	235

11

Using Helm with the Operator Framework   237

Technical requirements	238	Deploying the Guestbook application	250
Understanding Kubernetes operators	238	Using Helm to manage operators, CRDs, and CRs	252
Understanding the Guestbook operator control loop	239
Preparing a local development environment	240	Cleaning up	253
Scaffolding the operator file structure	242	Summary	254
Building the operator image	243	Further reading	254
Deploying the Guestbook operator	246	Questions	254

12
Helm Security Considerations 255

Technical requirements	255	Setting resource requests and limits	268
Data provenance and integrity	256	Handling secrets in Helm charts	270
Creating a GPG key pair	257	**Configuring RBAC rules**	**272**
Verifying Helm downloads	259	Accessing secure chart repositories	274
Signing and verifying Helm charts	263	Summary	276
Developing secure and stable Helm charts	**266**	Further reading	277
		Questions	277
Using secure images	266		

Index 279

Other Books You May Enjoy 288

Preface

Containerization is currently known to be one of the best ways to implement DevOps. While Docker introduced containers and changed the DevOps era, Google developed an extensive container orchestration system, Kubernetes, which is now considered the industry standard. With the help of this book, you'll explore the efficiency of managing applications running on Kubernetes using Helm.

Starting with a brief introduction to Helm and its impact on users working with containers and Kubernetes, you'll delve into the primitives of Helm charts and its overall architecture and use cases. From there, you'll learn how to write Helm charts in order to automate application deployment on Kubernetes and work your way toward more advanced strategies. These enterprise-ready patterns are focused on concepts beyond the basics so that you can get the most out of Helm, including topics related to automation, application development, delivery, life cycle management, and security.

By the end of this book, you'll have learned how to leverage Helm to build, deploy, and manage applications on Kubernetes.

Who this book is for

This book is for Kubernetes developers or administrators who are interested in learning Helm to provide automation for app development on Kubernetes. Although no prior knowledge of Helm is required, basic knowledge of Kubernetes application development will be useful.

What this book covers

Chapter 1, *Understanding Kubernetes and Helm*, is where you learn about the challenges involved in deploying Kubernetes applications and how Helm can be used to simplify the deployment process.

Chapter 2, *Preparing a Kubernetes and Helm Environment*, is where you learn how to configure a local development environment. In this chapter, you will download Minikube and Helm. You will also learn basic Helm configurations.

Chapter 3, *Installing Your First App with Helm*, teaches you the ins and outs of the main Helm commands by having you deploy your first Helm chart.

Chapter 4, *Scaffolding a New Helm Chart*, is about how Helm charts are structured and helps you scaffold your own Helm chart.

Chapter 5, *Helm Dependency Management*, is where you learn how to manage and use dependencies to build and manage complex application deployments.

Chapter 6, *Understanding Helm Templates*, explores Helm templates and how to dynamically generate Kubernetes resources.

Chapter 7, *Helm Lifecycle Hooks*, is about lifecycle hooks and how to deploy arbitrary resources at different Helm lifecycle phases.

Chapter 8, *Publishing to a Helm Chart Repository*, teaches you about Helm chart repositories and how they can be used to publish Helm charts.

Chapter 9, *Testing Helm Charts*, is about different strategies for testing Helm charts during Helm chart development.

Chapter 10, *Automating Helm with CD and GitOps*, looks at how to automate Helm deployments using continuous delivery and GitOps methodologies.

Chapter 11, *Using Helm with the Operator Framework*, covers how to create a Helm operator using the `operator-sdk` toolkit.

Chapter 12, *Helm Security Considerations*, is about different security topics as they relate to Helm releases, charts, and repositories.

To get the most out of this book

To get the most out of this book, you should install the technologies in the following table to follow along with the examples. While these are the versions that were used during writing, the latest versions should work as well.

Software/hardware covered in the book	Operating system requirements
Minikube v1.22.0	Windows, macOS, or Linux
VirtualBox 6.1.26	Windows, macOS, or Linux
Kubectl v1.21.2	Windows, macOS, or Linux
Helm v3.6.3	Windows, macOS, or Linux

If you are using the digital version of this book, we advise you to type the code yourself or access the code from the book's GitHub repository (a link is available in the next section). Doing so will help you avoid any potential errors related to the copying and pasting of code.

Download the example code files

You can download the example code files for this book from GitHub at https://github.com/PacktPublishing/Managing-Kubernetes-Resources-using-Helm. If there's an update to the code, it will be updated in the GitHub repository.

We also have other code bundles from our rich catalog of books and videos available at `https://github.com/PacktPublishing/`. Check them out!

Download the color images

We also provide a PDF file that has color images of the screenshots and diagrams used in this book. You can download it here: `https://packt.link/zeDY0`.

Conventions used

There are a number of text conventions used throughout this book.

`Code in text`: Indicates code words in text, database table names, folder names, filenames, file extensions, pathnames, dummy URLs, user input, and Twitter handles. Here is an example: "Notice that a space is missing between the colon and the `LearnHelm` string."

A block of code is set as follows:

```
configuration: |
  server.port=8443
  logging.file.path=/var/log
```

When we wish to draw your attention to a particular part of a code block, the relevant lines or items are set in bold:

```
$ cd ~
$ git clone <repository URI>
```

Any command-line input or output is written as follows:

```
$ helm dependency update chapter8/guestbook
$ helm package guestbook chapter8/guestbook
```

Bold: Indicates a new term, an important word, or words that you see onscreen. For instance, words in menus or dialog boxes appear in **bold**. Here is an example: "Click the **Generate Token** button to create the token."

> **Tips or Important Notes**
> Appear like this.

Get in touch

Feedback from our readers is always welcome.

General feedback: If you have questions about any aspect of this book, email us at `customercare@packtpub.com` and mention the book title in the subject of your message.

Errata: Although we have taken every care to ensure the accuracy of our content, mistakes do happen. If you have found a mistake in this book, we would be grateful if you would report this to us. Please visit `www.packtpub.com/support/errata` and fill in the form.

Piracy: If you come across any illegal copies of our works in any form on the internet, we would be grateful if you would provide us with the location address or website name. Please contact us at `copyright@packt.com` with a link to the material.

If you are interested in becoming an author: If there is a topic that you have expertise in and you are interested in either writing or contributing to a book, please visit `authors.packtpub.com`.

Share Your Thoughts

Once you've read *Managing Kubernetes Resources Using Helm, Second Edition*, we'd love to hear your thoughts! Scan the QR code below to go straight to the Amazon review page for this book and share your feedback.

`https://packt.link/r/1803242892`

Your review is important to us and the tech community and will help us make sure we're delivering excellent quality content.

Part 1: Introduction and Setup

Kubernetes is a robust system with complex configurations. In *Part 1*, you will learn how Helm addresses such complexities by providing a package manager interface. By the end of this part, you will have gained hands-on experience by deploying your first Helm chart.

In this part, we will cover the following topics:

- *Chapter 1, Understanding Kubernetes and Helm*
- *Chapter 2, Preparing a Kubernetes and Helm Environment*
- *Chapter 3, Installing Your First App with Helm*

1
Understanding Kubernetes and Helm

Thank you for choosing this book, *Learn Helm*. If you are interested in this book, you are probably aware of the challenges that modern applications bring. Teams face tremendous pressure to ensure that applications are lightweight and scalable. Applications must also be highly available and able to withstand varying loads. Historically, applications have most commonly been deployed as monoliths or large, single-tiered applications served on a single system. As time has progressed, the industry has shifted toward a microservice approach or small, multi-tiered applications served on multiple systems. Often deployed using container technology, the industry has started leveraging tools such as Kubernetes to orchestrate and scale their containerized microservices.

Kubernetes, however, comes with its own set of challenges. While it is an effective container orchestration tool, it presents a steep learning curve that can be difficult for teams to overcome. One tool that helps simplify the challenges of running workloads on Kubernetes is Helm. Helm allows users to more simply deploy and manage the life cycle of Kubernetes applications. It abstracts many of the complexities behind configuring Kubernetes applications and allows teams to be more productive on the platform.

In this book, you will explore each of the benefits offered by Helm and discover how Helm makes application deployment much simpler on Kubernetes. You will first assume the role of an end user, consuming Helm charts written by the community and learning the best practices behind leveraging Helm as a package manager. As this book progresses, you will assume the role of a chart developer and learn how to package Kubernetes applications in ways that are easily consumable and efficient. Toward the end of this book, you'll learn about advanced patterns around application management and security with Helm.

In this chapter, we will cover the following main topics:

- From monoliths to modern microservices
- What is Kubernetes?
- Deploying a Kubernetes application

- Approaches to resource management
- Resource configuration challenges
- Helm to the rescue!

From monoliths to modern microservices

Software applications are a fundamental component of most modern technology. Whether they take the form of a word processor, web browser, or streaming service, they enable user interaction to complete one or more tasks. Applications have a long and storied history, from the days of **Electronic Numerical Integrator and Computer** (**ENIAC**)—the first general-purpose computer—to taking man to the moon in the Apollo space missions, to the rise of the **World Wide Web** (**WWW**), social media, and online retail.

These applications can operate on a wide range of platforms and systems, leveraging either physical or virtual computing resources. Depending on their purpose and resource requirements, entire machines may be dedicated to serving the compute and/or storage needs of an application. Fortunately, thanks in part to the realization of Moore's law, the power and performance of microprocessors initially increased with each passing year, along with the overall cost associated with the physical resources used. This trend has subsided in recent years, but the advent of this trend and its persistence for the first 30 years of the existence of processors was instrumental to the advances in technology.

Software developers took full advantage of this opportunity and bundled more features and components into their applications. As a result, a single application could consist of several smaller components, each of which, on its own, could be written as its own individual services. Initially, bundling components together yielded several benefits, including a simplified deployment process. However, as industry trends began to change and businesses focused more on the ability to deliver features more rapidly, the design of a single deployable application brought with it a number of challenges. Whenever a change was required, the entire application and all of its underlying components needed to be validated once again to ensure the change had no adverse features. This process potentially required coordination from multiple teams, which slowed the overall delivery of the feature.

Delivering features more rapidly, especially across traditional divisions within organizations, was also something that organizations wanted. This concept of rapid delivery is fundamental to a practice called **development-operations** (**DevOps**), whose rise in popularity occurred around 2010. DevOps encouraged more iterative changes to applications over time, instead of extensive planning prior to development. In order to be sustainable in this new model, architectures evolved from being a single large application to instead favoring several smaller applications that could be delivered faster. Because of this change in thinking, the more traditional application design was labeled as **monolithic**. This new approach of breaking components down into separate applications coined a name for these components: **microservices**. The traits that were inherent in microservices applications brought with them several desirable features, including the ability to develop and deploy services concurrently from one another as well as to scale them (increase the number of instances) independently.

The change in software architecture from monolithic to microservices also resulted in re-evaluating how applications are packaged and deployed at runtime. Traditionally, entire machines were dedicated to either one or two applications. Now, as microservices resulted in the overall reduction of resources required for a single application, dedicating an entire machine to one or two microservices was no longer viable.

Fortunately, a technology called **containers** was introduced and gained popularity in filling in the gaps for many missing features needed to create a microservices runtime environment. Red Hat defines a container as "*a set of one or more processes that are isolated from the rest of the system and includes all of the files necessary to run*"(https://www.redhat.com/en/topics/containers/whats-a-linux-container#:~:text=A%20Linux%C2%AE%20container%20is,testing%2C%20and%20finally%20to%20production.). Containerized technology has a long history in computing, dating back to the 1970s. Many of the foundational container technologies, including **chroots** (the ability to change the root directory of a process and any of its children to a new location on the filesystem) and **jails**, are still in use today.

The combination of a simple and portable packaging model, along with the ability to create many isolated sandboxes on each physical machine or **virtual machine** (**VM**), led to the rapid adoption of containers in the microservices space. This rise in container popularity in the mid-2010s can also be attributed to Docker, which brought containers to the masses through simplified packaging and runtimes that could be utilized on Linux, macOS, and Windows. The ability to distribute container images with ease led to the increase in the popularity of container technologies. This was because first-time users did not need to know how to create images but instead could make use of existing images that were created by others.

Containers and microservices became a match made in heaven. Applications had a packaging and distribution mechanism, along with the ability to share the same compute footprint while taking advantage of being isolated from one another. However, as more and more containerized microservices were deployed, the overall management became a concern. How do you ensure the health of each running container? What do you do if a container fails? What happens if your underlying machine does not have the compute capacity required? Enter Kubernetes, which helped answer this need for container orchestration.

In the next section, we will discuss how Kubernetes works and provides value to an enterprise.

What is Kubernetes?

Kubernetes, often abbreviated as **k8s** (pronounced as *kaytes*), is an open source container orchestration platform. Originating from Google's proprietary orchestration tool, Borg, the project was open sourced in 2015 and was renamed Kubernetes. Following the v1.0 release on July 21, 2015, Google and the Linux Foundation partnered to form the **Cloud Native Computing Foundation** (**CNCF**), which acts as the current maintainer of the Kubernetes project.

The word *Kubernetes* is a Greek word, meaning *helmsman* or *pilot*. A helmsman is a person who is in charge of steering a ship and works closely with the ship's officer to ensure a safe and steady course, along with the overall safety of the crew. Having similar responsibilities with regard to containers and microservices, Kubernetes is in charge of the orchestration and scheduling of containers. It is in charge of *steering* those containers to proper worker nodes that can handle their workloads. Kubernetes will also help ensure the safety of those microservices by providing **high availability** (**HA**) and health checks.

Let's review some of the ways Kubernetes helps simplify the management of containerized workloads.

Container orchestration

The most prominent feature of Kubernetes is container orchestration. This is a fairly loaded term, so we'll break it down into different pieces.

Container orchestration is about placing containers on certain machines from a pool of compute resources based on their requirements. The simplest use case for container orchestration is for deploying containers on machines that can handle their resource requirements. In the following diagram, there is an application that requests 2 **Gibibytes** (**Gi**) of memory (Kubernetes resource requests typically use their *power-of-two* values, which in this case is roughly equivalent to 2 **gigabytes** (**GB**)) and one **central processing unit** (**CPU**) core. This means that the container will be allocated 2 Gi of memory and 1 CPU core from the underlying machine that it is scheduled on. It is up to Kubernetes to track which machines, or **nodes**, have the required resources available and to place an incoming container on that machine. If a node does not have enough resources to satisfy the request, the container will not be scheduled on that node. If none of the nodes in a cluster have enough resources to run the workload, the container will not be deployed. Once a node has enough resources free, the container will be deployed on the node with sufficient resources:

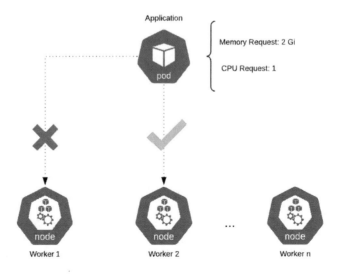

Figure 1.1 – Kubernetes orchestration and scheduling

Container orchestration relieves you of the effort required to track the available resources on machines. Kubernetes and other monitoring tools provide insight into these metrics. So, a developer can simply declare the number of resources they expect a container to use, and Kubernetes will take care of the rest on the backend.

HA

Another benefit of Kubernetes is that it provides features that help take care of redundancy and HA. HA is a characteristic that prevents application downtime. It's performed by a load balancer, which splits incoming traffic across multiple instances of an application. The premise of HA is that if one instance of an application goes down, other instances are still available to accept incoming traffic. In this regard, downtime is avoided, and the end user—whether a human or another microservice—remains completely unaware that there was a failed instance of the application. Kubernetes provides a networking mechanism, called a *service*, that allows applications to be load-balanced. We will talk about services in greater detail later on, in the *Deploying a Kubernetes application* section of this chapter.

Scalability

Given the lightweight nature of containers and microservices, developers can use Kubernetes to rapidly scale their workloads, both horizontally and vertically.

Horizontal scaling is the act of deploying more container instances. If a team running their workloads on Kubernetes were expecting increased load, they could simply tell Kubernetes to deploy more instances of their application. Since Kubernetes is a container orchestrator, developers would not need to worry about the physical infrastructure that those applications would be deployed on. It would simply locate a node within the cluster with the available resources and deploy the additional instances there. Each extra instance would be added to a load-balancing pool, which would allow the application to continue to be highly available.

Vertical scaling is the act of allocating additional memory and CPU to an application. Developers can modify the resource requirements of their applications while they are running. This will prompt Kubernetes to redeploy the running instances and reschedule them on nodes that can support the new resource requirements. Depending on how this is configured, Kubernetes can redeploy each instance in a way that prevents downtime while the new instances are being deployed.

Active community

The Kubernetes community is an incredibly active open source community. As a result, Kubernetes frequently receives patches and new features. The community has also made many contributions to documentation, both to the official Kubernetes documentation and to professional or hobbyist blog websites. In addition to documentation, the community is highly involved in planning and attending meetups and conferences around the world, which helps increase education about the platform and innovation surrounding it.

Another benefit of Kubernetes' large community is the number of different tools built to augment the abilities that are provided. Helm is one such tool. As we'll see later in this chapter and throughout this book, Helm—a tool built by members of the Kubernetes community—vastly improves a developer's experience by simplifying application deployments and life cycle management.

With an understanding of the benefits Kubernetes brings to managing containerized workloads, let's now discuss how an application can be deployed in Kubernetes.

Deploying a Kubernetes application

Deploying an application on Kubernetes is fundamentally similar to deploying an application outside of Kubernetes. All applications, whether containerized or not, must consider the following configuration details:

- Networking
- Persistent storage and file mounts
- Resource allocation
- Availability and redundancy
- Runtime configuration
- Security

Configuring these details on Kubernetes is done by interacting with the Kubernetes **application programming interface** (**API**). The Kubernetes API serves as a set of endpoints that can be interacted with to view, modify, or delete different Kubernetes resources, many of which are used to configure different details of an application.

There are many different Kubernetes API resources, but the following table shows some of the most common ones:

Resource Name	Definition
Pod	The smallest deployable unit in Kubernetes. Encapsulates one or more containers.
Deployment	Used to deploy and manage a set of Pods. Maintains the desired amount of Pod replicas (1 by default).
StatefulSet	Similar to a Deployment resource, except a StatefulSet maintains a sticky identity for each Pod replica and can also provision PersistentVolumeClaims resources (explained further down in this table) unique to each Pod.
Service	Used to load-balance between Pod replicas.
Ingress	Provides external access to services within the cluster.

`ConfigMap`	Stores application configuration to decouple configuration from code.
`Secret`	Used to store sensitive data such as credentials and keys. Data stored in Secrets resources are only obfuscated using Base64 encoding, so administrators must ensure that proper access controls are in place.
`PersistentVolumeClaim`	A request for storage by a user. Used to provide persistence for running Pods.
`Role`	Represents a set of permissions to be allowed against the Kubernetes API.
`RoleBinding`	Grants the permissions defined in a role to a user or set of users.

Table 1.1 – Common Kubernetes resources

Creating resources is central to deploying and managing an application on Kubernetes, but what does a user need to do to create them? We will explore this question further in the next section.

Approaches to resource management

In order to deploy an application on Kubernetes, we need to interact with the Kubernetes API to create resources. `kubectl` is the tool we use to talk to the Kubernetes API. `kubectl` is a **command-line interface** (**CLI**) tool used to abstract the complexity of the Kubernetes API from end users, allowing them to more efficiently work on the platform.

Let's discuss how `kubectl` can be used to manage Kubernetes resources.

Imperative and declarative configurations

The `kubectl` tool provides a series of subcommands to create and modify resources in an imperative fashion. Here is a small list of these commands:

- `create`
- `describe`
- `edit`
- `delete`

The `kubectl` commands follow a common format, as shown here:

```
kubectl <verb> <noun> <arguments>
```

The `verb` refers to one of the `kubectl` subcommands, and the `noun` refers to a particular Kubernetes resource. For example, the following command can be run to create a deployment:

```
kubectl create deployment my-deployment --image=busybox
```

This would instruct `kubectl` to talk to the Deployment API endpoint and create a new deployment called `my-deployment`, using the `busybox` image from Docker Hub.

You could use `kubectl` to get more information on the deployment that was created by using the `describe` subcommand, as follows:

```
kubectl describe deployment my-deployment
```

This command would retrieve information about the deployment and format the result in a readable format that allows developers to inspect the live `my-deployment` deployment on Kubernetes.

If a change to the deployment was desired, a developer could use the `edit` subcommand to modify it in place, like this:

```
kubectl edit deployment my-deployment
```

This command would open a text editor, allowing you to modify the deployment.

When it comes to deleting a resource, the user could run the `delete` subcommand, as illustrated here:

```
kubectl delete deployment my-deployment
```

This would call the appropriate API endpoint to delete the `my-deployment` deployment.

Kubernetes resources, once created, exist in the cluster as **JavaScript Object Notation** (**JSON**) resource files, which can be exported as **YAML Ain't Markup Language** (**YAML**) files for greater human readability. An example resource in YAML format can be seen here:

```yaml
apiVersion: apps/v1
kind: Deployment
metadata:
  name: busybox
spec:
  replicas: 1
  selector:
    matchLabels:
      app: busybox
  template:
    metadata:
```

```
      labels:
        app: busybox
    spec:
      containers:
        - name: main
          image: busybox
          args:
            - sleep
            - infinity
```

The preceding YAML format presents a very basic use case. It deploys the `busybox` image from Docker Hub and runs the `sleep` command indefinitely to keep the Pod running.

While it may be easier to create resources imperatively using the `kubectl` subcommands we have just described, Kubernetes allows you to directly manage the YAML resources in a declarative fashion to gain more control over resource creation. The `kubectl` subcommands do not always let you configure all the possible resource options, but creating YAML files directly allows you to more flexibly create resources and fill in the gaps that the `kubectl` subcommands may contain.

When creating resources declaratively, users first write out the resource they want to create in YAML format. Next, they use the `kubectl` tool to apply the resource against the Kubernetes API. While in imperative configuration developers use `kubectl` subcommands to manage resources, declarative configuration relies primarily on only one subcommand—`apply`.

Declarative configuration often takes the following form:

```
kubectl apply -f my-deployment.yaml
```

This command gives Kubernetes a YAML resource that contains a resource specification, although the JSON format can be used as well. Kubernetes infers the action to perform on resources (create or modify) based on whether or not they exist.

An application may be configured declaratively by following these steps:

1. First, the user can create a file called `deployment.yaml` and provide a YAML-formatted specification for the deployment. We will use the same example as before, as follows:

```
apiVersion: apps/v1
kind: Deployment
metadata:
  name: busybox
spec:
  replicas: 1
```

```yaml
  selector:
    matchLabels:
      app: busybox
  template:
    metadata:
      labels:
        app: busybox
    spec:
      containers:
        - name: main
          image: busybox
          args:
            - sleep
            - infinity
```

2. A deployment can then be created with the following command:

```
kubectl apply -f deployment.yaml
```

Upon running this command, Kubernetes will attempt to create a deployment in the way you specified.

3. If you wanted to make a change to the deployment by changing the number of replicas to 2, you would first modify the `deployment.yaml` file, as follows:

```yaml
apiVersion: apps/v1
kind: Deployment
metadata:
  name: busybox
spec:
  replicas: 2
  selector:
    matchLabels:
      app: busybox
  template:
    metadata:
      labels:
        app: busybox
    spec:
      containers:
```

```
            - name: main
              image: busybox
              args:
                - sleep
                - infinity
```

4. You would then apply the change with `kubectl apply`, like this:

   ```
   kubectl apply -f deployment.yaml
   ```

   After running that command, Kubernetes would apply the provided deployment declaration over the previously applied deployment. At this point, the application would scale up from a replica value of 1 to 2.

5. When it comes to deleting an application, the Kubernetes documentation actually recommends doing so in an imperative manner; that is, using the `delete` subcommand instead of `apply`, as illustrated here:

   ```
   kubectl delete -f deployment.yaml
   ```

   As you can see, the `delete` subcommand uses the `-f` flag to delete the resource from the given file.

With an understanding of how Kubernetes resources are created, let's now discuss some of the challenges involved in resource configuration.

Resource configuration challenges

In the previous section, we covered how Kubernetes has two different configuration methods—imperative and declarative. One question to consider is this: *What challenges do users need to be aware of when creating Kubernetes resources with imperative and declarative methodologies?*

Let's discuss some of the most common challenges.

The many types of Kubernetes resources

First of all, as described in the *Deploying a Kubernetes application* section, there are many different types of resources in Kubernetes. In order to be effective on Kubernetes, developers need to be able to determine which resources are required to deploy their applications, and they need to understand them at a deep enough level to configure them appropriately. This requires a lot of knowledge of and training on the platform. While understanding and creating resources may already sound like a large hurdle, this is actually just the beginning of many different operational challenges.

Keeping live and local states in sync

A method of configuring Kubernetes resources that we would encourage is to maintain their configuration in source control for teams to edit and share, which also allows the source control repository to become the source of truth. The configuration defined in source control (referred to as the *local state*) is then created by applying them to the Kubernetes environment, and the resources become *live* or enter what can be called a *live state*. This sounds simple enough, but what happens when developers need to make changes to their resources? The proper answer would be to modify the files in source control and apply the changes to synchronize the local state to the live state. However, this isn't what always ends up happening. It is often simpler, in the short term, to modify the live resource in place with `kubectl edit` or `kubectl patch` and completely skip over modifying the local files. This results in state inconsistency between local and live states and is an act that makes scaling on Kubernetes difficult.

Application life cycles are hard to manage

Life cycle management is a loaded term, but in this context, we'll refer to it as the concept of installing, upgrading, and rolling back applications. In the Kubernetes world, an installation would include API resources for deploying and configuring an application. The initial installation would create what we refer to here as version 1 of an application.

An upgrade, then, can be thought of as a modification to one or many of those Kubernetes resources. Each batch of edits can be thought of as a single upgrade. A developer could modify a single service resource, which would bump the version number to version 2. The developer could then modify a deployment, a configmap, and a service at the same time, bumping the version count to version 3.

As newer versions of an application continue to be rolled out onto Kubernetes, it becomes more difficult to keep track of changes that have occurred across relevant API resources. Kubernetes, in most cases, does not have an inherent way of keeping a history of changes. While this makes upgrades harder to keep track of, it also makes restoring a prior version of an application much more difficult. Say, for example, a developer previously made an incorrect edit on a particular resource. How would a team know where to roll back to? The `n-1` case is particularly easy to work out, as that is the most recent version. What happens, however, if the latest stable release was five versions ago? Teams often end up scrambling to resolve issues because they cannot quickly identify the latest stable configuration that worked previously.

Resource files are static

This is a challenge that primarily affects the declarative configuration style of applying YAML resources. Part of the difficulty in following a declarative approach is that Kubernetes resource files are not natively designed to be parameterized. Resource files are largely designed to be written out in full before being applied, and the contents remain the **source of truth** (**SOT**) until the file is modified. When dealing with Kubernetes, this can be a frustrating reality. Some API resources can be lengthy, containing many different customizable fields, and it can be quite cumbersome to write and configure YAML resources in full.

Static files lend themselves to becoming boilerplate. **Boilerplate** represents text or code that remains largely consistent in different but similar contexts. This becomes an issue if developers manage multiple different applications, where they could potentially manage multiple different deployment resources, multiple different services, and so on. In comparing the different applications' resource files, you may find large numbers of similar YAML configurations between them.

The following screenshot depicts an example of two resources with significant boilerplate configuration between them. The blue text denotes lines that are boilerplate, while the red text denotes lines that are unique:

```
apiVersion: v1                          apiVersion: v1
kind: Deployment                        kind: Deployment
metadata:                               metadata:
  name: my-k8s-app                        name: your-k8s-app
spec:                                   spec:
  replicas: 1                             replicas: 1
  selector:                               selector:
    matchLabels:                            matchLabels:
      app: my-k8s-app                         app: your-k8s-app
  strategy:                               strategy:
    rollingUpdate:                          rollingUpdate:
      maxSurge: 25%                           maxSurge: 25%
      maxUnavailable: 25%                     maxUnavailable: 25%
  template:                               template:
    metadata:                               metadata:
      labels:                                 labels:
        app: my-k8s-app                         app: your-k8s-app
    spec:                                   spec:
      containers:                             containers:
        - image: my-k8s-app:v1                  - image: your-k8s-app:v3
          imagePullPolicy: IfNotPresent           imagePullPolicy: IfNotPresent
          name: app                               name: app
```

Figure 1.2 – An example of two resources with boilerplate

Notice, in this example, that both files are almost exactly the same. When managing files that are as similar as this, boilerplate becomes a major headache for teams managing their applications in a declarative fashion.

Helm to the rescue!

Over time, the Kubernetes community discovered that creating and maintaining Kubernetes resources to deploy applications is difficult. This prompted the development of a simple yet powerful tool that would allow teams to overcome the challenges posed by deploying applications on Kubernetes. The tool that was created is called Helm. **Helm** is an open source tool used for packaging and deploying applications on Kubernetes. It is often referred to as the **Kubernetes package manager** because of its similarities to any other package manager you would find on your favorite **operating system** (**OS**). Helm is widely used throughout the Kubernetes community and is a CNCF graduated project.

Given Helm's similarities to traditional package managers, let's begin exploring Helm by first reviewing how a package manager works.

Understanding package managers

Package managers are used to simplify the process of installing, upgrading, reverting, and removing a system's applications. These applications are defined as packages that contain metadata around target software and its dependencies.

The idea behind package managers is simple. First, the user passes the name of a software package as an argument. The package manager then performs a lookup against a repository to see whether that package exists. If it is found, the package manager installs the application defined by the package and its dependencies to specified locations on the system.

Package managers make managing software very easy. As an example, let's imagine you wanted to install `htop`, a Linux system monitor, to a Fedora machine. Installing this would be as simple as typing a single command, as follows:

```
dnf install htop --assumeyes
```

This instructs `dnf`, the Fedora package manager, to find `htop` in the Fedora package repository and install it. `dnf` also takes care of installing the `htop` package's dependencies, so you don't have to worry about installing its requirements beforehand. After `dnf` finds the `htop` package from the upstream repository, it asks you whether you're sure you want to proceed. The `--assumeyes` flag automatically answers yes to this question and any other prompts that `dnf` may potentially ask.

Over time, newer versions of `htop` may appear in the upstream repository. `dnf` and other package managers allow users to efficiently upgrade to new versions of the software. The subcommand that allows users to upgrade using `dnf` is `upgrade`, as illustrated here:

```
dnf upgrade htop --assumeyes
```

This instructs `dnf` to upgrade `htop` to its latest version. It also upgrades its dependencies to the versions specified in the package's metadata.

While moving forward is often better, package managers also allow users to move backward and revert an application to a prior version if necessary. `dnf` does this with the `downgrade` subcommand, as illustrated here:

```
dnf downgrade htop --assumeyes
```

This is a powerful process because the package manager allows users to quickly roll back if a critical bug or vulnerability is reported.

If you want to remove an application completely, a package manager can take care of that as well. `dnf` provides the `remove` subcommand for this purpose, as illustrated here:

```
dnf remove htop --assumeyes
```

In this section, we reviewed how the `dnf` package manager on Fedora can be used to manage a software package. Helm, as the Kubernetes package manager, is similar to `dnf`, both in its purpose and functionality. While `dnf` is used to manage applications on Fedora, Helm is used to manage applications on Kubernetes. We will explore this in greater detail next.

The Kubernetes package manager

Given that Helm was designed to provide an experience similar to that of package managers, experienced users of `dnf` or similar tools will immediately understand Helm's basic concepts. Things become more complicated, however, when talking about the specific implementation details. `dnf` operates on **RPM Package Manager** (**RPM**) packages that provide executables, dependency information, and metadata. Helm, on the other hand, works with **charts**. A Helm chart can be thought of as a Kubernetes package. Charts contain the declarative Kubernetes resource files required to deploy an application. Similar to an RPM package, it can also declare one or more dependencies that the application needs in order to run.

Helm relies on repositories to provide widespread access to charts. Chart developers create declarative YAML files, package them into charts, and publish them to chart repositories. End users then use Helm to search for existing charts to deploy onto Kubernetes, similar to how end users of `dnf` will search for RPM packages to deploy to Fedora.

Let's go through a basic example. Helm can be used to deploy Redis, an in-memory cache, to Kubernetes by using a chart from an upstream repository. This can be performed using Helm's `install` command, as illustrated here:

```
helm install redis bitnami/redis --namespace=redis
```

This would install the `redis` chart from the `bitnami` repository to a Kubernetes namespace called `redis`. This installation would be referred to as the initial revision, or the initial installation of a Helm chart.

If a new version of the `redis` chart becomes available, users can upgrade to the new version using the `upgrade` command, as follows:

```
helm upgrade redis bitnami/redis --namespace=redis
```

This would upgrade `redis` to meet the specification defined by the newer `redis` chart.

With OSs, users should be concerned about rollbacks if a bug or vulnerability is found. The same concern exists with applications on Kubernetes, and Helm provides the `rollback` command to handle this use case, as illustrated here:

```
helm rollback redis 1 --namespace=redis
```

This command would roll `redis` back to its first revision.

Finally, Helm provides the ability to remove `redis` altogether with the `uninstall` command, as follows:

```
helm uninstall redis --namespace=redis
```

Compare `dnf` and Helm's subcommands, and the functions they serve in the following table. Notice that `dnf` and Helm offer similar commands that provide a similar **user experience** (**UX**):

dnf subcommands	Helm subcommands	Purpose
`install`	`Install`	Install an application and its dependencies.
`upgrade`	`Upgrade`	Upgrade an application to a newer version. Upgrade dependencies as specified by the target package.
`downgrade`	`rollback`	Revert an application to a previous version. Revert dependencies as specified by the target package.
`remove`	`uninstall`	Delete an application. Each tool has a different philosophy around handling dependencies.

Table 1.2 – Purpose of dnf and Helm subcommands

With an understanding of how Helm functions as a package manager, let's discuss in greater detail the benefits that Helm brings to Kubernetes.

The benefits of Helm

Earlier in this chapter, we reviewed how Kubernetes applications are created by managing Kubernetes resources, and we discussed some of the challenges involved. Here are a few ways Helm can overcome these challenges.

Abstracting the complexity of Kubernetes resources

Let's assume that a developer has been given the task of deploying a WordPress instance onto Kubernetes. The developer would need to create the resources required to configure its containers, network, and storage. The amount of Kubernetes knowledge required to configure such an application from scratch is high and is a big hurdle for new—and even intermediate Kubernetes users—to clear.

With Helm, a developer tasked with deploying a WordPress instance could simply search for WordPress charts from upstream chart repositories. These charts would have already been written by chart developers in the community and would already contain the declarative configuration required to deploy WordPress and a backing database. Vendor-owned chart repositories also tend to be well maintained, so teams using charts from them would not need to worry about keeping Kubernetes resources up to date. In this regard, developers with this kind of task would act as simple end users that consume Helm in a similar way to any other package manager.

Maintaining an ongoing history of revisions

Helm has a concept called **release history**. When a Helm chart is installed for the first time, Helm adds that initial revision to the history. The history is further modified as revisions increase via upgrades, keeping various snapshots of how the application was configured at varying revisions.

The following diagram depicts an ongoing history of revisions. The squares in blue illustrate resources that have been modified from their previous versions:

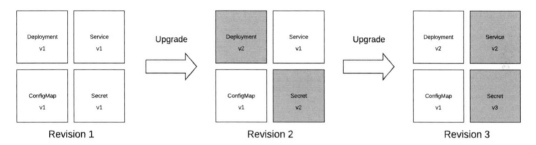

Figure 1.3 – An example of a revision history

The process of tracking each revision provides opportunities for rollback. Rollbacks in Helm are very simple. Users simply point Helm to a previous revision, and Helm reverts the live state to that of the selected revision. Helm allows users to roll back their applications as far as they desire, even back to the very first installation.

Configuring declarative resources in a dynamic fashion

One of the biggest hassles with creating resources declaratively is that Kubernetes resources are static and cannot be parameterized. As you may recall from earlier, this results in resources becoming boilerplate across applications and similar configurations, making it more difficult for teams to configure their applications as code. Helm alleviates these issues by introducing **values** and **templates**.

Values can be thought of as parameters for charts. Templates are dynamically generated files based on a given set of values. These two constructs give chart developers the ability to write Kubernetes resources that are generated based on values that end users provide. By doing so, applications managed by Helm become more flexible, have less boilerplate, and are easier to maintain.

Values and templates allow users to do things such as this:

- Parameterize common fields, such as the image name in a deployment and the ports in a service.
- Generate long pieces of YAML configuration based on user input, such as volume mounts in a deployment or the data in a ConfigMap.
- Include or exclude resources based on user input.

The ability to dynamically generate declarative resource files makes it simpler to create YAML-based resources while still ensuring that applications are deployed in an easily reproducible fashion.

Simplifying local and live state synchronization

Package managers prevent users from having to manage all of the intricate details of an application and its dependencies. The same idea holds true with Helm. Using Helm's `values` construct, users can provide configuration changes across an application's life cycle by managing a small number of parameters instead of multiple full-length YAML resources. When the local state (values/parameters) is updated, Helm propagates the configuration change out to the relevant resources in Kubernetes. This workflow keeps Helm in control of managing intricate Kubernetes details and encourages users to manage the state locally instead of updating live resources directly.

Deploying resources in an intelligent order

Helm simplifies application deployments by having a pre-determined order in which Kubernetes resources need to be created. This ordering exists to ensure that dependent resources are deployed first. For example, Secret instances and ConfigMap instances should be created before deployments, since a deployment would likely consume those resources as volumes. Helm performs this ordering without any interaction from the user, so this complexity is abstracted and prevents users from needing to understand the order in which resources should be applied.

Providing automated life cycle hooks

Similar to other package managers, Helm provides the ability to define life cycle hooks. Life cycle hooks are actions that take place automatically at different stages of an application's life cycle. They can be used to do things such as the following:

- Perform a data backup on an upgrade.
- Restore data on a rollback.
- Validate a Kubernetes environment prior to installation.

Life cycle hooks are valuable because they abstract complexities around tasks that may not be Kubernetes-specific. For example, a Kubernetes user may not be familiar with the best practices behind backing up a database or may not know when such a task should be performed. Life cycle hooks allow experts to write automation that handles various life cycle tasks and prevents users from needing to handle them on their own.

Summary

In this chapter, we began by exploring the trend of adopting microservice-based architectures to decompose monoliths into smaller applications. The creation of microservices that are more lightweight and easier to manage has led to utilizing containers as a packaging and runtime format to produce releases more frequently. By adopting containers, additional operational challenges were introduced and solved by using Kubernetes as a container orchestration platform to manage the container life cycle.

Our discussion turned to the various ways Kubernetes applications can be configured. These resources can be expressed using two distinct styles of application configuration: imperative and declarative. Each of these configuration styles contributes to a set of challenges involved in deploying Kubernetes applications, including the amount of knowledge required to understand how Kubernetes resources work and the challenge of managing application life cycles.

To better manage each of the assets that comprise an application, Helm was introduced as the package manager for Kubernetes. Through its rich feature set, the full life cycle of applications from installation, upgrading, and, rollback to deletion can be managed with ease.

In the next chapter, we'll walk through the process of installing Helm and preparing an environment that can be used for following along with this book's examples.

Further reading

For more information about the Kubernetes resources that make up an application, please see the *Understanding Kubernetes Objects* page from the Kubernetes documentation at https://kubernetes.io/docs/concepts/overview/working-with-objects/kubernetes-objects/.

To reinforce some of the benefits of Helm discussed in this chapter, please refer to the *Using Helm* page of the Helm documentation at https://helm.sh/docs/intro/using_helm/. (This page also dives into some basic usage around Helm, which will be discussed throughout this book in greater detail.)

Questions

Here are some questions to test your knowledge of the chapter:

1. What is the difference between a monolithic and a microservices application?
2. What is Kubernetes? What kinds of problems was it designed to solve?
3. What are some of the `kubectl` commands commonly used when deploying applications to Kubernetes?

4. What challenges are often involved in deploying applications to Kubernetes?
5. How does Helm function as a Kubernetes package manager? How does it address the challenges posed by Kubernetes?
6. Imagine you want to roll back an application deployed on Kubernetes. Which Helm command allows you to perform this action? How does Helm keep track of your changes to make this rollback possible?
7. What are the four primary Helm commands?

2
Preparing a Kubernetes and Helm Environment

Helm is a tool that provides a variety of benefits that help users deploy and manage **Kubernetes** applications easier. Before users can start experiencing these benefits, however, they must satisfy several prerequisites. First, a user must have access to a Kubernetes cluster. Next, a user should have the command-line tools for both Kubernetes and Helm. Finally, a user should be aware of Helm's basic configuration options to be productive with as little friction as possible.

In this chapter, we will outline the tools and concepts that are required to begin working with Helm. The following topics will be covered in this chapter:

- Preparing a local Kubernetes environment with minikube
- Setting up kubectl
- Setting up Helm
- Configuring Helm

Technical requirements

In this chapter, you must install the following technologies on your local workstation:

- minikube
- VirtualBox
- Helm
- kubectl

These tools can be installed with a package manager or by downloading them directly from the source. We will provide instructions for using the `Chocolatey` package manager on Windows, the `Homebrew` package manager on macOS, the `apt-get` package manager for Debian-based Linux distributions, and the `dnf` package manager for RPM-based Linux distributions.

Preparing a local Kubernetes environment with minikube

Helm won't be able to deploy applications without access to a Kubernetes cluster. For this reason, let's discuss one option where users can run a local cluster on their machine – **minikube**.

minikube is a community-driven tool that allows users to easily deploy a small, single-node Kubernetes cluster to their local machine. A cluster created with minikube is run inside either a container or a **virtual machine** (**VM**) so that it can easily be created and later discarded. minikube presents us with an excellent way to experiment with Kubernetes, and it can also be used to learn Helm alongside the examples provided throughout this book.

In the next few sections, we'll cover how minikube can be installed and configured so that you have a Kubernetes cluster available while learning how to use Helm. For more comprehensive instructions, please refer to the *Getting Started!* page of the official minikube website at `https://minikube.sigs.k8s.io/docs/start/`.

Installing minikube

minikube, like the other tools that will be installed within this chapter, has binaries compiled for the Windows, macOS, and Linux operating systems. The easiest way to install the latest version of minikube on Windows and macOS is via a package manager, such as `Chocolatey` for Windows and `Homebrew` for macOS. Linux users will find it easier to install the latest `minikube` binary by downloading it from minikube's GitHub releases page, though this method can also be used on Windows and macOS as well.

The following steps describe how to install minikube based on your machine and installation preference. Please note that minikube version v1.22.0 was used at the time of writing and for developing the examples that have been used throughout this book.

To install it via a package manager (on Windows and macOS), run one of the following commands based on your operating system:

- For Windows, run the following command:

    ```
    choco install minikube
    ```

- For macOS, run the following command:

    ```
    brew install minikube
    ```

The following steps show you how to install minikube using a direct download link (on Windows, macOS, and Linux):

1. Navigate to minikube's *releases* page on GitHub at `https://github.com/kubernetes/minikube/releases/`.

2. Find the **Assets** section, which contains the minikube binaries for a given release:

minikube-darwin-amd64	66 MB
minikube-darwin-amd64.sha256	65 Bytes
minikube-darwin-amd64.tar.gz	30.3 MB
minikube-darwin-arm64	64.9 MB
minikube-darwin-arm64.tar.gz	26 MB
minikube-installer.exe	27.5 MB
minikube-linux-386	58.7 MB
minikube-linux-amd64	66.5 MB
minikube-linux-amd64.sha256	65 Bytes
minikube-linux-amd64.tar.gz	32.5 MB
minikube-linux-arm	56.8 MB
minikube-linux-arm.sha256	65 Bytes

Figure 2.1 – A snippet of the minikube binaries from the GitHub releases page

3. Under the **Assets** section, download the binary that corresponds to your target platform. Once downloaded, you should rename the binary `minikube`. If you are downloading the Linux binary, for example, you would run the following command:

   ```
   mv minikube-linux-amd64 minikube
   ```

4. To execute minikube, Linux and macOS users may need to add the executable bit by running the `chmod` command:

   ```
   chmod u+x minikube
   ```

5. `minikube` should then be moved to a location that's managed by the `PATH` variable so that it can be executed from any location in your command line. The locations that the `PATH` variable contains vary, depending on your operating system. For macOS and Linux users, these locations can be determined by running the following command in the Terminal:

   ```
   echo $PATH
   ```

Windows users can determine the `PATH` variable's locations by running the following command in PowerShell:

```
$env:PATH
```

6. Move the `minikube` binary to a `PATH` location using the `mv` command. The following example moves `minikube` to a common `PATH` location on Linux:

```
mv minikube /usr/local/bin/
```

7. You can verify your minikube installation by running `minikube version` and ensuring that the displayed version corresponds with the version that was downloaded:

```
$ minikube version
minikube version: v1.22.0
commit: a03fbcf166e6f74ef224d4a63be4277d017bb62e
```

The next step involves installing a container or virtual machine manager to run your local Kubernetes cluster. In this book, we will choose to run Kubernetes in a VM using VirtualBox since it is flexible and available on the Windows, macOS, and Linux operating systems. We will explain how to install VirtualBox next.

Installing VirtualBox

Like minikube, VirtualBox can easily be installed via Chocolatey or Homebrew:

- Use the following command to install VirtualBox on Windows:

```
choco install virtualbox
```

- Use the following command to install VirtualBox on macOS:

```
brew install --cask virtualbox
```

VirtualBox can also be installed by Linux package managers, but you need to download a package first from VirtualBox's website (https://www.virtualbox.org/wiki/Linux_Downloads):

VirtualBox 6.1.26 for Linux

- ⇨ Oracle Linux 8 / Red Hat Enterprise Linux 8 / CentOS 8
- ⇨ Oracle Linux 7 / Red Hat Enterprise Linux 7 / CentOS 7
- ⇨ Oracle Linux 6 / Red Hat Enterprise Linux 6 / CentOS 6
- ⇨ Ubuntu 19.10 / 20.04 / 20.10 / 21.04
- ⇨ Ubuntu 18.04 / 18.10 / 19.04
- ⇨ Ubuntu 16.04
- ⇨ Debian 10
- ⇨ Debian 9
- ⇨ openSUSE 15.0
- ⇨ openSUSE 13.2 / Leap 42
- ⇨ Fedora 33 / 34
- ⇨ Fedora 32
- ⇨ All distributions (built on EL6 and therefore not requiring recent system libraries)

Figure 2.2 – VirtualBox package download links

Once you have downloaded your distribution's package, you can install VirtualBox via `apt-get` or `dnf`:

- Use the following command to install VirtualBox on Debian-based Linux:

```
apt-get install ./virtualbox-*.deb
```

- Use the following command to install VirtualBox on RPM-based Linux:

```
dnf install ./VirtualBox-*.rpm
```

Alternative methods of installing VirtualBox can be found at its official download page at https://www.virtualbox.org/wiki/Downloads.

With VirtualBox installed, minikube must be configured to leverage VirtualBox as its default hypervisor. We will configure this in the next section.

Configuring VirtualBox as the default driver

VirtualBox can be made the default driver in minikube by specifying the `driver` option as `virtualbox`:

```
minikube config set driver virtualbox
```

Note that this command may produce the following warning:

```
❗  These changes will take effect upon a minikube delete and then a minikube start
```

This message can be safely ignored if there are no active minikube clusters on your machine.

The change to VirtualBox can be confirmed by checking the value of the `driver` configuration option:

```
minikube config get driver
```

If the configuration change was successful, the following output will be displayed:

```
virtualbox
```

In addition to configuring the default driver, you can also configure the resources that are allocated to a minikube instance, which we will discuss in the next section.

Configuring minikube resource allocation

By default, minikube will allocate 2 CPUs and 2 GB of RAM to the VM, but we recommend increasing the memory allocation to 4 GB if your machine has the resources to spare. This is to prevent bumping into memory constraints as you run through the exercises.

Run the following command to increase the VM memory allocation to 4 GB:

```
minikube config set memory 4000
```

This change can be verified by running the following command:

```
minikube config get memory.
```

Let's continue exploring minikube by discussing its basic usage.

Exploring the basic usage of minikube

Throughout this book, it will be handy to understand the key commands that are used in a typical minikube operation. They will also be essential to understand while executing the examples provided throughout this book. Fortunately, minikube is an easy tool to get started with.

minikube has three key subcommands:

- start
- stop
- delete

The start subcommand is used to create a single-node Kubernetes cluster. It creates a VM and bootstraps a cluster within it. The command will terminate once the cluster is ready:

```
$ minikube start
😄  minikube v1.22.0 on Redhat 8.4
✨  Using the virtualbox driver based on user configuration
👍  Starting control plane node minikube in cluster minikube
🔥  Creating virtualbox VM (CPUs=2, Memory=4000MB,
```

```
    Disk=20000MB) ...
    🤚 Preparing Kubernetes v1.21.2 on Docker 20.10.6 ...
        ▪ Generating certificates and keys ...
        ▪ Booting up control plane ...
        ▪ Configuring RBAC rules ...
    🔍 Verifying Kubernetes components...
        ▪ Using image gcr.io/k8s-minikube/storage-provisioner:v5
    🌟 Enabled addons: storage-provisioner, default-storageclass
    🎉 Done! kubectl is now configured to use "minikube" cluster
    and "default" namespace by default
```

The `stop` subcommand is used to shut down the cluster and the VM. The state of the cluster and VM are saved to the disk, allowing users to run the `start` subcommand again to quickly begin resuming their work, rather than having to build a new VM from scratch. You should try to get into the habit of running `minikube stop` when you have finished working with a cluster that you would like to return to later:

```
$ minikube stop
✋ Stopping node "minikube"  ...
⬛ 1 nodes stopped.
```

The `delete` subcommand is used to delete a cluster and the VM. This command erases the state of the cluster and VM, freeing up the space on the disk that was previously allocated. The next time `minikube start` is executed, a fresh cluster and VM will be created:

```
$ minikube delete
🔥 Deleting "minikube" in virtualbox ...
💀 Removed all traces of the "minikube" cluster.
```

There are more minikube subcommands available, but these are the subcommands that you should be aware of.

With minikube installed and configured on a local machine, you can now install **kubectl**, the Kubernetes command-line tool, and satisfy the remaining prerequisite for working with Helm.

Setting up kubectl

As we mentioned in *Chapter 1*, *Understanding Kubernetes and Helm*, Kubernetes is a system that exposes different API endpoints. These API endpoints are used to perform various actions on a cluster, such as creating, viewing, or deleting resources. To provide a simpler user experience, developers need a way of interacting with Kubernetes without having to manage the underlying API layer.

While you will predominantly use the Helm command-line tool throughout this book to install and manage applications, kubectl is an essential tool for common tasks.

Read on to learn how to install kubectl on a local workstation. Note that the kubectl version that was used at the time of writing was v1.21.2.

Installing kubectl

kubectl can be installed using minikube, or it can be obtained via a package manager or through direct download. First, let's describe how to obtain kubectl using minikube.

Installing kubectl via minikube

Installing kubectl is straightforward with minikube. minikube provides a subcommand called `kubectl`, which downloads the kubectl binary for you. Begin by running a `kubectl` command using `minikube kubectl`:

```
minikube kubectl version
```

This command installs kubectl to the `$HOME/.minikube/cache/linux/v1.21.2` directory. Note that the version of kubectl that's included in the path will depend on the version of minikube that is being used. To access kubectl once it has been installed, use the following syntax:

```
minikube kubectl -- <subcommand> <flags>
```

Here's an example command:

```
$ minikube kubectl -- version --client
Client Version: version.Info{Major:"1",
Minor:"21", GitVersion:"v1.21.2",
GitCommit:"092fbfbf53427de67cac1e9fa54aaa09a28371d7",
GitTreeState:"clean", BuildDate:"2021-06-16T12:59:11Z",
GoVersion:"go1.16.5", Compiler:"gc", Platform:"linux/amd64"}
```

While invoking kubectl with `minikube kubectl` works, the syntax is more unwieldy than that of invoking kubectl directly. This can be overcome by copying the `kubectl` executable from the local minikube cache into a location that's managed by the `PATH` variable. Performing this action is similar on each operating system, but the following is an example of how it can be achieved on a Linux machine:

```
$ sudo cp ~/.minikube/cache/linux/v1.21.2/kubectl /usr/local/bin/
```

Once complete, `kubectl` can be invoked as a standalone binary, as illustrated here:

```
$ kubectl version -client
Client Version: version.Info{Major:"1",
Minor:"21", GitVersion:"v1.21.2",
GitCommit:"092fbfbf53427de67cac1e9fa54aaa09a28371d7",
GitTreeState:"clean", BuildDate:"2021-06-16T12:59:11Z",
GoVersion:"go1.16.5", Compiler:"gc", Platform:"linux/amd64"}
```

`kubectl` can also be installed without `minikube`, as we'll see in the following sections.

Installing kubectl without minikube

The Kubernetes upstream documentation provides several different mechanisms to do so for a variety of target operating systems, as described in https://kubernetes.io/docs/tasks/tools/install-kubectl/.

Using a package manager

Another way that kubectl can be installed without minikube is with a native package manager. The following list demonstrates how this can be accomplished on different operating systems:

- Use the following command to install kubectl on Windows:

    ```
    choco install kubernetes-cli
    ```

- Use the following command to install kubectl on macOS:

    ```
    brew install kubernetes-cli
    ```

- Use the following command to install kubectl on Debian-based Linux:

    ```
    sudo apt-get update
    sudo apt-get install -y apt-transport-https
    ca-certificates curl
    sudo curl -fsSLo /usr/share/keyrings/kubernetes-archive-keyring.gpg https://packages.cloud.google.com/apt/doc/apt-key.gpg
    echo "deb [signed-by=/usr/share/keyrings/kubernetes-archive-keyring.gpg] https://apt.kubernetes.io/ kubernetes-xenial main" | sudo tee /etc/apt/sources.list.d/kubernetes.list
    sudo apt-get update
    sudo apt-get install -y kubectl
    ```

- Use the following command to install kubectl on RPM-based Linux:

  ```
  cat <<EOF > /etc/yum.repos.d/kubernetes.repo[kubernetes]
  name=Kubernetesbaseurl=https://packages.cloud.google.com/
  yum/repos/kubernetes-el7-x86_64enabled=1gpgcheck=1repo_
  gpgcheck=1gpgkey=https://packages.cloud.google.com/yum/
  doc/yum-key.gpg https://packages.cloud.google.com/yum/
  doc/rpm-package-key.gpgEOF
  yum install -y kubectl
  ```

We will discuss the final kubectl installation method next.

Downloading directly from a link

kubectl can also be downloaded directly from a download link. The following list explains how version v1.21.2 can be downloaded, which is the version of kubectl that will be used throughout this book:

- Download kubectl for Windows from `https://storage.googleapis.com/kubernetes-release/release/v1.21.2/bin/windows/amd64/kubectl.exe`.
- Download kubectl for macOS from `https://storage.googleapis.com/kubernetes-release/release/v1.21.2/bin/darwin/amd64/kubectl`.
- Download kubectl for Linux from `https://storage.googleapis.com/kubernetes-release/release/v1.21.2/bin/linux/amd64/kubectl`.

The kubectl binary can then be moved to a location that's managed by the `PATH` variable. On the macOS and Linux operating systems, be sure to grant the file executable permission:

```
chmod u+x kubectl
```

The installation can be verified by running the following command.

```
$ kubectl version --client
Client Version: version.Info{Major:"1",
Minor:"21", GitVersion:"v1.21.2",
GitCommit:"092fbfbf53427de67cac1e9fa54aaa09a28371d7",
GitTreeState:"clean", BuildDate:"2021-06-16T12:59:11Z",
GoVersion:"go1.16.5", Compiler:"gc", Platform:"linux/amd64"}
```

Now that we've covered how to set up kubectl, we're ready to get into the key technology of this book – Helm.

Setting up Helm

Once minikube and kubectl have been installed, the next logical tool to configure is Helm. Note that the version of Helm that was used at the time of writing this book was v3.6.3.

Installing Helm

Packages for Helm exist for both `Chocolatey` and `Homebrew` to allow you to easily install it on Windows or macOS. On these systems, the following commands can be run to install Helm with the applicable package manager:

- Install Helm on Windows using the following command:

    ```
    > choco install kubernetes-helm
    ```

- Install Helm on macOS using the following command:

    ```
    $ brew install helm
    ```

Linux users, or users who would rather install Helm from a direct downloadable link, can download an archive from Helm's GitHub releases page by following these steps:

1. Find the **Installation and Upgrading** section on Helm's GitHub releases page at https://github.com/helm/helm/releases:

Installation and Upgrading

Download Helm v3.6.3. The common platform binaries are here:

- MacOS amd64 (checksum / 84a1ff17dd03340652d96e8be5172a921c97825fd278a2113c8233a4e8db5236)
- MacOS arm64 (checksum / a50b499dbd0bbec90761d50974bf1e67cc6d503ea20d03b4a1275884065b7e9e)
- Linux amd64 (checksum / 07c100849925623dc1913209cd1a30f0a9b80a5b4d6ff2153c609d11b043e262)
- Linux arm (checksum / 6918e573a70c309fbf6385a0a0d18d090c10b44d318724f1f73e47ede4809635)
- Linux arm64 (checksum / 6fe647628bc27e7ae77d015da4d5e1c63024f673062ac7bc11453ccc55657713)
- Linux i386 (checksum / e7bafc7dd870621a79f7f2ad0c92e45957817a371b738da4e590ccbc45983244)
- Linux ppc64le (checksum / 12ea5cdda8ee4a585230623254b997b28d4f9fb894ebf509b530af501366d0e9)
- Linux s390x (checksum / 1419787383c8062d5cb799d072c9ed10e1c3af66d0d2395832aafaf03d2d4bfb)
- Windows amd64 (checksum / 797d2abd603a2646f2fb9c3fabba46f2fabae5cbd1eb87c20956ec5b4a2fc634)

Figure 2.3 – The Installation and Upgrading section on the Helm GitHub releases page

2. Download the archive file associated with your operating system.

3. Once downloaded, the file will need to be unarchived. One way that this can be achieved is by using the `Expand-Archive` cmdlet on PowerShell or by using the `tar` utility on Bash:

   For Windows/PowerShell, use the following example code:

   ```
   Expand-Archive -Path helm-v3.6.3-windows-amd64.zip
   -DestinationPath $DEST
   ```

   For Linux, use the following example code:

   ```
   tar -zxvf helm-v3.6.3-linux-amd64.tar.gz
   ```

   For Mac, use the following example code:

   ```
   tar -zxvf helm-v3.6.3-linux-amd64.tar
   ```

The `helm` binary can be found in the unarchived folder. It should be moved to a location that's managed by the `PATH` variable.

The following example illustrates how to move the `helm` binary to the `/usr/local/bin` folder on a Linux system:

```
sudo mv ~/Downloads/linux-amd64/helm /usr/local/bin
```

Regardless of the method that Helm was installed with, verification can be performed by running the `helm version` command. If the resulting output is similar to that of the following code, then Helm has been successfully installed:

```
$ helm version
version.BuildInfo{Version:"v3.6.3",
GitCommit:"d506314abfb5d21419df8c7e7e68012379db2354",
GitTreeState:"clean", GoVersion:"go1.16.5"}
```

With Helm installed on your machine, let's learn about the basic Helm configuration topics.

Configuring Helm

Helm is a tool with sensible defaults that allow users to be productive without needing to perform a large number of tasks post-installation. With that being said, there are several different options users can change or enable to modify Helm's behavior. We will cover these options in the following sections, beginning with configuring upstream repositories.

Adding upstream repositories

One way that users can begin to configure their Helm installation is by adding upstream chart repositories. In *Chapter 1, Understanding Kubernetes and Helm*, we described how chart repositories contain Helm charts that are more broadly available for consumption. Helm, being the Kubernetes package manager, can connect to various chart repositories to install Kubernetes applications.

Helm provides the `repo` subcommand to allow users to manage configured chart repositories. This subcommand contains additional subcommands that can be used to perform actions against specified repositories.

Here are the five `repo` subcommands:

- `add`: To add a chart repository
- `list`: To list chart repositories
- `remove`: To remove a chart repository
- `update`: To update information on available charts locally from chart repositories
- `index`: To generate an index file, given a directory containing packaged charts

Using the preceding list as a guide, adding a chart repository can be accomplished using the `add repo` subcommand, as follows:

```
$ helm repo add $REPO_NAME $REPO_URL
```

Adding chart repositories is required before installing the charts contained within them. The specific steps to install charts from repositories will be discussed in detail throughout this book.

You can confirm whether a repository has been successfully added by leveraging the `list repo` subcommand:

```
$ helm repo list
NAME       URL
bitnami    https://charts.bitnami.com
```

Repositories that have been added to the Helm client will appear in this output. The preceding example shows that a chart repository called `bitnami` was previously added, so it appears in the list of repositories known by the Helm client. If additional repositories are added, they will also appear in this output.

Over time, updates to charts will be published and released to these repositories. Repository metadata is cached locally. As a result, Helm is not automatically aware of when a chart is updated. You can instruct Helm to check for updates from each configured repository by running the `update repo` subcommand. Once this command has been executed, you will be able to install the latest charts from each repository:

```
$ helm repo update
Hang tight while we grab the latest from your chart
repositories...
...Successfully got an update from the "bitnami" chart
```

```
repository
Update Complete. ⎈ Happy Helming!⎈
```

You may also need to remove repositories that have been configured previously. This can be accomplished by using the `repo remove` subcommand:

```
$ helm repo remove bitnami
"bitnami" has been removed from your repositories
```

The last remaining `repo` subcommand form is `index`. This subcommand is used by repository and chart maintainers to publish new or updated charts. This task will be covered more extensively in *Chapter 8, Publishing to a Helm Chart Repository*.

Next, we will discuss Helm plugin configurations.

Adding plugins

Plugins are add-on capabilities that can be used to provide additional features to Helm. Most users will not need to worry about plugins and plugin management with Helm. Helm is a powerful tool on its own and is complete with a full set of included features. With that being said, the Helm community maintains a variety of different plugins that can be used to enhance Helm's capabilities outside of the core code base. Some of the more popular Helm plugins are listed within the Helm documentation at `https://helm.sh/docs/community/related/`.

Helm provides a `plugin` subcommand for managing plugins, which contain further subcommands, as described in the following table:

Plugin Subcommand	Description	Usage
`install`	Installs one or more Helm plugins	`helm plugin install $URL`
`list`	Lists installed Helm plugins	`helm plugin list`
`uninstall`	Uninstalls one or more Helm plugins	`helm plugin uninstall $PLUGIN`
`update`	Updates one or more Helm plugins	`helm plugin update $PLUGIN`

Table 2.1 – Helm plugin subcommands

Plugins can provide a variety of different productivity enhancements.

The following are several examples of upstream plugins:

- **Helm Diff**: Performs a diff between a deployed release and proposed Helm upgrade
- **Helm Secrets**: Used to help conceal secrets from Helm charts

- **Helm Monitor**: Used to monitor a release and perform a rollback if certain events occur
- **Helm Unittest**: Used to perform unit testing on a Helm chart

We will continue discussing Helm configuration options by reviewing the different environment variables that can be set to change various aspects of Helm's behavior.

Environment variables

Helm relies on the existence of environment variables to configure some of the low-level options. There are many variables you can configure, each of which can be seen in the `helm help` output.

A few environment variables are used for storing Helm metadata:

- `HELM_CACHE_HOME` **or** `XDG_CACHE_HOME`: Sets an alternative location for storing cached files
- `HELM_CONFIG_HOME` **or** `XDG_CONFIG_HOME`: Sets an alternative location for storing Helm configuration
- `HELM_DATA_HOME` **or** `XDG_DATA_HOME`: Sets an alternative location for storing Helm data

Helm adheres to the **XDG Base Directory Specification**, which is designed to provide a standardized way of defining where different files are located on an operating system's filesystem. Based on the XDG specification, Helm automatically creates three different default directories on each operating system as required:

Operating System	Cache Path	Configuration Path	Data Path
Windows	`%TEMP%\helm`	`%APPDATA%\helm`	`%APPDATA%\helm`
macOS	`$HOME/Library/Caches/helm`	`$HOME/Library/Preferences/helm`	`$HOME/Library/helm`
Linux	`$HOME/.cache/helm`	`$HOME/.config/helm`	`$HOME/.local/share/helm`

Table 2.2 – Default locations for Helm metadata

Helm uses the **cache path** to store charts that are downloaded from upstream chart repositories. Installed charts are cached to the local machine to enable faster installation of the chart the next time it is referenced. The cache path also includes YAML files that are used to index the available Helm charts from each configured repository. These index files are updated when users run the `helm repo update` command.

The **configuration path** is used to save repository information, such as the URL and credentials for authentication, if required. When a chart is installed but is not located in the local cache yet, Helm uses the configuration path to look up the URL of the chart repository. The chart is then downloaded from this URL.

The **data path** is used to store plugins. When a plugin is installed using the `helm plugin install` command, the plugin itself is stored in this location.

Besides the Helm metadata paths, other environment variables are used for configuring regular Helm usage:

- **HELM_DRIVER**: Sets the backend storage driver. It is used to determine how the release state is stored in Kubernetes. The default value is `secret`, which Base64-encodes the state of a release in a Kubernetes `secret`. Other options include `configmap`, which stores state in a plaintext Kubernetes ConfigMap, `memory`, which stores the state in the local process's memory, and `sql`, which stores state in a relational database.

- **HELM_NAMESPACE**: Sets the namespace that's used for Helm operations. The `HELM_NAMESPACE` environment variable is used to set the namespace in which Helm operations take place. This is a convenient environment variable to use as it prevents you from needing to pass the `--namespace` or `-n` flag on each Helm invocation.

- **KUBECONFIG**: Sets an alternative Kubernetes configuration file. The `KUBECONFIG` environment variable is used to set the file that's used for authentication to the Kubernetes cluster. If unset, the default value will be `~/.kube/config`. In most cases, users won't need to modify this value.

Another component of Helm that can be configured is tab completion, as discussed next.

Tab completion

Bash, Zsh, and Fish users can enable tab completion to simplify Helm usage. Tab completion allows Helm commands to be auto-completed when the *Tab* key is pressed, enabling users to perform tasks faster and helping prevent input mistakes.

This process is similar to how most modern terminal emulators behave by default. When the *Tab* key is pressed, terminals try to guess what arguments are needed next by observing the state of the command and the environment. For example, the `cd /usr/local/b` input can be tab-completed to `cd /usr/local/bin` in a Bash shell. Similarly, an input such as `helm upgrade hello-` can be tab-completed to read `helm upgrade hello-world`.

Tab completion can be enabled by running one of the following commands, based on your shell of choice:

- For Bash users, run the following command:

```
source <(helm completion bash)
```

- For Zsh users, run the following command:

  ```
  source <(helm completion zsh)
  ```

- For Fish users, run the following command:

  ```
  helm completion fish | source
  ```

Note that auto-completion will only exist in terminal windows that execute one of the preceding commands, so other open windows will need to run this command as well to experience the auto-completion feature.

Authentication

Helm needs to be able to authenticate with a Kubernetes cluster to deploy and manage applications. It authenticates by referencing a `kubeconfig` file, which specifies different Kubernetes clusters and how to interact with them.

If you are using minikube, you will not need to configure authentication as minikube automatically configures a `kubeconfig` file each time a new cluster is created. If you are not running minikube, you will likely need to create a `kubeconfig` file or have one provided, depending on the Kubernetes distribution you are using. A `kubeconfig` file is comprised of three primary components:

- **clusters**: Hostnames or IP addresses, along with a certificate authority
- **users**: Authentication details
- **contexts**: Binding between a cluster, users, and an active namespace

A `kubeconfig` file, along with these three primary components, can be created by leveraging three different `kubectl` commands:

- The first command is `set-cluster`:

  ```
  kubectl config set-cluster
  ```

  The `set-cluster` command will define a `cluster` entry in the `kubeconfig` file. `set-context` is used to associate a credential with a cluster. Once an association between a credential and a cluster has been established, you will be able to authenticate to the specified cluster using the credential's authentication method.

- The next command is `set-credentials`:

  ```
  kubectl config set-credentials
  ```

  The `set-credentials` command will define the name of a user, along with its authentication method and details. This command can configure a username and password pair, client certificate, bearer token, or authentication provider to allow users and administrators to specify varying different methods of authentication.

- Then, we have the `set-context` command:

    ```
    kubectl config set-context
    ```

    The `set-context` command, as mentioned previously, specifies a name mapping between a `cluster`, `credential`, (user), and an active namespace. All invocations referencing a `kubeconfig` file target a specific context.

The `kubectl config view` command can be used to view the `kubeconfig` file. Notice how the `clusters`, `contexts`, and `user` stanzas of `kubeconfig` correspond to the previously described commands, as shown in the following example:

```
$ kubectl config view
apiVersion: v1
clusters:
- cluster:
    certificate-authority: /home/helm-user/.minikube/ca.crt
    extensions:
    - extension:
        last-update: Mon, 13 Dec 2021 17:26:45 EST
        provider: minikube.sigs.k8s.io
        version: v1.22.0
      name: cluster_info
    server: https://192.168.49.2:8443
  name: minikube
contexts:
- context:
    cluster: minikube
    extensions:
    - extension:
        last-update: Mon, 13 Dec 2021 17:26:45 EST
        provider: minikube.sigs.k8s.io
        version: v1.22.0
      name: context_info
    namespace: default
    user: minikube
  name: minikube
current-context: minikube
kind: Config
```

```
preferences: {}
users:
- name: minikube
  user:
    client-certificate: /home/helm-user/.minikube/profiles/minikube/client.crt
    client-key: /home/helm-user/.minikube/profiles/minikube/client.key
```

Starting the minikube instance will automatically populate the contents of the `kubeconfig` file. Once this file is present, kubectl and Helm will be able to interact with a Kubernetes cluster.

In the next section, we will discuss how authorization is handled against a Kubernetes cluster.

Authorization/RBAC

While authentication is a means of confirming identity, authorization defines the actions that an authenticated user is allowed to perform. Kubernetes uses **role-based access control** (**RBAC**) to perform authorization on Kubernetes. RBAC is a system for designing roles and privileges that can be assigned to a given user or group of users. The actions a user is permitted to perform on Kubernetes depends on the roles that the user has been assigned.

Kubernetes provides many different roles on the platform. Three common roles are listed here:

- `cluster-admin`: This allows a user to perform any action against any resource throughout the cluster.
- `edit`: This allows a user to read and write to most resources within a namespace or a logical grouping of Kubernetes resources.
- `view`: This prevents a user from modifying existing resources. It only allows users to read resources within a namespace.

Since Helm authenticates to Kubernetes using the credentials defined in the `kubeconfig` file, Helm is given the same level of access. If `edit` access is allowed, Helm can be assumed to have sufficient permission to install applications, in most cases. With view access, Helm will not be able to install applications, as this level of access is read-only. It may also be unable to list details related to installed releases since `secrets` are used as the default storage driver.

Users that run minikube are given `cluster-admin` by default after instance creation. While this level of access would not be a best practice in a production environment, it is acceptable for learning and experimenting. If you are running Minikube, you will not have to worry about configuring authorization to follow along with both the concepts and examples provided in this book. If you are working with Kubernetes users that aren't using minikube, you will need to make sure they are given at least the `edit` role to be able to deploy applications with Helm. This can be accomplished by asking an administrator to run the following command (where $USER is your Kubernetes user):

```
kubectl create clusterrolebinding $USER-edit --clusterrole=edit
--user=$USER
```

Best practices around RBAC will be discussed in *Chapter 12, Helm Security Considerations*, when we discuss, in greater detail, the concepts related to security, including how to appropriately apply roles to prevent mistakes and actions of malicious intent in the cluster.

Summary

There are a variety of different components you need to have available to start using Helm. In this chapter, you learned how to install minikube to provide a local Kubernetes cluster that can be used throughout this book. You also learned how to install kubectl, which is the official tool for interacting with the Kubernetes API. Finally, you learned how to install the Helm client and explored the various ways that Helm can be configured, including adding repositories and plugins, modifying environment variables, enabling tab completion, and configuring authentication and authorization against a Kubernetes cluster.

Now that you have the prerequisite tooling installed, you can begin learning how to deploy your first application with Helm. In the next chapter, you will install a Helm chart from an upstream chart repository, as well as learn about life cycle management and application configuration. After finishing that chapter, you will have an understanding of how Helm acts as the package manager for Kubernetes.

Further reading

Check out the following links to learn more about the installation options that are available for minikube, kubectl, and Helm:

- Minikube: https://kubernetes.io/docs/tasks/tools/install-minikube/
- kubectl: https://kubernetes.io/docs/tasks/tools/install-kubectl/
- Helm: https://helm.sh/docs/intro/install/

We covered various ways of configuring Helm post-installation. Check out the following links to learn more about these topics:

- Repository management: `https://helm.sh/docs/intro/quickstart/#initialize-a-helm-chart-repository`
- Plugin management: `https://helm.sh/docs/topics/plugins/`
- Environment variables and the `helm help` output: `https://helm.sh/docs/helm/helm/`
- Tab completion: `https://helm.sh/docs/helm/helm_completion/`
- Authentication and authorization via the `kubeconfig` file: `https://kubernetes.io/docs/tasks/access-application-cluster/configure-access-multiple-clusters/`

Questions

Answer the following questions to test your knowledge of this chapter:

1. How does Helm authenticate to a Kubernetes cluster?
2. What mechanism is in place to provide authorization to the Helm client? How can an administrator manage these privileges?
3. What is the purpose of the `helm repo add` command?
4. What are the three file paths that are used for storing Helm metadata? What does each path contain?
5. How does Helm manage the state? What options are available to change how the state is stored?

3
Installing Your First App with Helm

Earlier in this book, we referred to Helm as the **Kubernetes package manager** and compared it to an operating system's package manager. A package manager allows users to quickly and easily install applications of varying complexities and manage any dependencies that an application might have. Helm works similarly.

Users simply determine the application they want to deploy on Kubernetes and Helm does the rest of the work. A Helm chart – a packaging of Kubernetes resources – contains the logic and components required to install an application, allowing users to perform installations without needing to know the specific resources required. Users can also pass in parameters, called values, to a Helm chart to customize different aspects of the application. You will explore these features in this chapter by leveraging Helm as a package manager to deploy an instance of WordPress onto Kubernetes.

In this chapter, we will cover the following main topics:

- Understanding the WordPress application
- Finding a WordPress chart
- Creating a Kubernetes environment
- Installing a WordPress chart
- Choosing between `--set` and `--values`
- Accessing the WordPress application
- Upgrading the WordPress release
- Rolling back the WordPress release
- Uninstalling the WordPress release
- Shutting down your environment

Technical requirements

This chapter will use the following software technologies:

- minikube
- kubectl
- Helm

We assume that these components have already been installed on your system. For additional information on each of these tools, including their installation and configuration, please refer to *Chapter 2, Preparing a Kubernetes and Helm Environment*.

Understanding the WordPress application

WordPress is an open source **Content Management System** (**CMS**) used to create websites and blogs. Two different variants are available – WordPress.com and WordPress.org. WordPress.com is a **Software-as-a-Service** (**SaaS**) version of the CMS, meaning the WordPress application and its components are hosted and managed by WordPress. In this case, users do not need to worry about installing a WordPress instance as they can simply access instances that are already available. WordPress.org, on the other hand, is the self-hosted option. It requires users to deploy their WordPress instances and requires some level of expertise to maintain.

Since WordPress.com is easier to start with, it may sound like the more desirable option. This SaaS version of WordPress, however, has many disadvantages over the self-hosted WordPress.org, such as the following:

- It does not provide as many features as WordPress.org
- It does not give users full control over their website
- It requires users to pay for premium features
- It does not provide the ability to modify the backend code of a website

The self-hosted WordPress.org variation, on the other hand, gives users complete control over their website and WordPress instances. It provides the full WordPress feature set, from installing plugins to modifying backend code.

A self-hosted WordPress instance requires users to deploy a few different components. WordPress needs a MySQL or a MariaDB database to save the website and administrative data, and the WordPress UI is deployed as a PHP frontend. In Kubernetes, deploying these components means creating a variety of different resources:

- `Secrets` for database and admin console authentication
- A `ConfigMap` for externalized database configuration

- `Services` for networking
- A `PersistentVolumeClaim` for database storage
- A `StatefulSet` for deploying the database in a stateful fashion
- A `Deployment` for deploying the frontend

Creating these Kubernetes resources requires both WordPress and Kubernetes expertise. WordPress expertise is required because the user needs to know the required physical components, as well as how to configure them. Kubernetes expertise is required because users need to know how to deploy WordPress dependencies as Kubernetes resources. Given the complexity and number of components that are required, deploying WordPress on Kubernetes can be a daunting task.

The challenge presented by this task is a perfect use case for Helm. Rather than focusing on creating and configuring each of the Kubernetes resources we have described, users can leverage Helm as a package manager to deploy and configure WordPress on Kubernetes. To begin, we'll explore a platform called **Artifact Hub** to locate a suitable WordPress Helm chart. After that, we'll deploy WordPress to your Kubernetes cluster using Helm and explore basic Helm features along the way.

Finding a WordPress chart

Helm charts can be made available for consumption by publishing them to a chart repository. A chart repository is a location where packaged charts can be stored and shared. A repository is often hosted as an HTTP server and can take the form of various implementations, including GitHub pages, an Amazon S3 bucket, or a simple web server, such as Apache HTTPD. Recently, repositories can also take the form of OCI registries, allowing users to save and retrieve Helm charts from hosted services such as Docker Hub and Quay.

To use charts from a repository, Helm needs to be configured to use the repository. This can be accomplished by adding repositories using `helm repo add`. One challenge involved with adding repositories is that there are many different chart repositories available for consumption; it may be difficult to locate the particular repository that fits your use case. To make it easier to find chart repositories (and other Kubernetes-related artifacts), the Kubernetes community created a platform called Artifact Hub.

Artifact Hub is a centralized location for upstream Kubernetes artifacts, such as Helm charts, operators, plugins, and more. In this chapter, we will use the Artifact Hub platform to search for WordPress Helm charts. Once an appropriate chart is found, we will add the repository this chart belongs to so that it can be installed.

To begin, interaction with Artifact Hub can be accomplished either from the command line or from a web browser. When using the command line to search for Helm charts, the results that are returned provide a URL to Artifact Hub, which can be used to find additional information on the chart and instructions on how to add its chart repository.

Let's follow this workflow to add a chart repository containing a WordPress chart.

Searching for WordPress charts from the command line

In general, Helm contains two different search commands to assist us in finding Helm charts:

- To search for charts in Artifact Hub, use the following command:

  ```
  $ helm search hub
  ```

  Note that in prior versions of Helm, `helm search hub` referenced a centrally managed public repository of Helm charts maintained by the Helm community called Helm Hub instead of Artifact Hub. Backward compatibility has been retained through the use of the `--endpoint` parameter, which enables users to specify the location of any monocular-based instance, the web search and discovery web application backing Helm Hub.

- To search repositories for a keyword present in a chart, use the following command:

  ```
  $ helm search repo
  ```

  If repositories have not been added previously, users should run the `helm search hub` command to locate Helm charts available across all public chart repositories. Once a repository has been added, users can run `helm search repo` to search across these repositories.

Let's search Artifact Hub for any existing WordPress charts. Each chart in Artifact Hub has a set of keywords that can be searched against. Execute the following command to locate charts containing the `wordpress` keyword:

```
$ helm search hub wordpress
```

Upon running this command, an output similar to the following should be displayed:

```
URL                                                CHART VERSION    APP VERSION      DESCRIPTION
https://artifacthub.io/packages/helm/kube-wordp... 0.1.0            1.1              this is my word
https://artifacthub.io/packages/helm/bitnami/wo... 12.1.6           5.8.0            Web publishing
https://artifacthub.io/packages/helm/groundhog2... 0.4.1            5.8.0-apache     A Helm chart fo
https://artifacthub.io/packages/helm/bitnami-ak... 12.1.1           5.8.0            Web publishing
```

Figure 3.1 – The output from running helm search hub wordpress

Each line of the output returned by this command is a chart from Artifact Hub. The output displays the URL to each chart's Artifact Hub page. Also displayed is the chart version, which represents the latest version of the Helm chart, and the app version, which represents the version of the application that the chart deploys by default. The `helm search hub` command also prints a brief description of each chart.

As you may have noticed, some of the values returned are truncated. This is because the default output of `helm search hub` is `table`, causing the results to be returned in tabular format. By default, columns wider than 50 characters are truncated. This truncation can be avoided by using the `--max-col-width=0` flag.

Try running the following command by including the `--max-col-width` flag to view the untruncated results in tabular format:

```
$ helm search hub wordpress --max-col-width=0
```

Alternatively, users can pass the `--output` flag and specify either `yaml` or `json`, which will print the search results in full.

Try running the previous command again with the `--output yaml` flag:

```
$ helm search hub wordpress --output yaml
```

The result will be in YAML format, similar to the output shown here:

```
- app_version: "1.1"
  description: this is my wordpress package
  url: https://artifacthub.io/packages/helm/kube-wordpress/wordpress
  version: 0.1.0
- app_version: 5.8.0
  description: Web publishing platform for building blogs and websites.
  url: https://artifacthub.io/packages/helm/bitnami/wordpress
  version: 12.1.6
- app_version: 5.8.0-apache
  description: A Helm chart for Wordpress on Kubernetes
  url: https://artifacthub.io/packages/helm/groundhog2k/wordpress
  version: 0.4.1
```

Figure 3.2 – The output for the helm search hub wordpress --output yaml command

For this example, we will choose to install the second chart that was returned in the preceding sample output. To learn more about this chart and how it is installed, visit `https://artifacthub.io/packages/helm/bitnami/wordpress`. We'll explore this link in the next section.

Viewing the WordPress chart in a browser

Using `helm search hub` is the fastest way to search for charts on Artifact Hub. However, it does not provide all of the details needed for installation. Namely, users need to know a chart's repository URL to add its repository and install the chart. A chart's Artifact Hub page can provide this URL, along with other installation details.

Once you have entered the WordPress chart's URL into a browser window, a page similar to the following will be displayed:

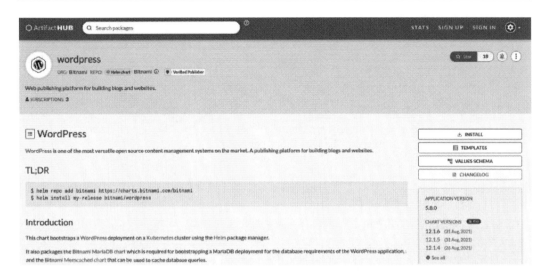

Figure 3.3 – A WordPress Helm chart from Artifact Hub

The WordPress chart's page from Artifact Hub provides many details, including the maintainer of the chart (**Bitnami**, which is a company that provides software packages that can be deployed to different environments) and a brief introduction to the chart (stating that this chart will deploy a WordPress instance to Kubernetes, along with a Bitnami MariaDB chart as a dependency). The web page also provides installation details, including the chart's supported values, which are used to configure the installation, along with Bitnami's chart repository URL. These installation details give users the ability to add this repository and install the WordPress chart.

Under the **TL;DR** heading, you should see a `helm repo add` command. This is the command that you need to run to add the Bitnami chart repository, which is the repository that contains the WordPress chart we are interested in installing.

Bitnami repository chart retention policy

Recent changes within the Bitnami Helm community have resulted in charts being removed from the Bitnami repository 6 months after their publication date. Aligning to the most recent versions of software packages is a recommended practice so that the most recent set of features and security remediations are included. However, since the remainder of the exercises specify specific chart versions to support the stability of the tested integrations, an alternate repository must be utilized.

Fortunately, another repository index has been provided that includes all of the Bitnami charts without the retention policy of the default index, which will be described in the next section. You will learn more about repository indexes by creating and managing your own repository in *Chapter 7, Helm Lifecycle Hooks*.

Adding the full Bitnami repository

With an understanding of the considerations as they relate to charts within the Bitnami repository, let's add the repository that allows us to specify specific chart versions without concerns that they may be removed in the future. The only difference in the `helm repo add` command is the URL of the repository.

Let's add the repository now and verify that we can interact with its contents:

1. Add the full Bitnami chart repository:

    ```
    $ helm repo add bitnami https://raw.githubusercontent.
    com/bitnami/charts/archive-full-index/bitnami
    ```

2. Verify that the chart has been added by running `helm repo list`:

    ```
    $ helm repo list
    NAME           URL
    bitnami        https://raw.githubusercontent.com/bitnami/
    charts/archive-full-index/bitnami
    ```

    We can do a little more now that we have added the repository.

3. Run the following command to view charts from locally configured repositories that contain the `bitnami` keyword:

    ```
    $ helm search repo bitnami --output yaml
    ```

A shortened list of the results returned is shown in the following output:

```
- app_version: 0.0.9
  description: DEPRECATED Chart with custom templates used in Bitnami charts.
  name: bitnami/bitnami-common
  version: 0.0.9
- app_version: 2.1.2
  description: Apache Airflow is a platform to programmatically author, schedule and
    monitor workflows.
  name: bitnami/airflow
  version: 10.3.1
- app_version: 2.4.48
  description: Chart for Apache HTTP Server
  name: bitnami/apache
  version: 8.6.3
- app_version: 2.0.5
  description: Declarative, GitOps continuous delivery tool for Kubernetes.
  name: bitnami/argo-cd
  version: 1.0.3
- app_version: 3.1.18
  description: ASP.NET Core is an open-source framework created by Microsoft for building
    cloud-enabled, modern applications.
  name: bitnami/aspnet-core
  version: 1.3.16
```

Figure 3.4 – The output for the helm search repo bitnami --output yaml command

Similar to the `helm search hub` command, the `helm search repo` command takes a keyword as an argument. Using `bitnami` as a keyword will return all the charts in the `bitnami` repository, as well as charts outside of that repository that may also contain the `bitnami` keyword.

To ensure that you now have access to the WordPress chart, run the following `helm search repo` command with the `wordpress` argument:

```
$ helm search repo wordpress
```

The output will display the WordPress chart that you found on Artifact Hub and observed in your browser:

```
NAME                    CHART VERSION    APP VERSION    DESCRIPTION
bitnami/wordpress       12.1.4           5.8.0          Web publishing
```

Figure 3.5 – The output for the helm search repo wordpress command

The value in the NAME field before the slash (/) indicates the name of the repository containing the Helm chart that was returned. The latest version of the WordPress chart from the `bitnami` repository, at the time of writing, is version `12.1.6`. This is the version that will be used for the installation. Previous versions can be queried by passing the `--versions` flag to the `search` command:

```
helm search repo wordpress --versions
```

You should then see a new line for each version of the available WordPress charts:

```
NAME                    CHART VERSION    APP VERSION    DESCRIPTION
bitnami/wordpress       12.1.6           5.8.0          Web publishing
bitnami/wordpress       12.1.5           5.8.0          Web publishing
bitnami/wordpress       12.1.4           5.8.0          Web publishing
bitnami/wordpress       12.1.3           5.8.0          Web publishing
```

Figure 3.6 – The version lists for WordPress charts in the bitnami repository

Now that a WordPress chart has been identified and the chart's repository has been added, we will explore how to use the command line to find out more about the chart so that you can install it.

Showing the WordPress chart information from the command line

You can find a lot of important details about a Helm chart on its Artifact Hub page. Once a chart's repository is added locally, this information (and more) can also be viewed from the command line with the following four `helm show` subcommands:

- Display the chart's metadata (or chart definition):

  ```
  helm show chart
  ```

- Display the chart's README file:

  ```
  helm show readme
  ```

- Display the chart's values:

  ```
  helm show values
  ```

- Display the chart's definition, README files, and values:

  ```
  helm show all
  ```

Let's use these commands with the Bitnami WordPress chart. In each of these commands, the chart should be referenced as `bitnami/wordpress`. Note that we will be passing the `--version` flag to retrieve information about version 12.1.6 of this chart. If this flag is omitted, information from the latest version of the chart will be returned.

Run the `helm show chart` command to retrieve the metadata for the chart:

```
$ helm show chart bitnami/wordpress --version 12.1.6
```

The result of this command will be the **chart definition** of the WordPress chart. A chart definition describes information such as the chart's version, its dependencies, keywords, and maintainers:

```
annotations:
  category: CMS
apiVersion: v2
appVersion: 5.8.0
dependencies:
- condition: mariadb.enabled
  name: mariadb
  repository: https://charts.bitnami.com/bitnami
  version: 9.x.x
- condition: memcached.enabled
  name: memcached
  repository: https://charts.bitnami.com/bitnami
  version: 5.x.x
- name: common
  repository: https://charts.bitnami.com/bitnami
  tags:
  - bitnami-common
  version: 1.x.x
description: Web publishing platform for building blogs and websites.
home: https://github.com/bitnami/charts/tree/master/bitnami/wordpress
icon: https://bitnami.com/assets/stacks/wordpress/img/wordpress-stack-220x234.png
keywords:
- application
- blog
- cms
- http
- php
- web
- wordpress
maintainers:
- email: containers@bitnami.com
  name: Bitnami
name: wordpress
sources:
- https://github.com/bitnami/bitnami-docker-wordpress
- https://wordpress.org/
version: 12.1.6
```

Figure 3.7 – The wordpress chart definition

Run the `helm show readme` command to view the chart's README file from the command line:

```
$ helm show readme bitnami/wordpress --version 12.1.6
```

The results of this command may look familiar since a chart's README file is also displayed on its Artifact Hub page. Using this option from the command line provides a quick way to view the README file without having to open a browser:

```
# WordPress

[WordPress](https://wordpress.org/) is one of the most versatile open source

## TL;DR

```console
$ helm repo add bitnami https://charts.bitnami.com/bitnami
$ helm install my-release bitnami/wordpress
```

Introduction

This chart bootstraps a [WordPress](https://github.com/bitnami/bitnami-docke

It also packages the [Bitnami MariaDB chart](https://github.com/bitnami/char
 application, and the [Bitnami Memcached chart](https://github.com/bitnami/c

Bitnami charts can be used with [Kubeapps](https://kubeapps.com/) for deploy
heus on top of the [BKPR](https://kubeprod.io/).
```

Figure 3.8 – The wordpress chart's README file shown in the command line

We can use `helm show values` to inspect a chart's values. Values serve as parameters that users can provide to customize a chart installation. We will run this command later in this chapter in the *Creating a values file for configuration* section when we install the WordPress chart.

Finally, `helm show all` aggregates all of the information from the previous three commands together. Use this command if you want to inspect all of a chart's details at once.

Now that we have found and inspected a WordPress chart, let's set up a Kubernetes environment where we can later install this chart.

Creating a Kubernetes environment

To create a Kubernetes environment in this chapter, we will use minikube. We learned how to install minikube in *Chapter 2, Preparing a Kubernetes and Helm Environment*.

Follow these steps to set up Kubernetes:

1. Start your Kubernetes cluster by running the following command:

   ```
   $ minikube start
   ```

2. After a short amount of time, you should see a line in the output that resembles the following:

   ```
   Done! kubectl is now configured to use "minikube" cluster
   and "default" namespace by default
   ```

3. Once the minikube cluster is up and running, create a dedicated namespace for this chapter's exercise. Run the following command to create a namespace called `chapter3`:

   ```
   $ kubectl create namespace chapter3
   ```

Now that the cluster setup is complete, let's begin the process of installing the WordPress chart to your Kubernetes cluster.

Installing a WordPress chart

Installing a Helm chart is a simple process that should begin with inspecting a chart's values. In the next section, we will inspect the values that are available in the WordPress chart and describe how to create a file that allows for customizing the installation. Finally, we will install the chart and access the WordPress application.

Creating a values file for configuration

You can override the values defined in charts by providing a YAML-formatted `values` file. To create a `values` file, you need to inspect the supported values that the chart provides. This can be done by running the `helm show values` command, as explained earlier.

Run the following command to inspect the WordPress chart's values:

```
$ helm show values bitnami/wordpress --version 12.1.6
```

The result of this command should be a long list of possible values that you can set, many of which already have default values set:

```
## @section WordPress Image parameters

## Bitnami WordPress image
## ref: https://hub.docker.com/r/bitnami/wordpress/tags/
## @param image.registry WordPress image registry
## @param image.repository WordPress image repository
## @param image.tag WordPress image tag (immutable tags are recommended)
## @param image.pullPolicy WordPress image pull policy
## @param image.pullSecrets WordPress image pull secrets
## @param image.debug Enable image debug mode
##
image:
  registry: docker.io
  repository: bitnami/wordpress
  tag: 5.8.0-debian-10-r24
  ## Specify a imagePullPolicy
  ## Defaults to 'Always' if image tag is 'latest', else set to 'IfNotPresent'
  ## ref: http://kubernetes.io/docs/user-guide/images/#pre-pulling-images
  ##
  pullPolicy: IfNotPresent
  ## Optionally specify an array of imagePullSecrets.
  ## Secrets must be manually created in the namespace.
  ## ref: https://kubernetes.io/docs/tasks/configure-pod-container/pull-image-
  ## e.g:
  ## pullSecrets:
  ##   - myRegistryKeySecretName
  ##
  pullSecrets: []
  ## Enable debug mode
  ##
  debug: false
```

Figure 3.9 – A list of values generated by running helm show values

The preceding output shows a portion of the WordPress chart's values. Many of these properties already have defaults set, meaning these values will represent how the chart is configured if they are not overridden. For example, if the values under the image map are not overridden, the WordPress chart will use the bitnami/wordpress container image from the docker.io registry against the 5.8.0-debian-10-r24 tag.

Lines in the chart's values that begin with a hash sign (#) are comments. Comments can be used to explain a value or a block of values, or they can be used to unset them. As shown in the preceding example, comments were used to document each of the image-related values.

If we explore the helm show values output further, we can find values that pertain to configuring the WordPress blog's metadata:

```
## @param wordpressUsername WordPress username
##
wordpressUsername: user
## @param wordpressPassword WordPress user password
## Defaults to a random 10-character alphanumeric string if not set
##
wordpressPassword: ""
## @param existingSecret Name of existing secret containing WordPress credentials
## NOTE: Must contain key `wordpress-password`
## NOTE: When it's set, the `wordpressPassword` parameter is ignored
##
existingSecret: ""
## @param wordpressEmail WordPress user email
##
wordpressEmail: user@example.com
## @param wordpressFirstName WordPress user first name
##
wordpressFirstName: FirstName
## @param wordpressLastName WordPress user last name
##
wordpressLastName: LastName
## @param wordpressBlogName Blog name
##
wordpressBlogName: User's Blog!
```

Figure 3.10 – The values returned by running the helm show values command

As you can see, these values are used to create a WordPress user and create a name for your blog. Let's override them by creating a `values` file. Create a new file on your machine called `wordpress-values.yaml`. In that file, enter the following content:

```
wordpressUsername: helm-user
wordpressPassword: my-password
wordpressEmail: helm-user@example.com
wordpressFirstName: Helm_is
wordpressLastName: Fun
wordpressBlogName: Learn Helm!
```

Feel free to get more creative with these values if you'd like. Continuing down the list of values from `helm show values`, there is one more important value that should be added to your `values` file before starting the installation, as shown here:

```
## @section Traffic Exposure Parameters

## WordPress service parameters
##
service:
  ## @param service.type WordPress service type
  ##
  type: LoadBalancer
```

Figure 3.11 – The LoadBalancer value returned after running helm show values

To simplify the installation, we are going to update this value (referred to as `service.type`) to `NodePort`. We could leave this set to `LoadBalancer`, but this would require you to use the `minikube tunnel` command to reach the service. By setting this to `NodePort` instead, you will be able to directly access WordPress against a local port.

Add this value to your `wordpress-values.yaml` file:

```
service:
  type: NodePort
```

Once this value has been added to your `values` file, your complete `wordpress-values.yaml` file should look as follows:

```
wordpressUsername: helm-user
wordpressPassword: my-password
wordpressEmail: helm-user@example.com
wordpressFirstName: Helm_is
wordpressLastName: Fun
wordpressBlogName: Learn Helm!
service:
  type: NodePort
```

Now that the `values` file is complete, let's run the installation.

Running the installation

We use `helm install` to install a Helm chart. The standard syntax is as follows:

```
helm install [NAME] [CHART] [flags]
```

The `NAME` parameter is the name you would like to give your Helm release. A **release** captures the Kubernetes resources that were installed with a chart and tracks an application's life cycle. We will explore how releases work throughout this chapter.

The `CHART` parameter is the name of the Helm chart that is installed. Charts from a repository can be installed using `<repo name>/<chart name>`.

The `flags` option in `helm install` allows you to further customize the installation. `flags` allows users to define and override values, specify the namespace to work against, and more. The list of flags can be viewed by running `helm install --help`. We can pass `--help` to other commands to view their usage and supported options.

Now that we have a proper understanding of the usage of `helm install`, let's run the following command:

```
$ helm install wordpress bitnami/wordpress --values=wordpress-values.yaml --namespace chapter3 --version 12.1.6
```

This command installs a new release called `wordpress` using the `bitnami/wordpress` Helm chart. It uses the values defined in the `wordpress-values.yaml` file to customize the installation, and the chart is installed in the `chapter3` namespace. Version `12.1.6` of the chart is deployed, as defined by the `--version` flag. Helm will install the latest cached version of the Helm chart without this flag.

If the chart's installation is successful, you should see the following output:

```
NAME: wordpress
LAST DEPLOYED: Mon Sep  6 13:03:45 2021
NAMESPACE: chapter3
STATUS: deployed
REVISION: 1
TEST SUITE: None
NOTES:
** Please be patient while the chart is being deployed **

Your WordPress site can be accessed through the following DNS name from within your

    wordpress.chapter3.svc.cluster.local (port 80)

To access your WordPress site from outside the cluster follow the steps below:

1. Get the WordPress URL by running these commands:

    export NODE_PORT=$(kubectl get --namespace chapter3 -o jsonpath="{.spec.ports[0].
    export NODE_IP=$(kubectl get nodes --namespace chapter3 -o jsonpath="{.items[0].s
    echo "WordPress URL: http://$NODE_IP:$NODE_PORT/"
    echo "WordPress Admin URL: http://$NODE_IP:$NODE_PORT/admin"

2. Open a browser and access WordPress using the obtained URL.

3. Login with the following credentials below to see your blog:

    echo Username: helm-user
    echo Password: $(kubectl get secret --namespace chapter3 wordpress -o jsonpath="{.
```

Figure 3.12 – The output of a successful WordPress chart installation

This output displays information about the installation, including the name of the release, the time it was deployed, the namespace it was installed to, the status of the deployment (which is `deployed`), and the revision number (which is set to `1` since this is the initial installation of the release).

The output also displays a list of notes related to the installation. Notes are used to provide users with additional information about their installation. In the case of the WordPress chart, these notes provide information about how to access the WordPress application. While these notes appear directly after installation, they can be retrieved at any time with the `helm get notes` command, as explained in the next section.

With your first Helm installation complete, let's inspect the release to observe the resources and configurations that were applied.

Inspecting your release

One of the easiest ways to inspect a release and verify its installation is to list all the Helm releases in a given namespace. For this to be achieved, Helm provides the `list` subcommand.

Run the following command to view the list of releases in the `chapter3` namespace:

```
$ helm list --namespace chapter3
```

You should see only one release in this namespace, as shown here:

```
NAME         NAMESPACE    REVISION    UPDATED
wordpress    chapter3     1           2021-09-06 13:03:45.905520214 -0500 CDT
```

Figure 3.13 – The output from the helm list command that lists the Helm releases

The `list` subcommand provides the following information:

- The release name
- The release namespace
- The latest revision number of the release
- A timestamp of the latest revision
- The release status
- The chart name
- The application version

Note that the status, chart name, and application version have been truncated in the preceding output.

While the `list` subcommand is useful for providing high-level release information, there are additional items that users may want to know about a particular release. Helm provides the `get` subcommand to provide more information about a release.

The following commands can be used to provide a set of detailed release information:

- To return all the hooks for a named release, run the following command:

    ```
    helm get hooks
    ```

- To return the manifest for a named release, run the following command:

  ```
  helm get manifest
  ```

- To return the notes for a named release, run the following command:

  ```
  helm get notes
  ```

- To return the values for a named release, run the following command:

  ```
  helm get values
  ```

- To return all the information about a named release, run the following command:

  ```
  helm get all
  ```

The first command from the preceding list, `helm get hooks`, is used to display the hooks for a given release. Hooks will be explored in more detail in *Chapter 7, Helm Lifecycle Hooks*, when you build and test a Helm chart. For now, hooks can be thought of as the actions that Helm performs during certain phases of an application's life cycle. This WordPress installation did not create any hooks, so let's move on to the next command.

The `helm get manifest` command can be used to get a list of the Kubernetes resources that were created as part of the installation. Run the following command:

```
$ helm get manifest wordpress --namespace chapter3
```

After you run this command, you'll see the following Kubernetes manifests:

- Two `Secrets` for MariaDB and WordPress credentials
- Two `ConfigMaps` (the first is used to configure the WordPress application, while the second is used for testing, which is performed by chart developers and so can be ignored).
- One `PersistentVolumeClaim` for persisting MariaDB data.
- Two `Services` for MariaDB and WordPress
- One `Deployment` for WordPress
- One `StatefulSet` for MariaDB
- One `ServiceAccount` for MariaDB

From this output, you can observe where your values had an effect when they configured the Kubernetes resources. One example to note is within the WordPress service, where `type` has been set to `NodePort`:

```
# Source: wordpress/templates/svc.yaml
apiVersion: v1
kind: Service
metadata:
  name: wordpress
  namespace: "chapter3"
  labels:
    app.kubernetes.io/name: wordpress
    helm.sh/chart: wordpress-12.1.6
    app.kubernetes.io/instance: wordpress
    app.kubernetes.io/managed-by: Helm
spec:
  type: NodePort
  externalTrafficPolicy: "Cluster"
  ports:
    - name: http
      port: 80
      protocol: TCP
      targetPort: http
    - name: https
      port: 443
      protocol: TCP
      targetPort: https
  selector:
    app.kubernetes.io/name: wordpress
    app.kubernetes.io/instance: wordpress
```

Figure 3.14 – Setting the Service type to NodePort

You can also observe the other values that we set for the WordPress user. These values are defined as environment variables in the WordPress deployment, as shown in the following screenshot:

```
- name: WORDPRESS_USERNAME
  value: "helm-user"
- name: WORDPRESS_PASSWORD
  valueFrom:
    secretKeyRef:
      name: wordpress
      key: wordpress-password
- name: WORDPRESS_EMAIL
  value: "helm-user@example.com"
- name: WORDPRESS_FIRST_NAME
  value: "Helm_is"
- name: WORDPRESS_LAST_NAME
  value: "Fun"
- name: WORDPRESS_HTACCESS_OVERRIDE_NONE
  value: "no"
- name: WORDPRESS_ENABLE_HTACCESS_PERSISTENCE
  value: "no"
- name: WORDPRESS_BLOG_NAME
  value: "Learn Helm!"
```

Figure 3.15 – Values set as environment variables

The rest of the default values provided by the chart were left untouched. Those defaults have been applied to the Kubernetes resources and can be observed through the `helm get manifest` command. If these values had been changed, the Kubernetes resources would have been configured differently.

Let's move on to the next `get` command. The `helm get notes` command is used to display the notes from a Helm release. As you may recall, the release notes were displayed when the WordPress chart was installed. Notes are chart-specific and, in the case of WordPress, provide important information about accessing the application and can be displayed once again by running the following command:

```
$ helm get notes wordpress --namespace chapter3
```

The next command is `helm get values`, and it is useful for recalling the values that were used for a given release. Run the following command to view the values that were provided in the `wordpress` release:

```
$ helm get values wordpress --namespace chapter3
```

The result of this command should look familiar as they should match the values specified in the `wordpress-values.yaml` file:

```
USER-SUPPLIED VALUES:
service:
  type: NodePort
wordpressBlogName: Learn Helm!
wordpressEmail: helm-user@example.com
wordpressFirstName: Helm_is
wordpressLastName: Fun
wordpressPassword: my-password
wordpressUsername: helm-user
```

Figure 3.16 – User-supplied values in the WordPress release

While recalling the user-supplied values is useful, it may be necessary to return all of the values used by a release, including the defaults. This can be accomplished by passing in an additional `--all` flag, as shown in the following command:

```
$ helm get values wordpress --all --namespace chapter3
```

For this chart, the output will be lengthy. The first several values are shown in the following output:

```
COMPUTED VALUES:
affinity: {}
allowEmptyPassword: true
allowOverrideNone: false
apacheConfiguration: ""
args: []
autoscaling:
  enabled: false
  maxReplicas: 11
  minReplicas: 1
  targetCPU: 50
  targetMemory: 50
clusterDomain: cluster.local
command: []
common:
  exampleValue: common-chart
  global:
    imagePullSecrets: []
    imageRegistry: ""
    storageClass: ""
```

Figure 3.17 – A subset of all the values for the WordPress release

Finally, Helm provides a `helm get all` command, which can be used to aggregate all of the information from the various `helm get` commands:

```
$ helm get all wordpress -n chapter3
```

In the preceding command, we snuck in the `-n` flag in place of `--namespace`. From here on out, we will use the `-n` flag to provide the namespace that Helm should operate within.

Besides the commands provided by Helm, the `kubectl` CLI can also be used to inspect an installation more closely. For example, you could return the deployments that Helm created by running the following command:

```
$ kubectl get deployments -l app.kubernetes.io/name=wordpress
-n chapter3
```

You'll find that the following deployment exists in the `chapter3` namespace:

```
NAME        READY   UP-TO-DATE   AVAILABLE   AGE
wordpress   1/1     1            1           3h3m
```

Figure 3.18 – The wordpress deployment in the chapter3 namespace

In the preceding command, we filtered the deployments by using the `-l app.kubernetes.io/name=wordpress` parameter. Many Helm charts add the `app.kubernetes.io/name` label (or a similar label) on the resources they create. You can use this label to filter resources using `kubectl` so that only resources that Helm created are returned.

Choosing between --set and --values

When we installed WordPress earlier, we used the `--values` flag to pass parameters to the Helm chart. However, there are two ways to pass values:

- To pass a value explicitly from the command line, use the following command:

    ```
    --set
    ```

- To specify values from a YAML file or URL, use the following command:

    ```
    --values
    ```

In this book, we will treat the `--values` flag as the preferred method of configuring chart values. The reason for this is that it is easier to configure multiple values when they are contained in a YAML file. Maintaining a `values` file also makes it simple to save these assets in a **Source Code Management** (**SCM**) system, such as `Git`, which allows installations to be easily reproducible. However, take note that sensitive values, such as passwords, should never be stored in a source control repository. When secrets need to be provided, the recommended approach is to use the `--set` flag to prevent them from being committed to source control. We will cover the topic of security in greater detail in *Chapter 12, Helm Security Considerations*.

The `--set` flag is used to pass values directly from the command line. This is an acceptable method for simple values, as well as for when there are only a small number of values that need to be configured. Complex values, such as lists and maps, can be challenging to input when using the `--set` flag, so it is not preferred. There are other related flags, such as `--set-file` and `--set-string`. The `--set-file` flag is used to pass along a file that has configured values in a `key1=val1` and `key2=val2` format, while the `--set-string` flag is used to set all the values provided in a `key1=val1` and `key2=val2` format as strings.

Now, let's explore the WordPress application that we just installed.

Accessing the WordPress application

The WordPress chart's release notes provided four commands that you can run to access your WordPress application (you can recall the full release notes using `helm get notes wordpress -n chapter3`). Run the four commands that were provided from the notes:

- For macOS or Linux, run the following:

  ```
  export NODE_PORT=$(kubectl get --namespace chapter3 -o jsonpath="{.spec.ports[0].nodePort}" services wordpress)
  export NODE_IP=$(kubectl get nodes --namespace chapter3 -o jsonpath="{.items[0].status.addresses[0].address}")
  echo "WordPress URL: http://$NODE_IP:$NODE_PORT/"
  echo "WordPress Admin URL: http://$NODE_IP:$NODE_PORT/admin"
  ```

- For Windows PowerShell, run the following:

  ```
  $NODE_PORT = kubectl get --namespace chapter3 -o jsonpath="{.spec.ports[0].nodePort}" services wordpress | Out-String
  $NODE_IP = kubectl get nodes --namespace chapter3 -o jsonpath="{.items[0].status.addresses[0].address}" | Out-String
  echo "WordPress URL: http://$NODE_IP:$NODE_PORT/"
  echo "WordPress Admin URL: http://$NODE_IP:$NODE_PORT/admin"
  ```

After defining the two environment variables based on the series of `kubectl` queries, the resulting `echo` commands will reveal the URLs to access WordPress. The first URL is to view the home page and is where visitors will access your site. The second URL is to reach the admin console, which is used by website administrators to configure and manage the site's content.

Paste the first URL into a browser. You should be presented with a page that looks similar to the following:

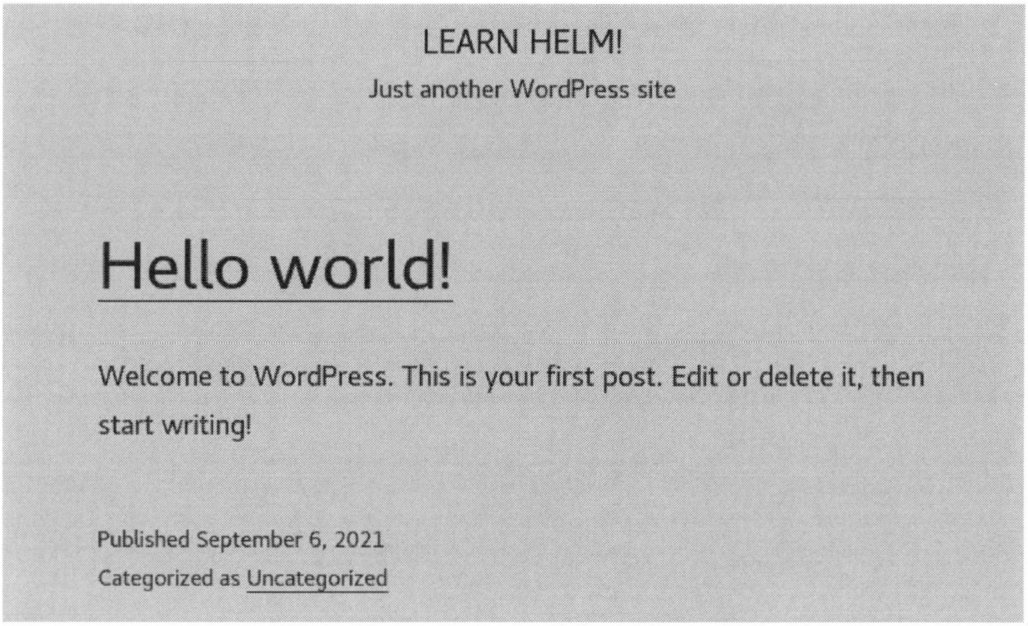

LEARN HELM!
Just another WordPress site

Hello world!

Welcome to WordPress. This is your first post. Edit or delete it, then start writing!

Published September 6, 2021
Categorized as Uncategorized

Figure 3.19 – The WordPress blog page

Several portions of this page may look familiar to you. First, at the top of the screen, the title of the blog is **Learn Helm!**, which is the string you gave the `wordpressBlogName` value previously during installation. You can also see this value at the bottom left-hand side of the page.

Another value that affected the customization of the home page is `wordpressUsername`. If you click on the **Hello world!** link, you'll find that the author of that post is `helm-user`:

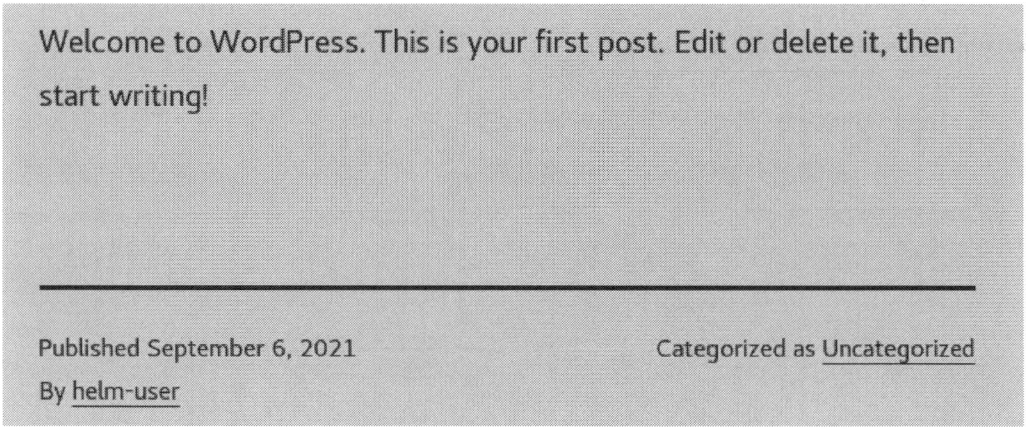

Welcome to WordPress. This is your first post. Edit or delete it, then start writing!

Published September 6, 2021   Categorized as Uncategorized
By helm-user

Figure 3.20 – The "Hello world!" post

If you had provided a different value for wordpressUsername, then the author here would appear differently as well.

The second link provided by the previous set of commands is for accessing the admin console. Paste the link from the second echo command into a browser. You should be presented with the following login screen:

Figure 3.21 – The WordPress admin console login page

To log into the admin console, enter the wordpressUsername and wordpressPassword values that you provided during the installation. If you used the same values we specified earlier, then the username will be helm-user and the password will be my-password.

Once you're authenticated, the admin console dashboard will be displayed, as shown here:

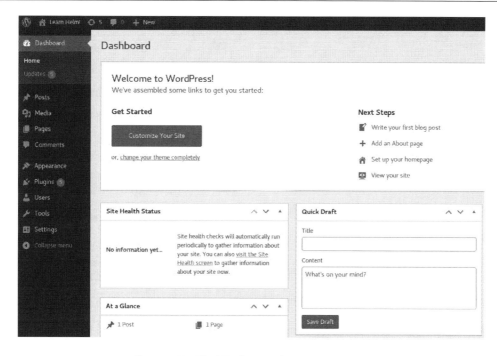

Figure 3.22 – The WordPress admin console page

If you were a WordPress administrator, this is where you could configure your site, write posts, and manage plugins. If you click on the top-right link that says **Howdy, helm-user** (not visible in the preceding screenshot), you will be directed to the `helm-user` profile page. From there, you can see several of the other values that you provided during the installation, as shown in the following screenshot:

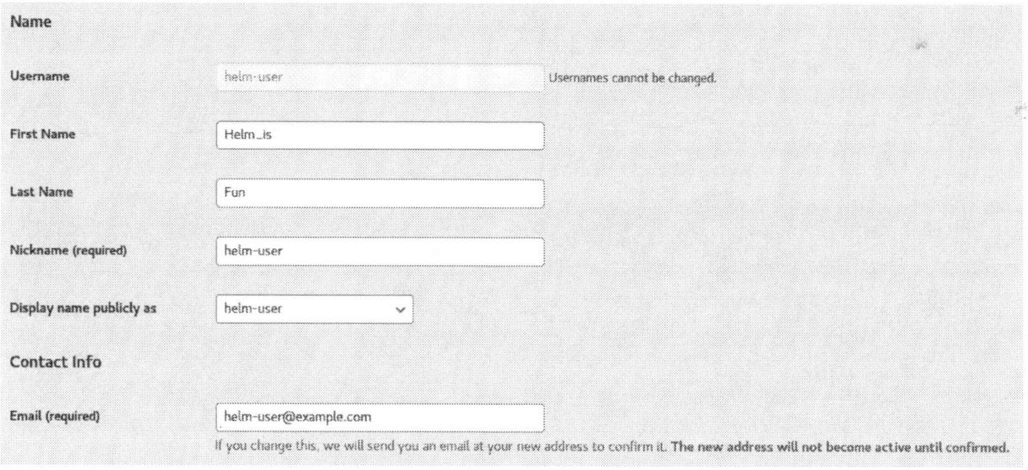

Figure 3.23 – The WordPress profile page

The **First Name**, **Last Name**, and **Email** fields refer to their corresponding `wordpressFirstname`, `wordpressLastname`, and `wordpressEmail` Helm values.

Feel free to continue exploring your WordPress instance. Once you are finished, continue to the next section to learn how to upgrade a Helm release.

Upgrading the WordPress release

Upgrading a release refers to the process of modifying the release's values or updating the chart to a newer version. In this section, we will upgrade the WordPress release by adding a couple more values to the installation.

Modifying the Helm values

Oftentimes, when deploying applications to Kubernetes, you will want to run multiple replicas of the application to provide high availability and reduce the load on a single instance. Helm charts often provide some sort of replica-related value for configuring the number of pod replicas to deploy. A quick browse through the output of the `helm show values bitnami/wordpress --version 12.1.6` command shows that you can increase WordPress replicas by using the `replicaCount` value:

```
## @param replicaCount Number of WordPress replicas to deploy
## NOTE: ReadWriteMany PVC(s) are required if replicaCount > 1
##
replicaCount: 1
```

Figure 3.24 – replicaCount in the helm show values command

Add the following line to your `wordpress-values.yaml` file to increase the number of replicas from 1 to 2:

```
replicaCount: 2
```

Let's add another value to set the resource requests. Looking through the `helm show values` output, you can see that this chart provides a `resources` map within its set of values:

```
## WordPress containers' resource requests and limits
## ref: http://kubernetes.io/docs/user-guide/compute-resources/
## @param resources.limits The resources limits for the WordPress container
## @param resources.requests [object] The requested resources for the WordPress container
##
resources:
  limits: {}
  requests:
    memory: 512Mi
    cpu: 300m
```

Figure 3.25 – The values under the resources stanza

Nested values such as `resources` are YAML maps (or objects), and they help provide a logical grouping of properties. Under the `resources` map is a `requests` map, which is used to configure the `memory` and `cpu` values that Kubernetes will allocate to the WordPress application. Let's modify these values to decrease the memory request to `256Mi` (256 mebibytes) and the `cpu` request to `100m` (100 millicores). Add these modifications to the `wordpress-values.yaml` file, as shown here:

```
resources:
  requests:
    memory: 256Mi
    cpu: 100m
```

After defining these two new values, your entire `wordpress-values.yaml` file will look as follows:

```
wordpressUsername: helm-user
wordpressPassword: my-password
wordpressEmail: helm-user@example.com
wordpressFirstName: Helm_is
wordpressLastName: Fun
wordpressBlogName: Learn Helm!
service:
  type: NodePort
replicaCount: 2
resources:
  requests:
    memory: 256Mi
    cpu: 100m
```

Once the `wordpress-values.yaml` file has been updated with these new values, you can run the `helm upgrade` command to upgrade the release, as we will discuss in the next section.

Running the upgrade

The `helm upgrade` command is almost identical to the `helm install` command in basic syntax, as illustrated in the following example:

```
helm upgrade [RELEASE] [CHART] [flags]
```

While `helm install` expects you to provide a name for a new release, `helm upgrade` expects you to provide the name of an already-existing release that should be upgraded. Alternatively, you can pass the `--install` flag, which instructs Helm to perform an installation instead if the release name you provide does not exist.

Values defined in a `values` file can be provided using the `--values` flag, identical to that of the `helm install` command. Run the following command to upgrade the WordPress release with the new set of values:

```
$ helm upgrade wordpress bitnami/wordpress --values wordpress-
values.yaml -n chapter3 --version 12.1.6
```

Once this command has been executed, you should see an output similar to that of `helm install`. You should also notice that the `REVISION` field now says 2:

```
Release "wordpress" has been upgraded. Happy Helming!
NAME: wordpress
LAST DEPLOYED: Mon Sep  6 19:15:17 2021
NAMESPACE: chapter3
STATUS: deployed
REVISION: 2
TEST SUITE: None
NOTES:
** Please be patient while the chart is being deployed **

Your WordPress site can be accessed through the following DNS name from within your cluster:

    wordpress.chapter3.svc.cluster.local (port 80)

To access your WordPress site from outside the cluster follow the steps below:

1. Get the WordPress URL by running these commands:

   export NODE_PORT=$(kubectl get --namespace chapter3 -o jsonpath="{.spec.ports[0].nodePort}
   export NODE_IP=$(kubectl get nodes --namespace chapter3 -o jsonpath="{.items[0].status.add
   echo "WordPress URL: http://$NODE_IP:$NODE_PORT/"
   echo "WordPress Admin URL: http://$NODE_IP:$NODE_PORT/admin"

2. Open a browser and access WordPress using the obtained URL.

3. Login with the following credentials below to see your blog:

   echo Username: helm-user
   echo Password: $(kubectl get secret --namespace chapter3 wordpress -o jsonpath="{.data.word
```

Figure 3.26 – The output for helm upgrade

You should also see that the `wordpress` pods have restarted if you run the following command:

```
$ kubectl get pods -n chapter3
```

In Kubernetes, new pods are created when their pod template is modified. The same behavior can be observed in Helm. The values that were added during the upgrade introduced a configuration change to the WordPress pod template. As a result, new WordPress pods were created with the updated configuration. These changes can be observed using the same `helm get manifest` and `kubectl get deployment` commands that were used earlier in this chapter.

In the next section, we'll perform a couple more upgrades to demonstrate how values can sometimes behave differently during an upgrade.

Reusing and resetting values during an upgrade

In addition to `--set` and `--values`, which are present in both `helm install` and `helm upgrade`, the `helm upgrade` command includes two additional values-related flags.

Let's look at these flags now:

- `--reuse-values`: When upgrading, reuse the last release's values
- `--reset-values`: When upgrading, reset the values to the chart defaults

If an upgrade is performed without providing values with the `--set` or `--values` flags, then the `--reuse-values` flag is applied by default. In other words, the same values that were used by the previous release will be used again during the upgrade if no values are provided. Alternatively, if at least one value is provided with `--set` or `--values`, then the `--reset-values` flag is applied by default. Let's run through an example:

1. Run another `upgrade` command without specifying any values:

   ```
   $ helm upgrade wordpress bitnami/wordpress -n chapter3
   --version 12.1.6
   ```

2. Run the `helm get values` command to inspect the values used in the upgrade:

   ```
   $ helm get values wordpress -n chapter3
   ```

   Notice that the values displayed are identical to the previous upgrade:

   ```
   USER-SUPPLIED VALUES:
   replicaCount: 2
   resources:
     requests:
       cpu: 100m
       memory: 256Mi
   service:
     type: NodePort
   wordpressBlogName: Learn Helm!
   wordpressEmail: helm-user@example.com
   wordpressFirstName: Helm_is
   wordpressLastName: Fun
   wordpressPassword: my-password
   wordpressUsername: helm-user
   ```

   Figure 3.27 – The output of the helm get values command

Different behavior can be observed when values are provided during an upgrade. If values are passed via the `--set` or `--values` flags, all of the chart's values that are not provided are reset to their defaults. Let's see this in action.

3. Run another upgrade by providing a smaller set of values with the `--set` flag:

   ```
   $ helm upgrade wordpress bitnami/wordpress --set
   replicaCount=1 --set wordpressUsername=helm-user --set
   wordpressPassword=my-password -n chapter3 --version
   12.1.6
   ```

4. After the upgrade, run the `helm get values` command:

   ```
   $ helm get values wordpress -n chapter3
   ```

The output will declare that you have only provided three values, as opposed to the many that you originally declared in the `wordpress-values.yaml` file:

```
USER-SUPPLIED VALUES:
replicaCount: 1
wordpressPassword: my-password
wordpressUsername: helm-user
```

Figure 3.28 – The updated user-supplied values

To prevent confusion during your upgrades and to simplify how values are managed, try to manage all of your values in a `values` file. This provides a more declarative approach, and it makes it clear which values will be applied each time you upgrade.

If you have been following along with each of the commands provided in this chapter, you should now have four revisions of the WordPress release in your environment. This fourth revision is not quite in the way we want the application to be configured since most of the values were set back to their defaults by the most recent upgrade. In the next section, we will explore how the WordPress release can be rolled back to the stable version that contained the set of desired values.

Rolling back the WordPress release

While moving forward is preferred, there are some occasions where it makes more sense to return to a previous version of the application. The `helm rollback` command exists to satisfy this use case. Let's describe how to roll back the WordPress release to a previous state.

Inspecting the WordPress history

Every Helm release has a history of **revisions**. A revision is used to track the values, Kubernetes resources, and the chart version that were used in a particular release version. A new revision is created when a chart is installed, upgraded, or rolled back. Revision data is saved in Kubernetes Secrets by default (other options are ConfigMaps, local memory, or a PostgreSQL database, as determined by the

`HELM_DRIVER` environment variable). This allows your Helm release to be managed and interacted with by different users on the Kubernetes cluster, provided they have the appropriate **Role-Based Access Control** (**RBAC**) permissions to view or modify resources in your namespace. `Secrets` containing the revisions can be observed by using `kubectl` to get them from the `chapter3` namespace:

```
$ kubectl get secrets -n chapter3
```

This command will return all of the secrets within the namespace, but you should see these four in the output:

```
sh.helm.release.v1.wordpress.v1
Sh.helm.release.v1.wordpress.v2
sh.helm.release.v1.wordpress.v3
sh.helm.release.v1.wordpress.v4
```

Each of these `Secrets` corresponds with an entry of the release's revision history, which can be viewed by running the `helm history` command:

```
$ helm history wordpress -n chapter3
```

This command will display a table of each revision, similar to the following (some columns have been omitted for readability):

REVISION	STATUS	DESCRIPTION
1	superseded	Install complete
2	superseded	Upgrade complete
3	superseded	Upgrade complete
4	deployed	Upgrade complete

Table 3.1 – Table caption

In this output, each revision has a number, along with the time it was updated, the status, the name of the chart, the app version, and the description. Revisions that have a status of `superseded` are no longer up to date, while the revision that says `deployed` is the currently deployed revision. Other statuses include `pending` and `pending_upgrade`, which means the installation or upgrade is currently in progress. `failed` refers to a particular revision that has failed to install or be upgraded and `unknown` means that you encountered a bug and may want to file an issue or notify the maintainers. It's unlikely you will ever encounter a release with a state of `unknown`.

The `helm get` commands described previously can be used against a revision number by specifying the `--revision` flag. For this rollback, let's determine the release that had the full set of desired values. As you may recall, the current revision, `revision 4`, only contains a subset of the values we need, but `revision 3` should contain all of our desired values. This can be verified by running the `helm get values` command with the `--revision` flag:

```
$ helm get values wordpress --revision 3 -n chapter3
```

The full list of values is presented by inspecting this revision:

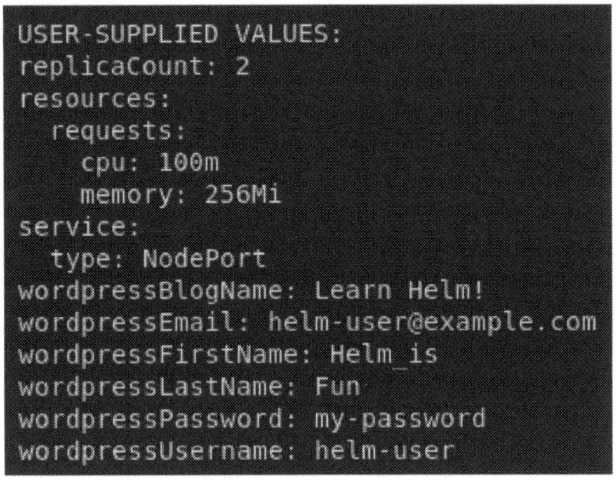

```
USER-SUPPLIED VALUES:
replicaCount: 2
resources:
  requests:
    cpu: 100m
    memory: 256Mi
service:
  type: NodePort
wordpressBlogName: Learn Helm!
wordpressEmail: helm-user@example.com
wordpressFirstName: Helm_is
wordpressLastName: Fun
wordpressPassword: my-password
wordpressUsername: helm-user
```

Figure 3.29 – The output of checking a specific revision

It is possible to execute other `helm get` commands against a revision number to perform a further inspection. If necessary, the `helm get manifest` command can also be executed against `revision 3` to check the state of the Kubernetes resources that would be restored.

In the next section, we will execute the rollback.

Running the rollback

The `helm rollback` command has the following syntax:

```
helm rollback <RELEASE> [REVISION] [flags]
```

Users provide the name of the release and the desired revision number to roll a Helm release back to a previous point in time. Execute the following command to roll back WordPress to `revision 3`:

```
$ helm rollback wordpress 3 -n chapter3
```

The `rollback` subcommand provides a simple output, printing the following message:

```
Rollback was a success! Happy Helming!
```

This rollback can be observed in the release history by running the `helm history` command:

```
$ helm history wordpress -n chapter3
```

In the release history, you will notice that a fifth revision was added with a status of `deployed` and a description of `Rollback to 3`. When an application is rolled back, it adds a new revision to the release history. This is not to be confused with an upgrade. The highest revision number simply denotes the currently deployed release. Be sure to check a revision's description to determine whether it was created by an upgrade or a rollback.

You can get this release's values to ensure that the rollback now uses the desired values by running `helm get values` again:

```
$ helm get values wordpress -n chapter3
```

The output will show the values from the latest stable release:

```
USER-SUPPLIED VALUES:
replicaCount: 2
resources:
  requests:
    cpu: 100m
    memory: 256Mi
service:
  type: NodePort
wordpressBlogName: Learn Helm!
wordpressEmail: helm-user@example.com
wordpressFirstName: Helm_is
wordpressLastName: Fun
wordpressPassword: my-password
wordpressUsername: helm-user
```

Figure 3.30 – The values from the latest revision

You may notice that we did not explicitly set the chart version or the release's values in the `rollback` subcommand. This is because the `rollback` subcommand is not designed to accept these inputs. It is designed to roll a chart back to a previous revision and leverage that revision's chart version and values. Note that the `rollback` subcommand should not be part of everyday Helm practices and that it should be reserved only for emergencies, where the current state of an application is unstable and must be reverted to a previously stable point.

If you have successfully rolled back the WordPress release, you are nearing the end of this chapter's exercise. The final step is to remove the WordPress application from the Kubernetes cluster by using the `uninstall` subcommand, which we will describe in the next section.

Uninstalling the WordPress release

Uninstalling a Helm release means deleting the Kubernetes resources that it manages. In addition, the `uninstall` command deletes the release's history. While this is often what we want, specifying the `--keep-history` flag will instruct Helm to retain the release history.

The syntax for the `uninstall` command is very simple:

```
helm uninstall RELEASE_NAME [...] [flags]
```

Uninstall the WordPress release by running the `helm uninstall` command:

```
$ helm uninstall wordpress -n chapter3
```

Once WordPress is uninstalled, you will see the following message:

```
release "wordpress" uninstalled
```

You will also notice that the `wordpress` release no longer exists in the `chapter3` namespace:

```
$ helm list -n chapter3
```

The output will be an empty table. You can also confirm that the release is no longer present by attempting to use `kubectl` to get the WordPress deployments:

```
$ kubectl get deployments -l app.kubernetes.io/name=wordpress
-n chapter3
No resources found in chapter3 namespace.
```

As expected, there are no more WordPress deployments available. However, there is still one `PersistentVolumeClaim` sticking around:

```
$ kubectl get pvc -n chapter3
NAME                      STATUS
data-wordpress-mariadb-0  Bound
```

`PersistentVolumeClaim` was not deleted because it was created in the background by the MariaDB StatefulSet. In Kubernetes, `PersistentVolumeClaim` resources that are created by StatefulSets are not automatically removed if the StatefulSet is deleted. During the `helm uninstall` process, the StatefulSet was deleted but the associated `PersistentVolumeClaim` was not, as expected. The `PersistentVolumeClaim` command can be deleted manually with the following command:

```
$ kubectl delete pvc data-wordpress-mariadb-0 -n chapter3
```

Now that we've finished running through an example of installing, upgrading, rolling back, and uninstalling an application using Helm, let's shut down the Kubernetes environment.

Shutting down your environment

First, you can remove this chapter's namespace by running the following command:

```
$ kubectl delete namespace chapter3
```

After the `chapter3` namespace has been deleted, stop the minikube VM:

```
$ minikube stop
```

This will shut down the VM but will retain its state so that you can quickly begin working again in the next exercise.

Summary

In this chapter, you learned how to install a Helm chart and manage its life cycle. We began by searching Artifact Hub for a WordPress chart to install. After locating a chart, the repository containing the chart was added by following the instructions from its Artifact Hub page. We then proceeded to inspect the WordPress chart to create a set of values that overrides their defaults. These values were saved to a `values` file called `wordpress-values.yaml`, which was then provided during the installation.

After the chart was installed, we used `helm upgrade` to upgrade the release by providing additional values. We then performed a rollback with `helm rollback` to restore the chart to a previous state. Finally, we removed the WordPress release at the end of the exercise with `helm uninstall`.

This chapter taught you how to leverage Helm as an end user, and how to use an already-written Helm chart. In the next chapter, we will explore the concepts and structure of a Helm chart in greater detail to begin learning how to create Helm charts of our own.

Further reading

To learn more about adding repositories locally, inspecting charts, and using the four life cycle commands used throughout this chapter (`install`, `upgrade`, `rollback`, and `uninstall`), go to https://helm.sh/docs/intro/using_helm/.

Questions

1. What is Artifact Hub? How can a user interact with it to find charts and chart repositories?
2. What is the difference between the `helm get` and `helm show` commands?
3. What is the difference between the `--set` and `--values` parameters in the `helm install` and `helm upgrade` commands? What are the benefits of using one over the other?
4. What command can be used to provide the list of revisions for a release?
5. What happens by default when you upgrade a release without providing any values? How does this behavior differ from when you do provide values for an upgrade?
6. Imagine that you have five revisions of a release. What would the `helm history` command show after you roll back the release to `revision 3`?
7. Imagine that you want to view all of the releases deployed to a Kubernetes namespace. What command should you run?
8. Imagine that you run `helm repo add` to add a chart repository. What command can you run to list all of the charts in that repository?

Part 2: Helm Chart Development

You've deployed your first Helm chart from a public repository. Now, it's time to develop your own Helm chart by learning the ins and outs of Helm templating and the Helm chart structure.

In this part, we will cover the following topics:

- *Chapter 4, Scaffolding a New Helm Chart*
- *Chapter 5, Helm Dependency Management*
- *Chapter 6, Understanding Helm Templates*
- *Chapter 7, Helm Lifecycle Hooks*
- *Chapter 8, Publishing to a Helm Chart Repository*
- *Chapter 9, Testing Helm Charts*

4
Scaffolding a New Helm Chart

In the previous chapter, you learned how to use Helm from an end user perspective, leveraging it as a package manager to install applications to Kubernetes. Leveraging Helm in this fashion required you to understand how to use the Helm life cycle commands (`install`, `upgrade`, `rollback`, and `uninstall`), but it did not require you to understand how the Helm chart itself was built. While an understanding of the Helm CLI commands is necessary to install and manage applications installed by Helm, that level of knowledge alone will not allow you to package your own applications into Helm charts.

In the second part of this book, starting with this chapter, we will switch gears away from being a Helm chart end user and transition into becoming a Helm chart developer. We will accomplish this by building a Helm chart from scratch over the next few chapters that deploys an instance of the Guestbook application, a commonly used sample application within the Kubernetes community. By the end of the second part, you will have an understanding of the concepts and experience required to write robust Helm charts.

In this chapter, we will begin to explore Helm chart development by discussing the following topics:

- Understanding the Guestbook application
- Understanding the YAML format
- Using `helm create` to scaffold a new Helm chart
- Deploying the scaffolded Guestbook chart
- Exploring the `Chart.yaml` file
- Updating the `Chart.yaml` file

Technical requirements

This section requires the `minikube` and `helm` binaries to be installed on your local machine. The installation and configuration of these tools are covered in *Chapter 2, Preparing a Kubernetes and Helm Environment*.

Understanding the Guestbook application

Since the second part of this book will be centered around developing a Helm chart to deploy the Guestbook application, let's first understand what this application does and what its architecture looks like.

The Guestbook application is a simple **PHP: Hypertext Preprocessor** (**PHP**) frontend designed to persist messages to a Redis backend. The frontend consists of a dialog box and a **Submit** button, as illustrated in the following screenshot:

Guestbook

[Messages]

[Submit]

Figure 4.1 – The Guestbook PHP frontend

To interact with this application, users can follow these steps:

1. Type a message in the **Messages** dialog box.
2. Click the **Submit** button.
3. When the **Submit** button is clicked, the message will be saved to the Redis database and displayed at the bottom of the page, as shown in the following screenshot:

Guestbook

[Messages]

[Submit]

Hello world!

Figure 4.2 – The Guestbook frontend after a new message has been submitted

Redis is an in-memory, key-value data store that, for our Helm chart, will be clustered to provide data replication. The cluster will consist of one leader node that the Guestbook frontend writes to. Once data is persisted, the leader will replicate across each of the follower nodes, from which Guestbook replicas will read, to retrieve and display the list of previously submitted messages.

The following diagram describes how the frontend interacts with Redis:

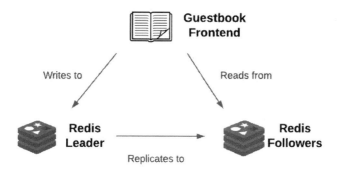

Figure 4.3 – Guestbook frontend and Redis interaction

With an understanding of how this application works, let's focus on starting our Guestbook Helm chart. We'll begin with a primer on the YAML format, since this format is ubiquitous among the files you will interact with as a Helm chart developer.

Understanding the YAML format

YAML Ain't Markup Language (YAML) is a file format used to create human-readable configuration. It is the file format most used to configure Kubernetes resources and is also the format used for many of the files in Helm charts.

YAML files follow a **key-value** format to declare configuration. Let's explore the YAML key-value construct.

Defining key-value pairs

One of the most basic examples of a YAML key-value pair is shown here:

```
name: LearnHelm
```

In the preceding example, the name key is given a LearnHelm value. In YAML, keys and values are separated by a colon (:). Characters written to the left of the colon represent the key, while characters written to the right of the colon represent the value.

Spacing matters in YAML format. The following line does not constitute a valid key-value pair:

```
name:LearnHelm
```

Note that a space is missing between the colon and the LearnHelm string. This would result in a parsing error. A space must exist between the colon and the value.

While the preceding example represents a simple key-value pair, YAML allows users to configure more complex pairings with nested elements, called maps. An example is shown here:

```
resources:
  limits:
    cpu: 100m
    memory: 512Mi
```

The preceding example demonstrates a `resources` object containing a map of two key-value pairs:

Key	Value
`resources.limits.cpu`	`100m`
`resources.limits.memory`	`512Mi`

Keys are determined by following the indentation under a YAML block. Each indentation adds a dot (`.`) separator to the name of the key. The value of the key has been reached when there are no longer any indentations remaining in the YAML block. By common practice, indentations in YAML should use two spaces, but users can provide as many spaces as they desire as long as the spacing is consistent throughout the document.

> **Important Note**
> **Tabs** are not supported by YAML, and their use will result in a parsing error.

With an understanding of YAML key-value pairs, let's now explore some of the common types that values can be defined as.

Value types

Values in a YAML file can be of different types. The most common type is a string, which is a text value. Strings can be declared by wrapping a value in quotation marks, but this is not always required. If a value contains at least one alphabetical letter or special character, the value is considered a string, with or without quotation marks. Multiline strings can be set by using the pipe (`|`) symbol, as shown:

```
configuration: |
  server.port=8443
  logging.file.path=/var/log
```

Values can also be integers. A value is an integer when it is a numeric character that is not wrapped in quotations. The following YAML declares an integer value:

```
replicas: 1
```

Compare this to the following YAML, which assigns `replicas` to a string value:

```
replicas: "1"
```

Boolean values are often used as well, which can be declared with either `true` or `false`:

```
ingress:
  enable: true
```

This YAML sets `ingress.enable` to the `true` Boolean value. Other acceptable Boolean values are `yes`, `no`, `on`, `off`, `y`, `n`, `Y`, and `N`.

Values can also be set to more complex types, such as lists. Items in a list in YAML are identified by the dash (`-`) symbol.

The following demonstrates a YAML list:

```
servicePorts:
  - 8080
  - 8443
```

This YAML sets `servicePorts` to a list of integers (such as `8080` and `8443`). This syntax can also be used to describe a list of objects:

```
deployment:
  env:
    - name: MY_VAR
      value: MY_VALUE
    - name: SERVICE_NAME
      value: MY_SERVICE
```

In this case, `env` is set to a list of objects containing the `name` and `value` fields. Lists are often used in both Kubernetes and Helm configuration, and understanding them is valuable to using Helm to its fullest potential.

While YAML is more commonly used in the worlds of Kubernetes and Helm for its ease of readability, the **JavaScript Object Notation (JSON)** format can be used as well. Let's briefly describe this format.

The JSON format

YAML is a superset of another widely used format—JSON. This is a string of key-value pairs, similar to YAML. The key difference is that while YAML relies on spacing and indentation to properly configure key-value pairs, JSON relies on braces and brackets.

The following example converts the previous YAML example into the JSON format:

```json
{
  "deployment": {
    "env": [
      {
        "name": "MY_VAR",
        "value": "MY_VALUE"
      },
      {
        "name": "SERVICE_NAME",
        "value": "MY_SERVICE"
      }
    ]
  }
}
```

All the keys in JSON are wrapped in quotation marks and positioned before a colon:

- Curly braces ({}) denote a block in a similar way to how indentations denote a block in YAML.
- Square brackets ([]) denote a list in a similar way to how dashes denote a list in YAML.

There are many more constructs to the YAML and JSON formats, but this introduction provides more than enough information to understand how they can be used in Helm charts.

In the next section, we will begin to develop our Guestbook Helm chart by first learning how to scaffold Helm charts.

Scaffolding the Guestbook Helm chart

When developing a new Helm chart from scratch, it is often useful to start by running the `helm create` command, which has the following syntax:

```
helm create NAME [flags]
```

The `helm create` command provides a new project folder for your Helm chart. Inside, the folder contains a basic Helm chart scaffolding that you can use to begin developing your chart.

Let's run the `helm create` command to scaffold our Guestbook Helm chart:

1. In your terminal, within a directory where you would like to store Helm charts, run the `helm create` command:

    ```
    $ helm create guestbook
    Creating guestbook
    ```

2. Review the list of files that have been created:

```
$ ls -al guestbook
.
..
charts/
Chart.yaml
.helmignore
templates/
values.yaml
$ ls -1 guestbook/templates/
deployment.yaml
_helpers.tpl
hpa.yaml
ingress.yaml
NOTES.txt
serviceaccount.yaml
service.yaml
tests/
```

As you can see, the `helm create` command generated a new folder for you called `guestbook`, which represents the name of the Helm chart. It is not necessarily required to call this folder `guestbook`, but since this is the name of the Helm chart we are creating, it is a good idea to make sure the folder name matches.

Under the `guestbook` folder, there are several different files and folders that make up your Helm chart. This may appear overwhelming at first, but we will dive deeper into each component as we develop the Guestbook chart over the next few chapters. By the end of the second part, each of these files will become clearer, and you will be able to jump into your next Helm chart with ease!

For now, let's take a high-level look at each of the files that `helm create` generated for us. As you'll see in the following table, some of the files are not strictly required for a new Helm chart, but `helm create` provided them for us as a best practice:

File/Directory	Definition	Required?
`charts/`	A directory that contains dependencies or Helm charts that the parent chart depends on.	No
`Chart.yaml`	A file that contains metadata about the Helm chart.	Yes

`.helmignore`	A file that contains a list of files and directories that should be omitted from the Helm chart's packaging.	No
`templates/`	A directory that contains Golang templates, which are primarily used for generating Kubernetes resources.	Yes, unless the chart contains dependencies
`templates/*.yaml`	A template file used to generate a Kubernetes resource.	Yes, unless the chart contains dependencies
`templates/_*.tpl`	A file that contains boilerplate helper templates.	No
`templates/NOTES.txt`	A template file that is used to generate usage instructions after chart installation.	No
`templates/tests/` (or more generically, `templates/*/`)	A folder used for grouping different templates. This is strictly for aesthetics and has no effect on how the Helm chart operates – for example, `templates/tests` is used to group templates that are used for testing.	No
`values.yaml`	A file that contains the chart's default values.	No, but every chart should contain this file as a best practice

Table 4.2 – Files created with the "helm create" command

In addition to the files listed in the preceding table, there are a few other files that a Helm chart can contain that `helm create` did not include for us. Let's take a high-level look at these files in the following table:

File/Directory	Definition	Required?
`Chart.lock`	A file used to save, or lock in, the previously applied dependency versions.	No
`crds/`	A directory that contains **Custom Resource Definition** (**CRD**) YAML resources. These CRD resources will be installed before those under `templates/`.	No
`README.md`	A file that contains installation and usage information about the Helm chart.	No, but every Helm chart should contain this file as a best practice

| `LICENSE` | A file that contains the chart's license, which provides information about usage and redistribution rights. | No |
| `values.schema.json` | A file that contains the chart's values schema in the JSON format. Used to provide input validation. | No |

Table 4.3– Additional Helm chart files

Again, we will explore each of these files in greater detail when they become relevant to the topics we will discuss later in this chapter and over the next few chapters.

For now, let's focus on the content in the `guestbook` directory that `helm create` generated for us. You may be surprised to know that, upon running `helm create`, you already have a fully functional Helm chart contained within your `guestbook` folder! Let's install the Guestbook chart in its current state to see what gets deployed.

Deploying the scaffolded Guestbook chart

Before we install the chart, let's set up your Kubernetes environment by following these steps:

1. Start Minikube by running the `minikube start` command:

   ```
   $ minikube start
   ```

2. Create a new namespace called `chapter4`:

   ```
   $ kubectl create namespace chapter4
   ```

   Now, let's proceed by installing your scaffolded chart and reviewing the deployed resources. In *Chapter 3, Installing Your First App With Helm*, we installed a Helm chart from a remote repository by providing the name `bitnami/wordpress`, which references the name of the remote repository and the chart contained within this repository. Alternatively, you can also install a chart by providing the local path to a valid Helm chart project folder. This makes it easy to test your Helm charts and see your progress without needing to publish the chart to a repository first.

3. Let's install your chart by running the following command, where `./guestbook` represents the folder generated by `helm create`:

   ```
   $ helm install guestbook ./guestbook -n chapter4
   NAME: guestbook
   LAST DEPLOYED: Sun Sep 19 10:39:40 2021
   NAMESPACE: default
   ```

```
STATUS: deployed
REVISION: 1
NOTES:
1. Get the application URL by running these commands:
  export POD_NAME=$(kubectl get pods --namespace default 
-l "app.kubernetes.io/name=guestbook,app.kubernetes.io/
instance=guestbook" -o jsonpath="{.items[0].metadata.
name}")
  export CONTAINER_PORT=$(kubectl get pod --namespace 
default $POD_NAME -o jsonpath="{.spec.containers[0].
ports[0].containerPort}")
  echo "Visit http://127.0.0.1:8080 to use your 
application"
  kubectl --namespace default port-forward $POD_NAME 
8080:$CONTAINER_PORT
```

4. Run `helm get manifest` to review the resources that were deployed:

```
$ helm get manifest guestbook -n chapter4
```

As denoted in the output, your scaffolded Guestbook chart (with the default values applied) contains one service account, one service, and one deployment. If you look carefully at the deployment, you'll find something interesting about the image that was deployed:

```
image: "nginx:1.16.0"
```

Sure enough, a new Helm chart that was scaffolded using `helm create` begins as a basic NGINX chart. **NGINX** is a popular open source web server and reverse proxy. Because its installation requires many of the same resources as many other Kubernetes applications, it serves as a great starting point when writing new Helm charts.

Let's continue by accessing the NGINX application to verify it was installed properly.

5. Since the Helm chart created a `ClusterIP` service, let's run `kubectl port-forward` so that we can access the NGINX pod. Keep in mind that, although our Guestbook chart has installed NGINX, the deployed resources are still called `guestbook`, since that is the name of our chart:

```
$ kubectl -n chapter4 port-forward svc/guestbook 8080:80
```

6. In a new terminal window (since the current one will block while the `kubectl port-forward` command is active), use the `curl` command to reach NGINX:

```
$ curl localhost:8080
<!DOCTYPE html>
```

```
<html>
<head>
<title>Welcome to nginx!</title>
<style>
    body {
        width: 35em;
        margin: 0 auto;
        font-family: Tahoma, Verdana, Arial, sans-serif;
    }
</style>
</head>
<body>
<h1>Welcome to nginx!</h1>
```

As you can see, we are able to reach NGINX successfully. Now, let's continue by cleaning up this Helm release.

7. Press *Ctrl + c* in the terminal window running the `kubectl port-forward` command. Alternatively, you can close the window.

8. Uninstall the `guestbook` Helm release:

```
$ helm uninstall guestbook -n chapter4
release "guestbook" uninstalled
```

9. Next, you can delete the `chapter4` namespace, since we won't need it for the remainder of the chapter:

```
$ kubectl delete namespace chapter4
namespace "chapter4" deleted
```

10. Finally, you can shut down your `minikube` cluster:

```
$ minikube stop
```

You may realize after this exercise that our Guestbook chart doesn't resemble the architecture we presented at the beginning of this chapter very much. However, by providing a scaffold that we will use as a starting point, we have already made great progress toward creating a Helm chart for deploying the desired architecture. We will continue making progress on our Guestbook chart in the next chapter when we learn about dependencies. At that time, we will declare a dependency to install Redis and the backend of our Guestbook architecture.

In the next section, we'll take a deeper dive into one of the most important Helm chart files, `Chart.yaml`. Then, at the end of the chapter, we will update this file to provide new settings that align with our Guestbook chart.

Understanding the Chart.yaml file

The `Chart.yaml` file, also referred to as the **chart definition**, is used for storing different pieces of metadata about a Helm chart. This file is required, and if it is not included within a chart, you'll receive the following error:

```
Error: Chart.yaml file is missing
```

A `Chart.yaml` file was created for you earlier when you ran `helm create`. Let's review this file by running the following command:

```
$ cat guestbook/Chart.yaml
```

An output like the following will be displayed:

```
apiVersion: v2
name: guestbook
description: A Helm chart for Kubernetes

# A chart can be either an 'application' or a 'library' chart.
#
# Application charts are a collection of templates that can be packaged into versioned archives
# to be deployed.
#
# Library charts provide useful utilities or functions for the chart developer. They're included as
# a dependency of application charts to inject those utilities and functions into the rendering
# pipeline. Library charts do not define any templates and therefore cannot be deployed.
type: application

# This is the chart version. This version number should be incremented each time you make changes
# to the chart and its templates, including the app version.
# Versions are expected to follow Semantic Versioning (https://semver.org/)
version: 0.1.0

# This is the version number of the application being deployed. This version number should be
# incremented each time you make changes to the application. Versions are not expected to
# follow Semantic Versioning. They should reflect the version the application is using.
# It is recommended to use it with quotes.
appVersion: "1.16.0"
```

Figure 4.4 – The Guestbook Chart.yaml file

A `Chart.yaml` file can contain many different fields, some of which are required, while most other fields are optional. Let's take a closer look at each of the fields provided in our Guestbook chart's `Chart.yaml` file.

Field	Description	Required?
`apiVersion`	The chart API version	Yes
`name`	The name of the Helm chart	Yes
`description`	A brief description of the Helm chart	No
`type`	The type of Helm chart (either `Application` or `Library`)	No
`version`	The version of the Helm chart, in SemVer format.	Yes
`appVersion`	The version of the application that the Helm chart deploys. This does not need to be in the SemVer format.	No

Table 4.4 – Fields from the generated Chart.yaml file

As you can see from Guestbook's chart definition, the `apiVersion` value for our chart is set to `v2`. Charts with an `apiVersion` value of `v2` are only compatible with Helm 3. The other possible `apiVersion` value is `v1`, but this is a legacy version that was geared towards Helm 2. Charts with an `apiVersion` value of `v1` handled dependencies differently and did not support library charts (topics that we will discuss in greater detail later in this book). Helm 3 is in fact backward-compatible with `apiVersion v1`, but in order to leverage Helm's latest features and to avoid deprecations, new Helm charts should be created using `apiVersion v2`.

The type of Helm chart we have scaffolded, according to the `Chart.yaml` file, is an `application` chart. A Helm chart can be either an `application` chart or a `library` chart. An application chart is used to deploy an application to Kubernetes, while a library chart is used to provide reusable helper templates. We will discuss library charts in greater detail in *Chapter 6, Understanding Helm Templates*. The `type` field in the `Chart.yaml` file is optional and defaults to `application`.

The other fields in our chart definition, `name`, `description`, `version`, and `appVersion`, are used to provide metadata that identifies our chart. As an example, think back to *Chapter 3, Installing Your First App with Helm*, when we searched Artifact Hub from the command line for WordPress charts. We ran the `helm search hub wordpress` command and saw an output like the following:

Figure 4.5 – An example of name, version, appVersion, and description

These fields are acquired from their corresponding fields in `Chart.yaml`. Note that you can also see this information on any chart's Artifact Hub page.

In addition to the fields included in our scaffolded `Chart.yaml` file, there are many other fields used to describe your chart, as shown in the following table:

Field	Description	Required?
`kubeVersion`	A range of compatible Kubernetes versions in the SemVer format.	No
`keywords`	A list of keywords used to describe the Helm chart. Keywords are also used to provide search terms for the `helm search` command.	No
`home`	The URL to the Helm chart's home page.	No
`sources`	A list of URLs that link to source code used by the Helm chart.	No
`dependencies`	A list of charts that your Helm chart is reliant on.	No
`maintainers`	A list of Helm chart maintainers.	No
`icon`	An icon in SVG or PNG format used to represent the Helm chart. Displayed on the chart's Artifact Hub page.	No
`deprecated`	Indicates whether the Helm chart has been deprecated.	No
`annotations`	A list of annotations used to provide custom metadata.	No

Table 4.5 – Additional Chart.yaml fields

The `kubeVersion` field is used to provide validation against the target Kubernetes cluster version. This is useful if your Helm chart uses resources that are only compatible with certain versions of Kubernetes. You could set `kubeVersion` to a string such as `>= 1.18.0 < 1.20.0`, and Helm will ensure that the chart is installed only if Kubernetes is greater than or equal to version `1.18.0` and less than (exclusive) `1.20.0`. You can also use the OR (`||`) operator, as in `>= 1.15.0 <= 1.17.0 || >= 1.18.0 < 1.20.0`.

The `dependencies` field is the most functional of these optional fields. Charts added under the `dependencies` field will be installed alongside your Helm chart's resources. We will explore dependencies more in the next chapter.

As shown earlier with the `name`, `version`, `appVersion`, and `description` fields, each of the other `Chart.yaml` properties also have an impact on how a Helm chart is displayed in Artifact Hub. Look at the following screenshot, taken from Bitnami's WordPress page in Artifact Hub:

Figure 4.6 – Chart.yaml metadata displayed on Artifact Hub

Let's compare this to WordPress's `Chart.yaml` file, retrieved by running `helm show values bitnami/wordpress`:

```yaml
annotations:
  category: CMS
apiVersion: v2
appVersion: 5.8.0
dependencies:
- condition: mariadb.enabled
  name: mariadb
  repository: https://charts.bitnami.com/bitnami
  version: 9.x.x
- condition: memcached.enabled
  name: memcached
  repository: https://charts.bitnami.com/bitnami
  version: 5.x.x
- name: common
  repository: https://charts.bitnami.com/bitnami
  tags:
  - bitnami-common
  version: 1.x.x
description: Web publishing platform for building blogs and websites.
home: https://github.com/bitnami/charts/tree/master/bitnami/wordpress
icon: https://bitnami.com/assets/stacks/wordpress/img/wordpress-stack-220x234.png
keywords:
- application
- blog
- cms
- http
- php
- web
- wordpress
maintainers:
- email: containers@bitnami.com
  name: Bitnami
name: wordpress
sources:
- https://github.com/bitnami/bitnami-docker-wordpress
- https://wordpress.org/
version: 12.1.4
```

Figure 4.7 – The Bitnami/WordPress Chart.yaml file

Note how `home`, `sources`, `maintainers`, `dependencies`, and `keywords` from `Chart.yaml` are also displayed in Artifact Hub.

It is not required to provide all the `Chart.yaml` fields in full, but it is a good thing to do if you are publishing your charts to Artifact Hub or another repository that can display chart metadata. Otherwise, feel free to use your discretion and provide the fields that you find relevant and necessary. Besides `apiVersion`, `name`, and `version`, we recommend providing at least `appVersion` and `description`, since these fields provide a good high-level glance at the application your Helm chart is packaging. If you are writing a Helm chart for public use, you should consider also adding `maintainers`, `home`, and `sources`, and if you are publishing to Artifact Hub, you should also include `keywords` so that the chart can be easily discovered.

With an understanding of the Chart.yaml fields, let's finish this chapter by updating our scaffolded chart definition to better suit our Guestbook application.

Updating the Guestbook Chart.yaml file

The scaffolded Chart.yaml file that helm create generated is catered around NGINX and not Guestbook as we would desire. Let's make a couple of quick changes to improve the content:

1. First, let's update the chart description to better describe the application our chart will deploy. Update the description field of Chart.yaml to the following (or feel free to provide your own):

   ```
   description: An application used for keeping a running
     record of guests
   ```

2. Next, let's provide a more appropriate appVersion setting that better suits the version of Guestbook that our chart will deploy. The latest version of Guestbook is v5, so let's use this as our appVersion:

   ```
   appVersion: v5
   ```

   Our Chart.yaml file should now look like this (with the comments removed):

   ```
   apiVersion: v2
   name: guestbook
   description: An application used for keeping a running record of guests
   type: application
   version: 0.1.0
   ```

   Figure 4.8 – The updated Chart.yaml file for Guestbook

Feel free to add any of the other Chart.yaml fields as well, but these changes, at a minimum, will put us in a good state where the Chart.yaml metadata accurately reflects the application that we will deploy.

We will revisit the Chart.yaml field in the next chapter when we add a chart dependency for deploying Redis.

Summary

In this chapter, we began to peek into the world of Helm chart development by introducing the Helm chart and chart definition structure. A Helm chart consists of a chart definition (a Chart.yaml file) and template files used for generating Kubernetes resources. A chart definition is used to provide an identity around the chart, including metadata such as the chart name, version, description, and the application version that the chart deploys.

We also introduced an application called Guestbook, and we began writing a Helm chart that will be used to deploy this application. We ran the `helm create` command to scaffold a new Helm chart, and we updated the `Chart.yaml` file to better reflect the application that our chart will deploy. In the next chapter, we will return to the `Chart.yaml` file when we add a dependency for installing Redis, the backend service that our Guestbook frontend relies on.

Further reading

To learn more about Helm chart structure and `Chart.yaml` files, visit the Helm documentation at https://helm.sh/docs/topics/charts/. For more information on the Guestbook application, visit https://kubernetes.io/docs/tutorials/stateless-application/guestbook/.

Questions

1. What is the file format most used in Kubernetes and Helm?
2. What is the command used to scaffold a new Helm chart?
3. Where is the Helm chart name and version defined?
4. What are the three required fields in the `Chart.yaml` file?
5. Helm charts can be made up of many different files. Which files are required?
6. Which folder of a Helm chart is used to contain Kubernetes resource templates?
7. Which `Chart.yaml` field is used to describe the application version that a Helm chart deploys?

5
Helm Dependency Management

As you may recall from *Chapter 4, Scaffolding a New Helm Chart*, the Helm chart we are developing, `guestbook`, will deploy two primary components. The first is a Redis backend, which is used to persist a list of messages. The second component is the frontend, where the user enters the messages in a text box. In this chapter, we will focus on updating our Helm chart to deploy the first major component – Redis.

To deploy Redis, you may assume that we will need to make vast modifications to our existing `guestbook` chart. However, this is not necessarily the case. There are many Redis Helm charts available in Artifact Hub, and as a result, we can use the dependency management features of Helm and declare one of those charts as a dependency. Then, when the `guestbook` chart has been installed in a Kubernetes cluster, the dependency is also installed. By declaring Redis as a dependency, we can reduce the amount of effort required to create the backend for our application.

In this chapter, we will explore how Helm manages dependencies. Then, we will use what we have learned to incorporate a Redis dependency in our Helm chart.

In this chapter, we will cover the following topics:

- Declaring chart dependencies
- The dependencies map
- Downloading chart dependencies
- Conditional dependencies
- Altering dependency names and values
- Updating the guestbook Helm chart
- Cleaning up

Technical requirements

For this chapter, you will require the following tools:

- `minikube`
- `kubectl`
- `helm`
- `git`

We will use minikube to explore several examples throughout this chapter, so now is a good time to start your minikube environment:

```
$ minikube start
```

Once minikube has started, create a new namespace for this chapter:

```
$ kubectl create namespace chapter5
```

Throughout this chapter, we will follow several examples to gain a better understanding of how chart dependencies work in practice. Ensure that you clone the sample repository to follow along with the examples. To clone the repository, run the following command:

```
$ git clone https://github.com/PacktPublishing/Managing-Kubernetes-Resources-using-Helm.git
```

With the repository cloned, let's continue to the next section to begin learning about Helm chart dependencies.

Declaring chart dependencies

Chart dependencies are used to install another chart's resources that a Helm chart (referred to as the **parent chart**) may depend on. We saw an example of chart dependencies in action when we installed WordPress in *Chapter 3, Installing Your First App with Helm*. When we installed WordPress, we used the `wordpress` chart to install both the WordPress application instance and a MariaDB backend. You may be surprised to learn that the MariaDB database that was installed was not a native WordPress chart resource – it was a dependency! We can confirm this fact by running the `helm show chart` command to view the dependencies declared in the `wordpress Chart.yaml` file:

```
$ helm show chart bitnami/wordpress --version 12.1.4
```

In the output, you'll see the `dependencies` map, as follows:

```
dependencies:
- condition: mariadb.enabled
  name: mariadb
  repository: https://raw.githubusercontent.com/bitnami/charts/
archive-full-index/bitnami
  version: 9.x.x
- condition: memcached.enabled
  name: memcached
  repository: https://raw.githubusercontent.com/bitnami/charts/
archive-full-index/bitnami
  version: 5.x.x
- name: common
  repository:  https://raw.githubusercontent.com/bitnami/
charts/archive-full-index/bitnami
  tags:
  - bitnami-common
  version: 1.x.x
```

Here, you can see that `mariadb` is the first dependency to be listed. The second dependency, `memcached`, is an in-memory key/value pair database and was not installed when we deployed WordPress in *Chapter 3, Installing Your First App With Helm*, as it depends on the `memcached.enabled` value being set to `true` (this value is `false` by default). The third dependency, `common`, is a library chart. We will explore library charts in greater detail in *Chapter 6, Understanding Helm Templates*.

The WordPress dependencies listed previously are examples of what you may see in other `Chart.yaml` files. Let's look at all possible dependency-related `Chart.yaml` fields to understand how to declare chart dependencies.

The dependencies map

The `dependencies` map within `Chart.yaml` supports many different fields for declaring dependencies and altering their behavior. Let's look at the fields that are included in this map:

Field	Description	Required?
Name	The name of the dependency chart	Yes
Repository	The location where the dependency chart resides	Yes
Version	The chart dependency version	Yes
Condition	A Boolean value that determines whether the dependency should be included or not	No
Tags	A list of Boolean values that determine whether the chart should be included or not	No
import-values	A mapping of source values to parent values	No
Alias	An alternative name to give the dependency	No

Table 5.1 – The dependencies fields in Chart.yaml

The minimum required fields in the `dependencies` map are `name`, `repository`, and `version`. We can see each of these being used in the WordPress `Chart.yaml` file, where the first dependency was called `mariadb`, the repository was `https://protect-eu.mimecast.com/s/ax_4C5lrwTkYXJhOWg2e?domain=raw.githubusercontent.com`, and the version was `9.x.x`. We will learn more about these three fields in the *Downloading chart dependencies* section.

The `condition` and `tags` fields are used to conditionally include dependencies based on the settings of specific values. `mariadb`, the first dependency of the WordPress chart, sets the condition field to `mariadb.enabled`, and its third dependency (`common`) uses a tag called `bitnami-common`. We will explore conditional dependencies with these settings in the *Conditional dependencies* section.

The remaining fields, `alias` and `import-values`, provide methods for manipulating the values of a dependency chart. We will learn more about these fields in the *Altering dependency names and values* section.

Now that we've provided a high-level overview of each of the dependency-related fields, let's learn how to download dependencies declared in `Chart.yaml`. Then, we will dive into using each field while covering several example scenarios.

Downloading chart dependencies

Chart dependencies can be viewed and downloaded using the `helm dependency` subcommands listed in the following table:

Command	Description
`helm dependency list`	Lists the dependencies for the given chart.
`helm dependency update`	Downloads the dependencies listed in `Chart.yaml` and generates a `Chart.lock` file.
`helm dependency build`	Downloads the dependencies listed in `Chart.lock`. If the `Chart.lock` file is not found, then this command will mirror the behavior of the `helm dependency update` command.

Let's explore these commands by using the example Helm charts located in the `chapter5/examples` folder of this book's GitHub repository; we cloned these at the beginning of this chapter. We'll start by using the `basic-fields` chart:

1. Using the `basic-fields` chart located in `chapter5/examples/basic-fields`, list the chart's declared dependencies:

    ```
    $ helm dependency list chapter5/examples/basic-fields
    ```

    You'll see an output similar to the following:

    ```
    NAME    VERSION REPOSITORY                                                              STATUS
    mariadb 9.5.0   https://raw.githubusercontent.com/bitnami/charts/archive-full-index/bitnami missing
    ```

    Figure 5.1 – An example helm dependency list output

    The `helm dependency list` command is used to give us a quick look at a chart's declared dependencies, as well as their download status. From the preceding output, you can see that the `basic-fields` chart declares one dependency, `mariadb`, and that its status is currently `missing`. When the status is labeled `missing`, it means that you have not downloaded that dependency yet, so the chart cannot be installed yet. Now, let's download the dependency.

2. Download the `basic-fields` chart's dependencies by using the `helm dependency update` command:

    ```
    $ helm dependency update chapter5/examples/basic-fields
    ```

    You'll see the following output:

    ```
    Hang tight while we grab the latest from your chart repositories...
    ...Successfully got an update from the "bitnami" chart repository
    Update Complete. *Happy Helming!*
    Saving 1 charts
    Downloading mariadb from repo https://raw.githubusercontent.com/bitnami/charts/archive-full-index/bitnami
    Deleting outdated charts
    ```

    Figure 5.2 – The output of helm dependency update

3. Run the `helm dependency list` command to confirm that the dependency has been downloaded. For brevity, you may want to run this command as `helm dep list` since `helm dep` is a shorthand spelling of `helm dependency`. We will continue to use `helm dependency` throughout this book for clarity, but feel free to use the shorthand spelling to reduce typing effort.

   Back to the task at hand, let's confirm that the download was successful by running the following command:

   ```
   $ helm dependency list chapter5/examples/basic-fields
   ```

   You will see an output similar to what we saw previously, except that the status has been updated to `ok`:

   ```
   NAME    VERSION REPOSITORY                                                              STATUS
   mariadb 9.5.0   https://raw.githubusercontent.com/bitnami/charts/archive-full-index/bitnami ok
   ```

   Figure 5.3 – The updated helm dependency list status

   When `helm dependency update` is successful, you will see the dependency's status turn to `ok`, but you will also see a couple of new files appear in your chart's directory. First, you will see that the dependency chart has been downloaded under a newly created `charts/` folder, and you will also see a `Chart.lock` file.

   Let's look at these new files.

4. Use the `ls` command to view the downloaded dependency:

   ```
   $ ls chapter5/examples/basic-fields/charts
   mariadb-9.5.0.tgz
   ```

   As you can see, dependencies are downloaded in the form of gzip archives with `.tgz` file extensions. The filename contains the dependency name as well as its version.

5. Use the `cat` command to view the generated `Chart.lock` file:

   ```
   $ cat chapter5/examples/basic-fields/Chart.lock
   ```

   You will see the following output:

   ```
   dependencies:
   - name: mariadb
     repository: https://raw.githubusercontent.com/bitnami/charts/archive-full-index/bitnami
     version: 9.5.0
   digest: sha256:6621adebbb98601072b13d904b11f42e31919298a590713229f6061795606fcd
   generated: "2022-07-17T18:34:20.093658-05:00"
   ```

   Figure 5.4 – The generated Chart.lock file

   The `Chart.lock` file is generated upon running `helm dependency update`, and it contains a list of dependencies, such as the `Chart.yaml` file. However, unlike `Chart.`

yaml, the `Chart.lock` file is used to lock in the dependency versions so that the same versions can be downloaded on other machines.

The impact that `Chart.lock` has is not profound in the `basic-fields` chart because the MariaDB version is already statically, set at 9.5.0. However, take a look at the `wildcard-version` chart located under `chapter5/examples/wildcard-version`. Within this directory, the version of MariaDB is set to 9.x.x, as shown in the following snippet:

```
dependencies:
  - name: mariadb
    repository: https://raw.githubusercontent.com/
bitnami/charts/archive-full-index/bitnami
    version: 9.x.x
```

The version, 9.x.x, is a wildcard, and it tells Helm to download the latest minor and patch versions under major release 9 while assuming a SemVer format of `major.minor.patch`. If the version was specified as 9.5.x, Helm would download the latest patch release under major version 9 and minor version 5.

Let's use the `wildcard-version` chart to understand how wildcards play a more important role in the `Chart.lock` file.

6. Use the `helm dependency update` command to download the `wildcard-version` chart's dependencies:

```
$ helm dependency update chapter5/examples/wildcard-version
```

7. View the generated `Chart.lock` file:

```
$ cat chapter5/examples/wildcard-version/Chart.lock
```

Notice that the MariaDB version in `Chart.lock`, 9.8.1, is different than the version in `Chart.yaml`, which was 9.x.x:

```
dependencies:
- name: mariadb
  repository: https://raw.githubusercontent.com/bitnami/charts/archive-full-index/bitnami
  version: 9.8.1
digest: sha256:07240684a9a393cbe1a7c7d8e9905c25f97e7d82139677e0c1df8af1c7c9bbd6
generated: "2022-07-17T18:37:02.86214-05:00"
```

Figure 5.5 – The Chart.lock file when using a wildcard dependency version

Here, you can see the impact that `Chart.lock` has more clearly. Since version 9.x.x was specified in the `Chart.yaml` file, Helm downloads the latest 9.x.x release, and the resulting `Chart.lock` was generated to lock in version 9.8.1, which was the latest at the time `helm dependency update` was run. However, what happens if dependencies need to be redownloaded or if the `charts/` folder needs to be regenerated? If you run `helm dependency update` again, you run the risk that the latest 9.x.x release is different than 9.8.2, which may cause incompatibility issues. To address this risk, you can use the `helm dependency build` command. Let's see this command in action:

1. Delete the `charts/` directory under `wildcard-version`:

   ```
   $ rm -rf chapter5/examples/wildcard-version/charts
   ```

2. Run `helm dependency build` to redownload the MariaDB version specified in `Chart.lock`:

   ```
   $ helm dependency build chapter5/examples/wildcard-version
   ```

3. Verify that version 9.8.1 was redownloaded to the `charts/` directory:

   ```
   $ ls chapter5/examples/wildcard-version/charts
   mariadb-9.8.1.tgz
   ```

In this section, we walked through downloading dependencies using the `helm dependency` subcommands. However, the examples we have seen so far have always resulted in dependencies being downloaded. Sometimes, you will want to conditionally include or exclude dependencies based on user input. We will explore this concept in the next section.

Creating conditionals

Conditional dependencies can be created by using the `condition` and `tags` fields of the dependencies map. The `condition` field is used to list `Boolean` values that, if present, toggle the inclusion of the dependency. Let's explore this field first by looking at the `condition-example` chart located under `chapter5/examples/condition-example`:

1. Observe the `Chart.yaml` file located at `chapter5/examples/condition-example/Chart.yaml`:

   ```
   $ cat chapter5/examples/condition-example/Chart.yaml
   <output omitted>
   dependencies:
     - name: mariadb
       repository: https://raw.githubusercontent.com/bitnami/charts/archive-full-index/bitnami
       version: 9.5.0
       condition: mariadb.enabled
   ```

Notice that the last line of `Chart.yaml` in the preceding snippet uses the `condition: mariadb.enabled` setting. This setting allows users to set a value called `mariadb.enabled` to either `true` or `false`. If the value evaluates to `true`, the MariaDB dependency will be included. If `false`, MariaDB will not be included. By default, if `mariadb.enabled` does not exist, then this condition will have no effect, and MariaDB will be included.

The best practice for setting a condition is to follow a `chartname.enabled` value format, where each dependency has a unique condition, depending on the dependency's name. This allows for a more intuitive values schema. However, if necessary, you can specify multiple values for a condition by using a comma-separated expression, like so:

```
condition: example.enabled, example2.enabled
```

When a condition is a comma-delimited list, the first value is used if it exists, and the rest are ignored. Otherwise, if the first value does not exist, then subsequent values in the list are used to fall back on.

Let's continue with this example to see the use of the `condition` property in action.

2. Observe the `condition-example` chart's `values.yaml` file, which includes the `mariadb.enabled` value by default:

```
$ cat chapter5/examples/condition-example/values.yaml
<output omitted>
mariadb:
  enabled: true
```

As you can see, `mariadb.enabled` defaults to `true`, so we can expect to see MariaDB resources created in Helm's output. Let's verify that this is the case.

3. Download the `condition-example` chart's dependencies using the `helm dependency update` command:

```
$ helm dependency update chapter5/examples/condition-
example
```

4. Install the `condition-example` chart in your minikube cluster:

```
$ helm install conditional-example chapter5/examples/
condition-example -n chapter5
```

5. Verify that the MariaDB-related resources were created during the installation:

```
$ helm get manifest conditional-example -n chapter5 |
grep mariadb
```

You should see a lengthy output of strings containing `mariadb`.

As expected, MariaDB was installed because the `mariadb.enabled` value was set to `true`. Let's set this value to `false` next and verify that MariaDB has been excluded.

6. Upgrade the `conditional-example` release by setting `mariadb.enabled` to `false`:

   ```
   $ helm upgrade conditional-example chapter5/examples/
   condition-example --set mariadb.enabled=false -n chapter5
   ```

7. Verify that the MariaDB-related resources were excluded after the upgrade:

   ```
   $ helm get manifest conditional-example -n chapter5 |
   grep mariadb
   ```

   You should not see any output.

   The `condition` setting is the most common way to conditionally include dependencies within your Helm charts. However, there is a second setting you can use as well that we will showcase called `tags`. Whereas `condition` is best used for enabling individual dependencies using the `chartname.enabled` format, `tags` is used to enable or disable one or more dependencies by associating each dependency with descriptive labels.

   Let's use the `tags-example` chart located in `chapter5/examples/tags-example` to understand how tags can define conditional dependencies.

8. Observe the `Chart.yaml` file for the `tags-example` chart located in `chapter5/examples/tags-example/Chart.yaml`:

   ```
   <output omitted>
   dependencies:
     - name: mariadb
       repository: https://raw.githubusercontent.com/bitnami/charts/archive-full-index/bitnami
       version: 9.5.0
       tags:
         - backend
         - database
     - name: memcached
       repository: https://raw.githubusercontent.com/bitnami/charts/archive-full-index/bitnami
       version: 5.15.6
       tags:
         - backend
         - cache
   ```

As you can see, the `tags-example` chart defines two different dependencies: `mariadb` and `memcached`. Both `mariadb` and `memcached` share the `backend` tag, while `mariadb` also has the `database` tag; `memcached` has the `cache` tag separately. Let's explore how these tags are used by checking the chart's `values.yaml` file.

9. Observe the `tags-example` chart's `values.yaml` file. Notice the usage of the `tags` map at the end of the file:

```
$ cat chapter5/examples/tags-example/values.yaml
<output omitted>
tags:
  backend: true
```

Given the values file for the `tags-example` chart, you can see that the backend tag has been enabled. Since both `mariadb` and `memcached` share the same `backend` tag, both dependencies are enabled by default (similarly, if the `tags` map was omitted, both dependencies would also be included). To verify this ascertain, we can upgrade our previous `conditional-example` release using the `tags-example` chart.

10. Use the `helm upgrade` command to upgrade `conditional-example` using the contents from the `tags-example` chart:

```
$ helm upgrade conditional-example chapter5/examples/
tags-example -n chapter5
```

11. Verify that both `mariadb` and `memcached` were installed:

```
$ helm get manifest conditional-example -n chapter5 |
grep mariadb
$ helm get manifest conditional-example -n chapter5 |
grep memcached
```

While both commands should show large amounts of output, the presence of a match confirms that both dependencies were installed.

By using the same tag across multiple dependencies, you can conveniently include or exclude dependencies within your chart. Imagine, however, that you only wanted to include `mariadb` within the `tags-example` chart. While it would be intuitive to believe you could simply set `tags.database` to `true` and `tags.cache` to `false`, this would not have any effect because `tags.backend` already defaults to `true`. If one tag is true, then the dependency is included, even if the other tags are set to false.

To address this issue, you can override `tags.backend` to `false`.

12. Upgrade the `conditional-example` release so that it includes `mariadb` and excludes `memcached`:

```
$ helm upgrade conditional-example chapter5/examples/
tags-example --set tags.backend=false --set tags.
database=true -n chapter5
```

Notice that we have passed `--set tags.backend=false` first to ensure that none of the `memcached` conditions evaluate to true.

13. Verify that `mariadb` was included during the upgrade:

```
$ helm get manifest conditional-example -n chapter5 |
grep mariadb
```

This command should return a large amount of output.

14. Verify that `memcached` was excluded during the upgrade:

```
$ helm get manifest conditional-example -n chapter5 |
grep memcached
```

This command should not return any output.

The `condition` and `tags` fields both provide a robust set of options for conditionally including dependencies within your Helm charts. Keep in mind that you can also use both of these options together, but `condition` always overrides `tags`. This means that if all tags evaluate to true, and if any condition evaluates to false, then the condition will override the tags, and the dependency will not be included.

As a final step before advancing to the next topic, uninstall the `conditional-example` release:

```
$ helm uninstall conditional-example -n chapter5
```

Next, let's discuss the options available for altering how dependencies and their values are referenced.

Altering dependency names and values

When you include a dependency within a chart, you will most likely need to alter some of its values. One way to alter a dependency's values is to override them under a map whose root has the same name as the dependency.

For example, consider the `basic-fields` chart located under `chapter5/examples/basic-fields`. This chart contains one dependency in the `Chart.yaml` file:

```
dependencies:
  - name: mariadb
    repository: https://raw.githubusercontent.com/bitnami/
```

```
      charts/archive-full-index/bitnami
        version: 9.5.0
```

To override the values from the `mariadb` chart, you could incorporate a values structure, similar to the following:

```
mariadb:
  image:
    registry: my-registry.example.com
    repository: my-mariadb
    tag: my-tag
```

This will override the `image.registry`, `image.repository`, and `image.tag` values from the `mariadb` chart.

Let's experiment with overriding dependency values by completing a hands-on example:

1. Install the `basic-fields` chart located in `chapter5/examples/basic-fields`. Override MariaDB's `image.tag` value to deploy a different tag for the `mariadb` image than the default:

   ```
   $ helm install override-example chapter5/examples/basic-
   fields --set mariadb.image.tag=latest -n chapter5
   ```

2. Verify that the `latest` tag was applied:

   ```
   $ helm get manifest override-example -n chapter5 | grep
   latest
   image: docker.io/bitnami/mariadb:latest
   ```

3. Uninstall the Helm release:

   ```
   $ helm uninstall override-example -n chapter5
   ```

Nesting values in this fashion is the simplest and most common way to override the values of dependencies. However, the `dependencies` map provides a configuration for altering the root's name – `alias`.

Let's run through an example to understand how `alias` can be used.

Observe the `Chart.yaml` file of the `alias-example` chart located in `chapter5/examples/alias-example/Chart.yaml`:

```
$ cat chapter5/examples/alias-example/Chart.yaml
<output omitted>
```

```yaml
dependencies:
  - name: mariadb
    repository: https://raw.githubusercontent.com/bitnami/charts/archive-full-index/bitnami
    version: 9.5.0
    alias: db1
  - name: mariadb
    repository: https://raw.githubusercontent.com/bitnami/charts/archive-full-index/bitnami
    version: 9.5.0
    alias: db2
```

From the preceding `Chart.yaml` snippet, you can see that `alias-example` has two nearly identical MariaDB dependencies. This is the best use case for using `alias`. Since there are multiple MariaDB dependencies, Helm needs to be able to distinguish between the two. By using `alias`, you can give each identical dependency a unique name. Then, you can override values from each specific dependency. Let's explore `alias`:

1. Install the Helm chart by overriding the `image.tag` value for each MariaDB instance:

    ```
    $ helm install alias-example chapter5/examples/alias-example --set db1.image.tag=latest --set db2.image.tag=10.4 -n chapter5
    ```

2. Verify that each database's tag was applied:

    ```
    $ helm get manifest alias-example -n chapter5 | grep latest
    image: docker.io/bitnami/mariadb:latest
    $ helm get manifest alias-example -n chapter5 | grep 10.4
    image: docker.io/bitnami/mariadb:10.4
    ```

3. Uninstall the Helm release:

    ```
    $ helm uninstall alias-example -n chapter5
    ```

In general, when you are working with unique dependencies, you will not need to use `alias`. However, when you are working with multiple invocations of the same dependency, `alias` is an excellent way to manage and override values from each invocation.

Besides `alias`, the `dependencies` map in the `Chart.yaml` file provides one additional property for altering how values are managed for dependencies – `import-values`. The `import-values` setting is used to alter how dependency values are propagated to a parent chart. It comes in two different formats: `exports` and `child-parent`. The `exports` format is only applicable when dependency charts contain the `exports` map within its values file. Imagine that a dependency chart contains the following values:

```
exports:
  image:
    registry: my-registry
    repository: my-repository
    tag: my-tag
```

Using the `import-values` setting on the parent chart, you could import each of the image-related values underneath `exports`:

```
dependencies:
  - name: dependency
    repository: http://localhost:8080
    version: 1.0.0
    import-values:
      - image
```

Using `import-values` in `exports` format would result in the image-related values being propagated, as follows:

```
registry: my-registry
repository: my-repository
tag: my-tag
```

Compare this with the way these dependency values would be propagated by default, without `import-values`:

```
dependency:
  exports:
    image:
      registry: my-registry
      repository: my-repository
      tag: my-tag
```

As you can see, using `import-values` resulted in a less complex propagation with fewer deeply nested values.

The other format of `import-values` is the `child-parent` format. This format does not require dependency charts (referred to as **child** charts) to use `exports`, and it is especially useful for importing deeply nested values. Consider the following dependency chart, which contains the following values:

```
common:
  deployment:
    image:
      registry: my-registry
      repository: my-repository
      tag: my-tag
```

In the parent chart, you can import the image-related values using the `child-parent` format of `import-values`:

```
dependencies:
  - name: dependency
    repository: http://localhost:8080
    version: 1.0.0
    import-values:
      - child: common.deployment.image
        parent: image
```

This will propagate the dependency values so that each value under `common.deployment.image` is mapped directly under `image` in the parent chart:

```
image:
  registry: my-registry
  repository: my-repository
  tag: my-tag
```

Once again, by using the `import-values` setting, you can simplify how dependency values are propagated into the parent chart.

One important detail to note is that, when using `import-values`, you cannot override the values that you are importing. If you need to override values from the dependency, those values should not be imported using `import-values`.

Now that we have explored each of the different settings involved in Helm dependency management, let's finish this chapter by updating our `guestbook` chart with a Redis dependency to create the backend.

Updating the guestbook Helm chart

Similar to how we searched Artifact Hub to locate a WordPress chart in *Chapter 3, Installing Your First App with Helm*, we need to search for a Redis chart so that it can be used as a dependency. Let's search for a Redis chart:

1. Execute the following command to search for Redis charts from Artifact Hub:

   ```
   $ helm search hub redis
   ```

2. The first chart that's displayed is Bitnami's Redis chart. We'll use this chart as our dependency. If you didn't add the `bitnami` chart repository in *Chapter 3, Installing Your First App with Helm*, add this chart repository now by using the `helm repo add` command:

   ```
   $ helm repo add bitnami https://raw.githubusercontent.com/bitnami/charts/archive-full-index/bitnami
   ```

3. Next, determine the Redis chart version you would like to use. A list of version numbers can be found by running the following command:

   ```
   $ helm search repo redis --versions
   ```

   You will see an output similar to the following:

   ```
   NAME                CHART VERSION    APP VERSION    DESCRIPTION
   bitnami/redis       15.5.1           6.2.6          Open source,
   bitnami/redis       15.5.0           6.2.6          Open source,
   bitnami/redis       15.4.2           6.2.6          Open source,
   bitnami/redis       15.4.1           6.2.6          Open source,
   bitnami/redis       15.4.0           6.2.5          Open source,
   bitnami/redis       15.3.3           6.2.5          Open source,
   ```

   Figure 5.6 – Redis chart versions

   For our dependency, let's use the wildcard version `15.5.x` so that we can lock in the latest patch that is currently available, `15.5.1`, but also so that we can easily download newer patch releases as they become available in the future.

   Let's also use the `condition` property so that Redis can be toggled to enabled or disabled. While our `guestbook` chart does require Redis, `condition` will allow a user to disable the built-in Redis option so that they can use their own if they desire.

4. Update your `guestbook` chart's `Chart.yaml` file to declare the Redis dependency. An updated `Chart.yaml` file is located in this book's GitHub repository in `chapter5/guestbook/Chart.yaml` for reference:

   ```
   dependencies:
     - name: redis
   ```

```
      repository: https://raw.githubusercontent.com/
bitnami/charts/archive-full-index/bitnami
      version: 15.5.x
      condition: redis.enabled
```

Your full `Chart.yaml` file should look as follows:

```
apiVersion: v2
name: guestbook
description: An application used for keeping a running
record of guests
type: application
version: 0.1.0
appVersion: v5
dependencies:
  - name: redis
    repository: https://raw.githubusercontent.com/
bitnami/charts/archive-full-index/bitnami
    version: 15.5.x
    condition: redis.enabled
```

Now that the `Chart.yaml` file has been updated, download the Redis dependency by using `helm dependency update`. Now, we can deploy the `guestbook` chart to ensure that the dependency has been installed properly.

5. Download the latest Redis `15.5.x` release by running `helm dependency update`:

   ```
   $ helm dependency update guestbook
   ```

6. Install the `guestbook` chart in your minikube environment:

   ```
   $ helm install guestbook guestbook -n chapter5
   ```

7. Verify that the Redis StatefulSets have been created:

   ```
   $ kubectl get statefulsets -n chapter5
   NAME                        READY   AGE
   guestbook-redis-master      1/1     3m24s
   guestbook-redis-replicas    3/3     3m24s
   ```

If you see a similar output for the StatefulSets shown here, then you have successfully created the Redis dependency! As you can see, by using Helm's dependency management, the effort required to deploy the backend was relatively low. In the next chapter, we'll continue developing the `guestbook` chart by writing templates for creating the frontend resources.

Before we wrap up, let's clean up the minikube environment.

Cleaning up

First, delete the `chapter5` namespace:

```
$ kubectl delete namespace chapter5
```

Now, you can shut down your minikube environment.

```
$ minikube stop
```

Now, let's summarize this chapter.

Summary

Dependencies can greatly reduce the effort required to deploy complex applications in Kubernetes. As we saw with our `guestbook` chart, to deploy a Redis backend, we only needed to add five lines of YAML to our `Chart.yaml` file. Compare this to the effort required to write an entirely separate Redis chart from scratch, which would have required both a high level of Kubernetes and Redis expertise.

Helm dependency management supports several different configurations to declare, as well as configure dependencies. To declare a dependency, you can specify the chart's `name`, `version`, and `repository` under the `dependencies` map in the `Chart.yaml` file. You can allow users to toggle whether to enable or disable each dependency using the `condition` and `tags` properties. When incorporating multiple instances of the same dependency, you can use `alias` to provide each with a unique identifier, and when working with dependencies with complex values, you can use `import-values` to simplify how values are propagated from a dependency to a parent chart. To list and download dependencies, Helm provides a set of `helm dependency` subcommands that are used regularly when managing chart dependencies.

In the next chapter, we will dive deep into the next crucial topic in the world of Helm chart development – templates.

Further reading

To learn more about Helm dependency management, visit the Helm documentation's *Chart Dependencies* section at `https://helm.sh/docs/topics/charts/#chart-dependencies`.

Questions

Answer the following questions to test your knowledge of this chapter:

1. What file is used to declare chart dependencies?
2. What is the difference between the `helm dependency update` and `helm dependency build` commands?
3. What is the difference between the `Chart.yaml` and `Chart.lock` files?
4. Imagine that you want to allow users to enable or disable dependencies within your chart. What `dependencies` properties can you use?
5. What `dependencies` properties should you use if you need to declare multiple invocations of the same dependency?
6. If you have a dependency with complex values, which `dependencies` property can you use to simplify the propagated values?
7. How do you override the values of a dependency?
8. As a chart developer, what is the value of using a chart dependency?

6
Understanding Helm Templates

One of the fundamental features of Helm is to create and maintain the Kubernetes resources that comprise an application. Helm accomplishes this with a concept called **templates**. Templates represent the core component comprising Helm charts, as they are used to configure Kubernetes resources based on a given set of **values**.

In *Chapter 4, Scaffolding a New Helm Chart*, you scaffolded a new Helm chart by using the `helm create` command, which created basic templates under the chart's `templates/` folder. In this chapter, we will dive deep into the world of Helm templates, and at the end, we will revisit the scaffolded templates to make improvements and deploy the Guestbook frontend. By the end of the chapter, your Helm chart will be able to deploy the full Guestbook architecture—from the Redis backend added in *Chapter 5, Helm Dependency Management*, to the frontend that we will add later in this chapter.

Here are the main topics for this chapter:

- Helm template basics
- Template values
- Built-in objects
- Helm template functions
- Helm template control structures
- Generating release notes
- Helm template variables
- Helm template validation
- Enabling code reuse with named templates and library charts
- Creating **custom resource definitions (CRDs)**
- Post rendering
- Updating and deploying the Guestbook chart

Technical requirements

This chapter requires the following tools:

- minikube
- kubectl
- Helm
- Git

We will use minikube to explore several examples throughout this chapter, so feel free to start your minikube environment by running the following command:

```
$ minikube start
```

Once minikube has started, create a new namespace for this chapter, like so:

```
$ kubectl create namespace chapter6
```

If you have not already cloned the example Git repository in previous chapters, do so by running the following command:

```
$ git clone https://github.com/PacktPublishing/Managing-Kubernetes-Resources-using-Helm.git
```

Now that your environment is set up, let's explore this chapter's first topic—Helm templating.

Helm template basics

Helm templates are used to dynamically generate Kubernetes **YAML Ain't Markup Language** (**YAML**) (or **JavaScript Object Notation** (**JSON**)) resources. They consume a set of default and user-provided values to generate resources that comprise a Kubernetes application. You've had some exposure to templates already in *Chapter 4, Scaffolding a New Helm Chart*, when you ran the `helm create` command, which generated a set of starter templates. In the Git repository cloned previously, these templates are located at `chapter6/guestbook/templates/`. Here's a short snippet of the `deployment.yaml` Helm template, located within the `chapter6/guestbook/templates/deployment.yaml` file:

```
apiVersion: apps/v1
kind: Deployment
metadata:
  name: {{ include "guestbook.fullname" . }}
  labels:
```

```
      {{- include "guestbook.labels" . | nindent 4 }}
spec:
  {{- if not .Values.autoscaling.enabled }}
  replicas: {{ .Values.replicaCount }}
  {{- end }}
  selector:
    matchLabels:
      {{- include "guestbook.selectorLabels" . | nindent 6 }}
  template:
    metadata:
      {{- with .Values.podAnnotations }}
      annotations:
        {{- toYaml . | nindent 8 }}
      {{- end }}
      labels:
        {{- include "guestbook.selectorLabels" . | nindent 8 }}
```

You may find the syntax from the preceding code snippet to be odd, as it resembles a YAML file, but it contains characters that are invalid per the YAML specification. To understand this syntax, we must first talk about **Go**. Go is a programming language developed by Google in 2009. It is the programming language used by Kubernetes, Helm, and many other tools in the container community. A core component of the Go programming language is **templates**, which are used to generate files of many different formats. Helm's template engine is built off of Go and can be thought of as a superset of Go templates. Go templates provide the fundamental syntax and control, while Helm adds extra capabilities to enhance the template engine's capabilities.

Helm templates contain various different actions, or strings, that begin with two opening curly braces ({{) and end with accompanying two closing curly braces (}}). Actions mark locations where data processing occurs or where control structures such as conditionals and loops are implemented. You can see different actions located throughout the code snippets and in other Helm chart templates under the `templates/` directory. While actions appear in local template files, they are processed and removed during processing, such as during an installation or upgrade, to produce a valid Kubernetes YAML resource.

There are many different components such as objects, functions, and control structures that you can leverage to write actions throughout your Helm chart templates. We will explore each of these throughout this chapter. Let's begin by discussing how the `values` component can be used within chart templates.

Template values

In previous chapters, we described values as parameters that are used to configure a Helm chart. Now, we will gain an understanding of how values are integrated into chart templates to dynamically generate Kubernetes resources.

Here is a basic `ConfigMap` template from the Git repository at `chapter6/examples/values-example/templates/configmap.yaml`:

```
apiVersion: v1
kind: ConfigMap
metadata:
  name: values-example
data:
  config.properties: |-
    chapterNumber={{ .Values.chapterNumber }}
    chapterName={{ .Values.chapterName }}
```

The last two lines of this template contain `{{ .Values.chapterNumber }}` and `{{ .Values.chapterName }}` actions, which are used as placeholders for the `chapterNumber` and `chapterName` values. This allows the ConfigMap to be parameterized based on the default chart values and the values the user provides during installation or upgrade.

Let's take a look at the default chart values located at `chapter6/examples/values-example/values.yaml`. You can see these here:

```
chapterNumber: 6
chapterName: Understanding Helm Templates
```

Given this `Values` file, we would expect the default ConfigMap to be rendered like this:

```
apiVersion: v1
kind: ConfigMap
metadata:
  name: values-example
data:
  config.properties: |-
    chapterNumber=6
    chapterName=Understanding Helm Templates
```

You could verify this on your own by running the `helm install` command, as we have demonstrated in previous chapters, but it may be more convenient to leverage a new command, `helm template`, which is used to render template resources locally, but not install them to the Kubernetes cluster. The `helm template` command, as shown here, has the same syntax as `helm install`:

```
helm template <RELEASE_NAME> <CHART_NAME> [flags]
```

Let's use this command to render the `values-example` chart templates locally. Proceed as follows:

1. Run the `helm template` command, pointing the `<CHART_NAME>` parameter to the `values-example` folder, as follows:

    ```
    $ helm template example chapter6/examples/values-example
    ```

2. You should see the ConfigMap rendered as shown previously, with the actions replaced by `chapterNumber` and `chapterName` values, as illustrated in the following code snippet:

    ```
    <skipped for brevity>
    data:
      config.properties: |-
        chapterNumber=6
        chapterName=Understanding Helm Templates
    ```

Unless we intend to install resources to the minikube environment, we will use the `helm template` command to quickly demonstrate templating constructs throughout this chapter. That way, you won't have to worry about cleaning up after each exercise. We will return to using `helm install` at the end of this chapter when we install an updated version of the Guestbook Helm chart.

As you saw in the preceding example, templates that reference values refer to a construct called `.Values` each time an action is being used as a placeholder for chart values. `.Values` is one of several built-in objects that are at your disposal as a Helm chart developer. Let's explore these built-in objects next.

Built-in objects

Built-in objects are essential building blocks that you can use to write your own Helm charts. As mentioned previously, they provide access to chart values by using the `.Values` object, but there are many more objects to explore that provide access to additional information and features.

The following table lists these built-in objects:

Object	Definition
.Values	Used to access values in the values.yaml file or values that were provided using the --values and --set flags
.Release	Used to access metadata about the Helm release, such as its name, namespace, and revision number
.Chart	Used to access metadata about the Helm chart, such as its name and version
.Template	Used to access metadata about chart templates, such as their filename and path
.Capabilities	Used to access information about the Kubernetes cluster
.Files	Used to access arbitrary files within a Helm chart directory
.	The root object

Table 6.1 – Built-in Helm objects

Each object contains fields and functions that are accessible by using dot notation. Dot notation is used to access an object's properties. For example, imagine the following Values file is provided:

```
books:
  harryPotter:
    - The Sorcerer's Stone
    - The Chamber of Secrets
    - The Prisoner of Azkaban
  lotr:
    - The Fellowship of the Ring
    - The Two Towers
    - Return of the King
```

The .Values object would now contain the following properties:

- .Values.books.harryPotter (list of strings)
- .Values.books.lotr (list of strings)

In Helm (and Go templates), a dot (.) is also used to represent object scope. The dot represents global scope, from which all objects are accessible. A dot followed by an object name limits the scope of that object. For example, the .Values scope limits visibility to the chart's values, and the .Release scope limits visibility to the release's metadata. Scopes play a significant role in loops and control structures, which we will explore later in this chapter.

While the `.Values` object is the most common object that you will use throughout Helm chart development, there are other built-in objects that we will discuss. We'll start with the `.Release` object next.

The .Release object

The `.Release` object is used to retrieve metadata about the Helm release being installed. Two common attributes that are used from within the `.Release` object are `.Release.Name` and `.Release.Namespace`, which allow chart developers to substitute the release name and namespace in their chart templates.

Consider the following example template, located at `chapter6/examples/release-example/templates/configmap.yaml` in the Git repository:

```
apiVersion: v1
kind: ConfigMap
metadata:
  name: {{ .Release.Name }}
data:
  config.properties: |-
    namespace={{ .Release.Namespace }}
```

In the template, we are setting the ConfigMap's name to the name of the Helm release, and we are setting the namespace property to the release namespace.

When running the Helm `install`, `upgrade`, or `template` commands, you can see the `{{ .Release.Name }}` and `{{ .Release.Namespace }}` actions get replaced with their actual values, as illustrated in the following code snippet:

```
$ helm template release-example chapter6/examples/release-example
---
# Source: release-example/templates/configmap.yaml
apiVersion: v1
kind: ConfigMap
metadata:
  name: release-example
data:
  config.properties: |-
    namespace=default
```

As you can see, the ConfigMap name has been generated as `release-example`, and the `namespace` property has been generated as `default` (if we had selected a different namespace using the `-n` flag, that value would have been reflected instead). By using the `.Release` object, we were able to leverage the name and namespace that were provided when invoking Helm rather than creating repetitive values in `values.yaml` for the name and namespace.

There are several more objects besides `name` and `namespace` under `.Release` that you can leverage in your chart templates. The following table lists each `.Release` object, with the descriptions quoted from the Helm documentation at `https://helm.sh/docs/chart_template_guide/builtin_objects/#helm`:

Object	Description
.Release.Name	The release name
.Release.Namespace	The namespace to be released into
.Release.IsUpgrade	This is set to `true` if the current operation is an upgrade or rollback
.Release.IsInstall	This is set to `true` if the current operation is an install
.Release.Revision	The revision number for this release
.Release.Service	The service that is rendering the template (this is always equivalent to the `"Helm"` string)

Table 6.2 – .Release objects

We will explore the `.Chart` object next.

The .Chart object

The `.Chart` object is used to retrieve metadata from the `Chart.yaml` file of the Helm chart that is being installed. It is commonly used for labeling chart resources with the chart name and version. Let's take a look at the example template at `chapter6/examples/chart-example/templates/configmap.yaml` from the Git repository. You can view this here:

```
apiVersion: v1
kind: ConfigMap
metadata:
  name: {{ .Release.Name }}
  labels:
    helm.sh/chart: {{ .Chart.Name }}-{{ .Chart.Version }}
    app.kubernetes.io/version: {{ .Chart.AppVersion }}
```

```
data:
  config.properties: |-
    chapterNumber={{ .Values.chapterNumber }}
    chapterName={{ .Values.chapterName }}
```

As you can see in the `metadata.labels` section, the template is using the `{{ .Chart.Name }}`, `{{ .Chart.Version }}`, and `{{ .Chart.AppVersion }}` actions, which retrieve the name, version, and appVersion fields from the `Chart.yaml` file. Here, you can see the `Chart.yaml` file for this example chart:

```
apiVersion: v2
name: chart-example
description: A Helm chart for Kubernetes
type: application
version: 1.0.0
appVersion: 0.1.0
```

When we use the `helm template` command to render this template locally, we see the fields from the `Chart.yaml` file are used in the ConfigMap resource, as illustrated here:

```
$ helm template chart-example chapter6/examples/chart-example
---
# Source: chart-example/templates/configmap.yaml
apiVersion: v1
kind: ConfigMap
metadata:
  name: chart-example
  labels:
    helm.sh/chart: chart-example-1.0.0
    app.kubernetes.io/version: 0.1.0
data:
  config.properties: |-
    chapterNumber=6
    chapterName=Understanding Helm Templates
```

The `.Chart` object can reference any field from the `Chart.yaml` file. For a full list of `Chart.yaml` fields, please refer to *Chapter 4, Scaffolding a New Helm Chart*.

The .Template object

The `.Template` object is used to retrieve metadata about the current template that is being rendered. It is the simplest built-in object (besides `.Values`) and contains only two objects underneath, as outlined here:

- `.Template.Name`—The file path to the template being rendered (such as `mychart/templates/mytemplate.yaml`)
- `.Template.BasePath`—The path leading up to the `templates` directory (such as `mychart/templates`)

In our experience, the `.Template` object is rarely used, but it can be useful if you need to reference the template's file path in your chart.

The .Capabilities object

The `.Capabilities` object is used for getting information about the target Kubernetes cluster. There are many objects underneath `.Capabilities`, but the most common are `.Capabilities.APIVersions.Has` and `.Capabilities.KubeVersion`.

The `.Capabilities.APIVersions.Has` object is a function that returns a Boolean based on whether or not the Kubernetes cluster has a given **application programming interface (API)** version. Here is an example invocation:

```
{{ .Capabilities.APIVersions.Has "batch/v1" }}
```

This action would return `true` or `false` based on whether or not the cluster contains the "batch/v1" API version. `.Capabilities.APIVersions.Has` is most commonly used in conditional logic to install a resource only if the cluster contains a particular API version. Conditional logic will be covered in the *Helm template control structures* section later in this chapter.

The other commonly used `.Capabilities` object is `.Capabilities.KubeVersion`. Use this property to retrieve the version of the Kubernetes cluster. For example, the following action would return a `v1.21.2` string (or similar, based on the version of Kubernetes being used):

```
{{ .Capabilities.KubeVersion }}
```

Other `.Capabilities` objects, such as `.Capabilities.KubeVersion.Major` and `.Capabilities.KubeVersion.Minor`, allow chart developers to get only the major or minor version of the Kubernetes cluster (as opposed to the whole **Semantic Versioning (SemVer)** version). For a full list of objects under `.Capabilities`, visit the Helm documentation at https://helm.sh/docs/chart_template_guide/builtin_objects/#helm.

The .Files object

Occasionally, you may encounter use cases where you need to include contents from files in your chart templates. You can include file contents by using the `.Files` object. This is used primarily with ConfigMap and Secret resources, where the `data` section is provided or supplemented by a separate configuration file. Note that files must be located within the Helm chart directory (but outside of the `templates/` folder) in order to be referenced with `.Files`.

The `.Files` object contains several other objects underneath. The most basic is `.Files.Get`, which is a function that retrieves the contents of the provided filename. Imagine a ConfigMap template such as this (this template is also located in the Git repository at `chapter6/examples/files-example/get`):

```
apiVersion: v1
kind: ConfigMap
metadata:
  name: {{ .Release.Name }}
data:
  config.properties: |-
    {{ .Files.Get "files/config.properties" }}
```

The `.Files.Get` function in the example is being used to get the contents of the `files/config.properties` file, which is a path relative to the Helm chart root. This file is located at `chapter6/examples/files-example/get/files/config.properties` in the Git repository and contains the following:

```
chapterNumber=6
```

Now, when we render this template, we will see the following output:

```
$ helm template basic-files-example chapter6/examples/files-example/get
---
# Source: files-example/templates/configmap.yaml
apiVersion: v1
kind: ConfigMap
metadata:
  name: basic-files-example
data:
  config.properties: |-
    chapterNumber=6
```

Three other important objects under `.Files` are `.Files.Glob`, `.Files.AsConfig`, and `.Files.AsSecret`. First, `.Files.Glob`, is a function that returns a list of file objects that match a provided **global** (**glob**) pattern. A glob pattern is a set of names with wildcard characters (`*`). For example, the `files/*` glob would match each file under the `files/` folder.

The `.Files.Glob` object is commonly used with `.Files.AsConfig` and `.Files.AsSecrets` objects. `.Files.AsConfig` is a function used to return the file as a YAML dictionary, where the key is the name of the file and the value is the file contents. It is called `AsConfig` because it is useful when formatting different ConfigMap data entries. The `.Files.AsSecrets` function is similar, but in addition to returning files as a YAML map, `AsSecrets` also Base64-encodes the contents of the file—this is useful for creating data for Kubernetes Secrets. Do keep in mind that sensitive files should never be checked into a Git repository in plaintext (though we have one such file in the example Git repository for demonstration purposes).

The following templates demonstrate the usage of these objects and are also located in the Git repository at `chapter6/examples/files-example/glob`:

```
---
apiVersion: v1
kind: ConfigMap
metadata:
  name: {{ .Release.Name }}
data:
{{ (.Files.Glob "files/chapter*").AsConfig | indent 2 }}
---
kind: Secret
<skipped for brevity>
Data:
{{ (.Files.Glob "files/secret*").AsSecrets | indent 2 }}
```

The `files` folder contains the following files:

- `chapter.properties`
- `secret.properties`

When this template is rendered, the contents of both files are generated as YAML maps under the ConfigMap's `data`, as illustrated in the following code snippet:

```
$ helm template glob-example chapter6/examples/files-example/glob
---
```

```
# Source: files-example/templates/configmap.yaml
apiVersion: v1
kind: ConfigMap
metadata:
  name: glob-example
data:
  chapter.properties: |
    chapterNumber=6
    chapterName=Understanding Helm Templates
---
# Source: files-example/templates/secret.yaml
apiVersion: v1
kind: Secret
<skipped for brevity>
  secret.properties:
dXNlcm5hbWU9bXl1c2VyMTIzCnBhc3N3b3JkPW15cGFzczEyMwo=
```

In the previous example, you likely noticed the usage of | indent 2. This represents a pipeline and function that will be explored thoroughly in the next section, *Helm template functions*. For now, all you need to worry about is that the output is indented by two spaces in order to produce properly formatted ConfigMap and Secret resources.

Other .Files objects are .Files.GetBytes, which returns a file as an array of bytes, and .Files.Lines, which is used to iterate over each line of a file.

Helm template functions

One of the common traits of any templating language is the ability to transform data. Thus far, when referring to .Values or any of the other built-in objects within Helm, we have only made reference to the resource as-is, without any form of data manipulation. Where Helm really begins to shine and show its true power is its ability to perform complex data processing within templates through the use of template functions and pipelines.

Since Helm uses Go as the basis for its own templating language, it inherits the capabilities provided by functions. A Go template function is comparable to any other function that you may have interacted with in another programming language. Functions contain logic designed to consume certain inputs and provide an output based on the inputs that were provided.

When using Go templates, functions make use of the following syntax:

```
functionName arg1 arg2 . .
```

A function that is commonly used within Helm charts is the `quote` function, as it encompasses quotation marks surrounding an input string. Take the following ConfigMap located in `chapter6/examples/functions-example/templates/configmap.yaml` from the Git repository:

```yaml
apiVersion: v1
kind: ConfigMap
metadata:
  name: {{ .Release.Name }}
  labels:
    helm.sh/chart: {{ .Chart.Name }}-{{ .Chart.Version }}
    app.kubernetes.io/version: {{ .Chart.AppVersion }}
  annotations:
    {{- toYaml .Values.annotations | nindent 4 }}
data:
  path: {{ .Values.fs.path }}
  config.properties: |-
    {{- (.Files.Get "files/chapter-details.cfg") | nindent 4}}
```

The `path` property in the preceding ConfigMap represents a filesystem location that is consumed by an application, as shown in the following code snippet. The value referenced by this property is located in the `values.yaml` file:

```yaml
fs:
  path: /var/props/../configs/my app/config.cfg
```

The resulting template would be rendered as follows (some fields were omitted for brevity):

```yaml
...
data:
  path: /var/props/../configs/my app/config.cfg
...
```

A potential downstream issue within a consuming application could result if it did not contain logic to appropriately manage whether spaces could be present within the input.

To avoid these potential issues, add the `quote` function that will surround the property with quotation marks, as shown in the following code snippet:

```yaml
apiVersion: v1
kind: ConfigMap
metadata:
```

```
  name: {{ .Release.Name }}
  labels:
    helm.sh/chart: {{ .Chart.Name }}-{{ .Chart.Version }}
    app.kubernetes.io/version: {{ .Chart.AppVersion }}
  annotations:
    {{- toYaml .Values.annotations | nindent 4 }}
data:
  path: {{ quote .Values.fs.path }}
...
```

Use the `helm template` command to render the chart locally to see the function in action, as follows:

```
$ helm template functions-example chapter6/examples/functions-
example
```

The result upon template rendering produces a /var/props/../configs/my app/config.cfg string that not only enhances the readability of the property but protects any consuming application.

`quote` is just one of over 60 functions included within Helm. While some of the functions are sourced from Go templates, the majority are part of the Sprig template library. The Sprig library includes functions to implement more complex capabilities within charts, such as the ability to perform mathematical formulas, conversion operations, and the management of data structures, including lists and dictionaries.

The functions inherited from Go and Sprig can be found in the Go documentation at https://pkg.go.dev/text/template#hdr-Functions and in the Sprig template library at http://masterminds.github.io/sprig/.

One of the more recent functions added to Helm is the ability to query resources from a running Kubernetes environment through the use of the `lookup` function. Helm chart developers can make reference to a single resource or references of a given type across a namespace or cluster and inject the results within their templates.

The `lookup` function takes the following form:

```
lookup <apiVersion> <kind> <namespace> <name>
```

For example, to query a ConfigMap called `props` in the `chapter6` namespace, use the following function:

```
lookup "v1" "ConfigMap" "chapter6" "props"
```

The result from the `lookup` function is a dictionary that can be further navigated as necessary to retrieve individual properties on the returned resource.

So, to extract a property defined on a ConfigMap called `author` containing the default name of the author for all WordPress posts, the following code would be added within a Helm template:

```
{{ (lookup "v1" "ConfigMap" "chapter6" "props").data.author }}
```

As you can see, we are first retrieving a dictionary of values containing the `props` ConfigMap and then navigating to the `author` property on the ConfigMap data structure.

You are not limited to querying for a single resource when using the `lookup` function and can instead search for all resources of a given type within a single namespace or within all namespaces. This can be accomplished by substituting empty quotes for either the namespace and/or resource name, as shown in the following template:

```
lookup "v1" "ConfigMap" "chapter6" ""
```

One final important note when working with the `lookup` function is that it can only be used when resources are being deployed to a Kubernetes cluster, such as through the `helm install` and `helm upgrade` commands. This is due to the requirement that there be an active connection to a Kubernetes cluster as part of the execution process being performed. For commands such as `helm template`, where templates are being rendered locally and there is no interaction with a Kubernetes cluster, the `lookup` function will not return any meaningful results.

Helm functions and their ability to influence Helm template commands are just the first steps toward adding more dynamic mechanisms to chart templates. Multiple template commands can also be chained together to perform a series of complex actions through the use of **pipelines**.

Pipelines are a borrowed concept from Unix where the result from one command is fed in as the input of another command. You can see an illustration of this in the following code snippet:

```
cat file.txt | grep helm
```

Commands are separated by the pipe (`|`) character (hence the name *pipeline*) where in this case, the output of the contents of the `file.txt` file is provided as an input to the `grep` command. `grep` processes the input, filters out any presence of the word `helm` from the input, and provides it as an output that is printed to the screen.

Pipelines can be applied to Helm in a similar fashion. Let's return to the prior example where we introduced the `quote` function to add quotation marks to a filesystem path. Instead of using the `value` property as a function argument, inverse the order to pipe the contents of the value into the `quote` function, as follows:

```
{{ .Values.fs.path | quote }}
```

The end result remains the same whether calling the function directly or using the pipeline approach. However, in practice, you will find that pipelines are the preferred option over directly invoking functions, given the extensibility of chinning template commands.

You may also have noticed that the `fs.path` value includes a reference to a relative path (denoted by ..). This may be difficult for some to read and or understand if they are unfamiliar with the syntax. Fortunately, there is a function included in the Sprig library called `clean` that can resolve the path fully and remove any relative paths automatically. This function can be added to the existing pipeline, as shown here:

```
{{ .Values.fs.path | clean | quote }}
```

In the ConfigMap within the `functions-example` Helm chart from the Git repository, apply the preceding changes and then use the `helm template` command to see the changes in action. Upon instantiation, the rendered template would look like this:

```
"/var/configs/my app/config.cfg"
```

Functions and pipelines are both extensively used within Helm, and it is important that as a chart developer, you have insights into the available options in order to design charts effectively. Let's take a moment to look at a few more commonly used functions.

`Values` files, as we have seen, contain a dictionary of key/value pairs. While individual key/value pairs can be referenced, there are plenty of situations where a deeply nested structure would want to be injected instead. Fortunately, several Helm functions can help in this situation.

As you recall, the YAML language is very particular about the specific indentation and spacing of content. To account for this, Helm provides the `toYaml` function, which allows a dictionary of values to be provided, and for it to be formatted appropriately, regardless of how deeply nested it is. An example of this can be found within the ConfigMap that we have been using thus far in this section where a dictionary of annotations is injected from properties defined in the `Values` file, as illustrated in the following code snippet:

```
apiVersion: v1
kind: ConfigMap
metadata:
  name: {{ .Release.Name }}
  labels:
    helm.sh/chart: {{ .Chart.Name }}-{{ .Chart.Version }}
    app.kubernetes.io/version: {{ .Chart.AppVersion }}
  annotations:
    {{- toYaml .Values.annotations | nindent 4 }}
data:
  ...
```

The following content is defined within the chart `values.yaml` file:

```
annotations:
  publisher: "Packt Publishing"
  title: "Managing Kubernetes Resources Using Helm"
```

You may also notice that the result of the `toYaml` function is then piped to another function called `nindent`. The use of this function is a necessary requirement to manage the formatting of the content; otherwise, a rendering error would occur. Both `indent` and `nindent` provide formatting capabilities by indenting content a certain number of spaces, crucial when working with YAML. The difference between `indent` and `nindent` is that `nindent` will add a newline character after each line of input, a required step in our use case as there are multiple annotation properties defined within the `Values` file.

Process the chart using the `helm template` command to visualize how these values would be rendered, as follows:

```
$ helm template functions-example chapter6/examples/functions-example
apiVersion: v1
kind: ConfigMap
metadata:
  name: functions-example
  labels:
    helm.sh/chart: functions-example-0.1.0
    app.kubernetes.io/version: 1.16.0
  annotations:
    publisher: Packt Publishing
    title: Managing Kubernetes Resources Using Helm
```

The final Helm function that we will look at in detail is used when performing more complex rendering of templates. Earlier in this chapter, you learned how external files can be referenced within charts and their values injected into templates using the built-in `.Files` object. While Helm's templating capabilities can be used to evaluate resources within template files, there are cases where there is a need to perform evaluation against externally sourced files. Take a look here at the ConfigMap once again and note the `config.properties` key:

```
config.properties: |-
  {{- (.Files.Get "files/chapter-details.cfg") | nindent 4}}
```

Instead of including the values directly within the ConfigMap, they are instead sourced from a file located at `files/chapter-details.cfg`, as illustrated in the following code snippet:

```
chapterNumber={{ .Values.book.chapterNumber }}
chapterName={{ .Values.book.chapterName }}
```

However, when the chart is rendered using `helm template`, the desired values are not substituted as we would expect, as we can see here:

```
  config.properties: |-
    chapterNumber={{ .Values.book.chapterNumber }}
    chapterName={{ .Values.book.chapterName }}
```

This situation occurs since template processing only occurs by default, within files in the `templates` folder and not in any externally sourced content. To apply templating to external sources that are brought into templates, the `tpl` function can be used, as shown here:

```
...
  config.properties: |-
    {{- tpl (.Files.Get "files/chapter-details.cfg") . | nindent 4}}
```

What you may be wondering about when looking at the updated content of the ConfigMap is the presence of the period (.) before the pipe. This character indicates the scope that will be passed to the templating engine. We will cover this topic in detail in the next section.

Use the `helm template` command to confirm that values are substituted appropriately thanks to the inclusion of the `tpl` function, as follows:

```
$ helm template functions-example chapter6/examples/functions-example
...
  config.properties: |-
    chapterNumber=6
    chapterName=Understanding Helm Templates
```

The template functions addressed in this section only scratch the surface of the functions provided by Helm. The following table lists a few other important functions that chart developers should be aware of in order to fully take advantage of what Helm has to offer:

Function	Description	Example
`printf`	Returns a string based upon a formatting string and arguments	`printf "A cat named %s has %d lives." $name $numLives`
`default`	Assigns a string "placeholder" if the content of `$value` is `nil` or empty	`default "placeholder" $value`
`list`	Returns a new list based upon a series of inputs	`list "ClusterIP" "NodePort" "LoadBalancer"`
`has`	Determines if an element is present in a list	`has 4 $list`
`b64enc/b64dec`	Encodes or decodes with Base64. Useful when working with Secrets.	`b64enc $mySecret`
`atoi`	Convert a string to an integer	`atoi $myIntegerString`
`add`	Adds a list of integers	`add 1 2 3`
`upper/lower`	Convert the entire string to uppercase or lowercase	`upper $myString`
`now`	Gets the current date and time	`Now`
`date`	Formats a date in the specified format	`now	date "2006-01-02"`

Table 6.3 – A list of common Helm functions

With a better understanding of the ways that Helm can be used to manipulate and format content within templates using functions, let's turn to how we can introduce flow control to manage the content that will be rendered.

Helm template control structures

The way in which templates are generated can be managed by chart developers thanks to the functionality provided by control structures. Included in the `actions` component of the `Go` templates, control structures enable fine-grained flow control for determining the types of resources that should be generated and how they are rendered.

The following control-structure keywords are available:

- `if/else`—Creating conditional blocks for resource generation
- `with`—Modifying the *scope* of resources being generated
- `range`—Looping over a set of resources

There are occasions where portions of a template would need to be included or excluded based on some sort of condition. In this situation, an `if/else` action can be used. Here is a basic example for conditionally determining whether to include a readiness probe as part of a deployment resource:

```
{{- if .Values.readinessProbe.enabled }}
readinessProbe:
  httpGet:
    path: /healthz
    port: 8080
    scheme: HTTP
  initialDelaySeconds: 30
  periodSeconds: 10
{{- end }}
```

The `readinessProbe` section will only be included when the condition evaluates to `true`. However, it is important to note that the condition is actually a pipeline where multiple statements can be chained together to aid in the creation of complex conditionals. The logic behind the `if/else` action can also be interpreted as follows:

```
{{ if PIPELINE }}
    # Do something
{{ else if OTHER PIPELINE }}
    # Do something else
{{ else }}
    # Default case
{{ end }}
```

The conditional statements and their associated `if/else` action should look familiar to anyone with prior programming experience. But what is the logic behind determining whether a pipeline is `true` or `false`?

A pipeline fails to evaluate to `true` when the following is returned:

- A `false` Boolean
- A numeric 0
- An empty string
- `nil` (whether it be empty or `null`)
- An empty collection

So, in the previous scenario where conditional logic is applied to the readiness probe, the probe would only be included if the value is `readinessProbe.enabled=true`.

Nesting of conditionals can also be applied within templates. The following code snippet illustrates how conditionals can be used to determine the type of probe that should be applied to `readinessProbe`:

```
{{- if .Values.readinessProbe.enabled }}
readinessProbe:
{{- if eq .Values.readinessProbe.type "http" }}
  httpGet:
    path: /healthz
    port: 8080
    scheme: HTTP
  initialDelaySeconds: 30
  periodSeconds: 10
{{- else }}
  tcpSocket:
    port: 8080
{{- end }}
{{- end }}
```

An `httpGet` probe type will be applied when the `readinessProbe.type` property is equal to `"http"`. Otherwise, a **Transmission Control Protocol** (**TCP**) probe will be used.

`eq` (short for *equals*) within the `if` statement is one of the available Boolean functions that test the equality of the two arguments. When the `readinessProbe.type` is equal to `http`, the `httpGet` probe type will be applied. Otherwise, a TCP probe type will be used.

A full list of available Boolean functions is provided here:

- `and`
- `or`
- `not`
- `eq` (short for *equals*)
- `ne` (short for *not equals*)
- `lt` (short for *less than*)
- `le` (short for *less than or equal to*)
- `gt` (short for *greater than*)
- `ge` (short for greater than or *equal to*)

Another method of flow control available for chart developers is the ability to modify the scope of the resources being rendered. A period (.) represents the *current scope*, and thus far, we have been operating at the root or top-level scope. Each of the built-in objects that were covered earlier in this chapter is available at this level. However, when working with objects with deeply nested structures, there may be a desire to modify the scope being applied to avoid rather unwieldy property references.

The `with` action provides these necessary capabilities to modify the current scope.

Take a look at the `flowcontrol-example` Helm chart located at `chapter6/examples/flowcontrol-example` within the Git repository. Included within the `values.yaml` file is a deeply nested dictionary of properties, as illustrated here:

```yaml
book:
  chapter6:
    props:
      chapterNumber: 6
      chapterName: Understanding Helm Templates
```

These values should look familiar given that they have been used several times in this chapter, but note that they are now placed into a deeply nested dictionary. They could be referenced in the following manner:

```
chapterNumber: {{ .Values.book.chapter6.props.chapterNumber }}
chapterName: {{ .Values.book.chapter6.props.chapterName }}
```

However, by using the `with` action, the current scope is changed so that references within the block begin at `.Values.book.chapter6.props`, greatly increasing the readability and reducing the complexity. You can see an illustration of this in the following code snippet:

```
{{- with .Values.book.chapter6.props }}
  chapterNumber: {{ .chapterNumber }}
  chapterName: {{ .chapterName }}
{{- end }}
```

This is illustrated within the ConfigMap located at `chapter6/examples/flowcontrol-example/templates/configmap.yaml`. Render the chart using the `helm template` command to confirm that values within the ConfigMap are generated properly, as follows:

```
$ helm template flowcontrol-example chapter6/examples/
flowcontrol-example
```

One very important note when modifying scope is that chart developers may be caught off guard when attempting to reference any built-in objects such as `.Release` or `.Chart` within a block where the current scope has changed.

Attempting to use the following templating within the ConfigMap would result in an error upon instantiation:

```
{{- with .Values.book.chapter6.props }}
  chapterNumber: {{ .chapterNumber }}
  chapterName: {{ .chapterName }}
  ChartName: {{ .Chart.Name }}
{{- end }}
Error: template: flowcontrol-example/templates/configmap.
yaml:12:22: executing "flowcontrol-example/templates/configmap.
yaml" at <.Chart.Name>: nil pointer evaluating interface
{}.Name
```

This is due to the fact that the current scope within the `with` statement is no longer at the root scope where the built-in objects reside. Fortunately, Helm provides a way to reference the root scope by using `$`. By adding `$` to the `.Chart.Name` reference, a rendering error will no longer occur. You can see this in use in the following code snippet:

```
{{- with .Values.book.chapter6.props }}
  chapterNumber: {{ .chapterNumber }}
  chapterName: {{ .chapterName }}
  ChartName: {{ $.Chart.Name }}
{{- end }}
```

The final flow-control action that chart developers need to be aware of is `range`—this is useful when performing `foreach` style iteration over lists and dictionaries. Similar to the `with` action, the `range` action also modifies the scope of resources being rendered.

For example, say the following were included as values within a `values.yaml` file to represent ports associated with a Service resource:

```
service:
  ports:
    - name: http
      port: 80
      targetPort: 8080
    - name: https
      port: 443
      targetPort: 8443
```

By using the `range` action, these values can be then applied to the Service, as shown in the following example:

```yaml
apiVersion: v1
kind: Service
metadata:
  name: {{ .Release.Name }}
  labels:
    helm.sh/chart: {{ .Chart.Name }}-{{ .Chart.Version }}
    app.kubernetes.io/version: {{ .Chart.AppVersion }}
spec:
  type: ClusterIP
  ports:
  {{- range .Values.service.ports }}
    - port: {{ .port }}
      targetPort: {{ .targetPort }}
      protocol: TCP
      name: {{ .name }}
  {{- end }}
  selector:
    app: {{ .Release.Name }}
```

The `range` action modifies the scope in a similar fashion as the `with` action so that within the block, the current scope represents each port within the `ports` list during each iteration of the loop and can be referenced accordingly. An example of this in practice can be found in the `flowcontrol-example` chart within the Git repository located at `chapter6/examples/flowcontrol-example`.

Generating release notes

One special type of Helm template is called the `NOTES.txt` file, located in a Helm chart's `templates/` folder. This file is used to dynamically generate usage instructions (or other details) for applications once they are installed with Helm.

A `NOTES.txt` file uses the same exact templating syntax as Kubernetes resource templates and can be seen in the following example:

```
Follow these instructions to access your application.
{{- if eq .Values.serviceType "NodePort" }}
export NODE_PORT=$(kubectl get --namespace {{ .Release.Namespace }} -o jsonpath="{.spec.ports[0].nodePort}" services
```

```
{{ .Release.Name }})

export NODE_IP=$(kubectl get nodes --namespace {{ .Release.
Namespace }} -o jsonpath="{.items[0].status.addresses[0].
address}")

echo "URL: http://$NODE_IP:$NODE_PORT
{{- else }}
export SERVICE_IP=$(kubectl get svc --namespace {{ .Release.
Name }} wordpress --template "{{ range (index .status.
loadBalancer.ingress 0) }}{{.}}{{ end }}")

echo "URL: http://$SERVICE_IP"
{{- end }}
```

These examples would provide instructions on how to access applications deployed by the chart. They would be displayed during the install, upgrade, and rollback phases, and can be recalled by running the `helm get notes` command. By providing a `NOTES.txt` file, chart developers can provide additional insight on how to better use applications that have just been deployed.

In the next section, we will discuss Helm template variables.

Helm template variables

In addition to leveraging values and other built-in objects, chart developers can create variables of their own within chart templates to provide additional processing options. A common use case for this approach is flow control, but template variables can serve other use cases as well.

A variable in a chart template is defined as follows:

```
{{ $myvar := "Hello World!" }}
```

The preceding example creates a variable called `myvar` and sets the value to a string equaling to `Hello World!`. Variables can be assigned to objects as well, such as a chart's values, as illustrated here:

```
{{ $myvar := .Values.greeting }}
```

Once a variable is defined, it can be referenced in the following way:

```
data:
  greeting.txt: |-
    {{ $myvar }}
```

Another example of using variables is in a `range` block, where variables capture the index and value of list iterations, as illustrated in the following code snippet:

```
data:
  greetings.txt
{{- range $index, $value := .Values.greetings }}
    Greeting {{ $index }}: {{ $value }}
{{- end }}
```

`index` represents the current loop iteration number and `value` represents the value from the list for the iteration. The previous snippet is rendered as follows:

```
data:
  greetings.txt
    Greeting 0: Hello
    Greeting 1: Hola
    Greeting 2: Hallo
```

Variables can also simplify the processing of map iterations, as shown here:

```
data:
  greetings.txt
{{- range $key, $val := .Values.greetings }}
    Greeting in {{ $key }}: {{ $val }}
{{- end }}
```

A possible result might look like this:

```
data:
  greetings.txt
    Greeting in English: Hello
    Greeting in Spanish: Hola
    Greeting in German: Hallo
```

Another common use case for Helm variables is to refer to values outside of the current scope.

Consider the following `with` block:

```
{{- with .Values.application.configuration }}
My application is called {{ .Release.Name }}
{{- end }}
```

A template such as this one would fail to process since `.Release.Name` is not under the scope of `.Values.application.configuration`. One way this can be remedied is by setting a variable to `.Release.Name` above the `with` block, as follows:

```
{{ $appName := .Release.Name }}
{{- with .Values.application.configuration }}
My application is called {{ $appName }}
{{- end }}
```

While this is a possible solution to this problem, the approach of using a dollar sign ($) to refer to the global scope is preferred as it requires fewer lines to configure and is easier to read as the complexity increases. In this case, this template could be rewritten like so:

```
{{- with .Values.application.configuration }}
My application is called {{ $.Release.Name }}
{{- end }}
```

We will explore template validation next.

Helm template validation

When working with Kubernetes and Helm, input validation is automatically performed by the Kubernetes API server when a new resource is created. This means that if an invalid resource is created by Helm, an error message will be returned by the API server, resulting in a failed installation. Although Kubernetes performs input validation, there may still be cases in which chart developers will want to perform validation before the resources reach the API server, such as to return a simple error message or to limit the range of possibilities to the user.

In Helm, input validation refers to validating user-provided values to ensure that users have provided a proper set of values. You can perform this validation in three different ways (or a combination of these three), as follows:

- Using the `fail` function
- Using the `required` function
- Using a `values.schema.json` file

Let's begin exploring input validation by first looking at the `fail` function.

The fail function

The `fail` function is used to immediately fail the Helm installation and is often used in cases where users have provided an invalid value. In this section, we'll explore an example use case of the `fail` function that restricts user input and halts the installation if the user has provided a value outside of the expected set of values.

Many Helm charts support values for setting the Kubernetes Service type. There are many different Service types that a user could choose from, but here are a few:

- `ClusterIP`: Assigns an **Internet Protocol** (**IP**) address to the Service. Reachable only from within the cluster.
- `NodePort`: Exposes a port on each Kubernetes node. Reachable from outside the cluster.
- `LoadBalancer`: Creates a load balancer on the cloud provider where Kubernetes is deployed, if applicable.

Let's assume that we want to restrict users to be able to only create a `ClusterIP` or `NodePort` Service. We can use the `fail` function to fail and provide an error message if the Service type is not one of these two types.

The example in the Git repository, located at `chapter6/examples/fail-example`, demonstrates this use case. In the `values.yaml` file, we see the following value:

```
service:
  type: ClusterIP
```

In the `service.yaml` template (located in the chart's `templates/` folder), we see the following lines of code:

```
{{- $serviceTypes := list "ClusterIP" "NodePort" }}
{{- if has .Values.service.type $serviceTypes }}
  type: {{ .Values.service.type }}
{{- else }}
  {{- fail "value 'service.type' must be either 'ClusterIP' or 'NodePort'" }}
{{- end }}
```

In the previous template snippet, we first created a variable called `serviceTypes` and set it to a list of strings, containing the `ClusterIP` and `NodePort` types. Then, in an `if` action, we used the `has` function to determine whether or not the `service.type` value was included in the `serviceTypes` list, representing the set of permitted values. If the value provided was found, then we assume that the input was valid and render the service type and proceed with the installation. Otherwise, the `fail` function would be invoked, failing the installation and displaying to the user a message that explains the reason for the failure.

Since the default service is already `ClusterIP` (as seen in the `values.yaml` file), we know that running `helm template` or `helm install` without providing any additional values would be successful. But let's see what happens if we try to set the `service.type` value to an invalid setting, such as `LoadBalancer`. This is what we'd see:

```
$ helm template fail-example chapter6/examples/fail-example
--set service.type=LoadBalancer
Error: execution error at (fail-example/templates/service.
yaml:10:6): value 'service.type' must be either 'ClusterIP' or
'NodePort'
```

As you can see in the error message, the `fail` function caused rendering to fail early and displays an error message that was coded in the Service template.

Let's look at the next way to perform input validation—the `required` function.

The required function

The `required` function, as with `fail`, is also used to halt template rendering. The difference is that, unlike `fail`, the `required` function is used to ensure that a value is not left blank when a chart's templates are rendered. It is named as such because it requires a user to provide a value when specified.

Take a look at this snippet of the `values.yaml` file from the chart at `chapter6/examples/required-example`:

```
service:
  type:
```

In the `service.yaml` template for this chart, we see the following output:

```
spec:
  type: {{ required "value 'service.type' is required" .Values.
service.type }}
```

This invocation of `required` checks to see if the string represented by the `service.type` value is empty. If it is empty, rendering fails and an error message is displayed. Otherwise, it renders the `service.type` value.

We can see this in action by using the `helm template` command, as follows:

```
$ helm template required-example chapter6/examples/required-
example
Error: execution error at (required-example/templates/service.
yaml:6:11): value 'service.type' is required
```

As expected, we receive an error message stating that the `service.type` value is required. The user can then remedy this error by providing a value for `service.type` by using either the `--set` or `--values` flags.

Let's explore the final validation method that we will touch upon—the `values.schema.json` file.

The values.schema.json file

The `values.schema.json` file is used to define and enforce a schema for your chart's values. Whereas the `required` and `fail` functions are invoked from within chart templates, the `values.schema.json` file allows you to set value requirements and constraints in a single location. This file also adds additional validation capabilities, such as setting minimums and maximums for integer values.

The `values.schema.json` file is based on the **JSON Schema** vocabulary. An exhaustive overview of JSON Schema is out of scope for this book, but you can explore the vocabulary yourself by visiting `http://json-schema.org/specification.html`.

Let's review an example `values.schema.json` file, located in the chart at `chapter6/examples/schema-example` within the Git repository. You can see a representation of this here:

```
{
    "$schema": "http://json-schema.org/draft-07/schema",
    "required": [
        "image",
        "service"
    ],
    "properties": {
        "image": {
            "type": "object",
            "required": [
                "repository",
                "tag"
            ],
            "properties": {
                "repository": {
                    "type": "string"
                },
                "tag": {
                    "type": "string"
                }
            }
        },
        "service": {
            "type": "object",
            "required": ["type", "port"],
            "properties": {
              "type": {
                "type": "string",
                "enum": ["ClusterIP", "NodePort"]
              },
              "port": {
                "type": "integer",
                "minimum": 8080
              }
            }
        }
    }
}
```

Figure 6.1 – Sample values.schema.json file

This schema provides validation for the following objects under `.Values`:

Object	Validation
`.Values.image`	Ensures that the image object exists
`.Values.image.repository`	Ensures that the `image.repository` value exists and is a string
`.Values.image.tag`	Ensures that the `image.tag` value exists and is a string
`.Values.service`	Ensures that the service object exists
`.Values.service.type`	Ensures that the `service.type` value exists and is set to either `ClusterIP` or `NodePort`
`.Values.service.port`	Ensures that the `service.port` value exists and is greater than or equal to `8080`

Table 6.4 – Values that are validated in the example values.schema.json file

As shown in the preceding table, there is a lot of robust validation being performed by providing the `values.schema.json` file. More values could be added to the schema file, but we've only included a small amount for demonstration purposes. Sometimes, it is useful to include all supported values in the `values.schema.json` file for purposes of self-documentation or to ensure that all values are strictly validated.

When using a `values.schema.json` file, error messages are handled for you automatically. For example, let's see what happens if we try to set `service.type` to `LoadBalancer` (which is not supported in the **enumerator** (**enum**) defined in the schema). Here's the result:

```
$ helm template schema-example chapter6/examples/schema-example
--set service.type=LoadBalancer
Error: values don't meet the specifications of the schema(s) in
the following chart(s):
schema-example:
- service.type: service.type must be one of the following:
"ClusterIP", "NodePort"
```

Notice we did not have to specify the specific error message to return to the user—the JSON Schema library provided it for us.

In this section, we reviewed three different input validation strategies. Next, we'll look at enabling template reuse with named templates and library charts.

Enabling code reuse with named templates and library charts

When creating template files, there may be boilerplate or repetitive blocks of YAML among the different Kubernetes resources in a chart.

For example, you may strive to use a consistent set of labels for each resource, as illustrated here:

```
labels:
  "app.kubernetes.io/instance": {{ .Release.Name }}
  "app.kubernetes.io/managed-by": {{ .Release.Service }}
  "helm.sh/chart": {{ .Chart.Name }}-{{ .Chart.Version }}
  "app.kubernetes.io/version": {{ .Chart.AppVersion }}
```

The preceding labels could be copy-pasted manually throughout your templates, but this would be cumbersome, especially if you wanted to make updates to these labels in the future. To help reduce the amount of boilerplate code and to enable reuse, Helm provides a construct called **named templates**.

Named templates, as with regular Kubernetes templates, are defined under the `templates/` directory. They begin with an underscore and end with the `.tpl` file extension. Many charts (including our Guestbook chart) leverage a file called `_helpers.tpl` that contains these named templates, though the file does not need to be called `helpers`. When creating a new chart with the `helm create` command, this file is included in the scaffolded set of resources.

To create a named template, chart developers can leverage the `define` action. The following example creates a named template that can be used to encapsulate resource labels:

```
{{- define "mychart.labels" }}
labels:
  "app.kubernetes.io/instance": {{ .Release.Name }}
  "app.kubernetes.io/managed-by": {{ .Release.Service }}
  "helm.sh/chart": {{ .Chart.Name }}-{{ .Chart.Version }}
  "app.kubernetes.io/version": {{ .Chart.AppVersion }}
{{- end }}
```

The `define` action takes a template name as an argument. In the preceding example, the template name is called `mychart.labels`. The common convention for naming a template is `$CHART_NAME.$TEMPLATE_NAME`, where `$CHART_NAME` is the name of the Helm chart and `$TEMPLATE_NAME` is a short, descriptive name that describes the purpose of the template. The `mychart.labels` name implies that the template is native to the `mychart` Helm chart and will generate labels for resources it is applied to.

To use a named template in a Kubernetes YAML template, you can use the `include` function, which has the following usage:

```
include [TEMPLATE_NAME] [SCOPE]
```

The `TEMPLATE_NAME` parameter is the name of the named template that should be processed. The `SCOPE` parameter is the scope in which values and built-in objects should be processed. Most of the time, this parameter is a dot (`.`) to denote the current top-level scope, but any scope could be provided including the dollar-sign (`$`) symbol, which should be used if the named template references values outside of the current scope.

The following example demonstrates how the `include` function is used to process a named template:

```
metadata:
  name: {{ .Release.Name }}
{{- include "mychart.labels" . | indent 2 }}
```

This example begins by setting the name of the resource to the name of the release. It then uses the `include` function to process the labels and indents each line by two spaces, as declared by the pipeline. When processing is finished, a rendered resource may appear as follows for a release called `template-demonstration`:

```
metadata:
  name: template-demonstration
  labels:
    "app.kubernetes.io/instance": template-demonstration
    "app.kubernetes.io/managed-by": Helm
    "helm.sh/chart": mychart-1.0.0
    "app.kubernetes.io/version": 1.0
```

Helm also provides a `template` action that can also expand named templates. This action has the same usage as `include`, but with one major limitation—it cannot be used in a pipeline to provide additional formatting and processing capabilities. The `template` action is used to simply display data inline. Because of this limitation, chart developers should use the `include` function over the `template` action since `include` has feature parity with `template` but also provides additional processing options.

Named templates are excellent for reducing boilerplate in a single Helm chart, but imagine you want to share common boilerplate (such as labels) across multiple Helm charts. To do this, you can leverage **library charts**. Library charts are similar in structure to application charts, but their `type` field in `Chart.yaml` is set to `library`. Library charts also differ in that they cannot be installed—a library chart's purpose is to provide a set of helper templates that can then be imported among different application charts by using dependency management.

An example of a library chart is Bitnami's `common` chart, which can be seen at the following link: `https://github.com/bitnami/charts/tree/master/bitnami/common`. There, you will find that each of the chart's templates is actually a `tpl` file that contains named templates within. Here is an abbreviated list from Bitnami's common library chart:

- `_affinities.tpl`
- `_capabilities.tpl`
- `_errors.tpl`
- `_images.tpl`

These named templates can be used by adding the following dependency to any application Helm chart:

```
dependencies:
  - name: common
    version: 0.x.x
    repository: https://raw.githubusercontent.com/bitnami/charts/archive-full-index/bitnami
```

Then, any chart importing this dependency can leverage any template by referencing the template name with the `include` function—for example, `{{ include "common.names.fullname" . }}`.

In the next section, we will explore how Helm can handle the creation of Kubernetes **custom resources** (**CRs**).

Creating CRDs

While Helm is often used to create traditional Kubernetes resources, it can also be used to create CRDs and CRs. CRDs are used to define resources that are not native to the Kubernetes API. You may want to use this functionality to augment the abilities that Kubernetes provides. CRs are resources that implement the CRD's specification. As a result, it's important to ensure that a CRD is always created before the CRs that implement it.

Helm is able to ensure CRDs are created and registered to Kubernetes before CRs are included in a Helm chart when CRDs are included in the chart's `crds/` folder. All CRDs defined under this folder are created before those in `templates/`.

An example `crds/` folder is shown here:

```
crds/
  my-custom-resource-crd.yaml
```

The `my-custom-resource-crd.yaml` file may have the following contents:

```
apiVersion: apiextensions.k8s.io/v1
kind: CustomResourceDefinition
metadata:
  name: my-custom-resources.learnhelm.io
spec:
  group: learnhelm.io
  names:
    kind: MyCustomResource
    listKind: MyCustomResourceList
    plural: MyCustomResources
    singular: MyCustomResource
  scope: Namespaced
  version: v1
```

Then, the `templates/` directory can contain an instance of the `MyCustomResource` resource (that is, the CR), as illustrated here:

```
templates/
  my-custom-resource.yaml
```

There are a few important caveats to note when creating CRDs with Helm. First, CRDs cannot be templated, so they are created exactly as defined under the CRDs folder. Second, CRDs cannot be deleted with Helm, and as a result, they also cannot be upgraded or rolled back. Third, creating CRDs requires `cluster-admin` privileges within the Kubernetes cluster. Note that these caveats apply to CRDs, not CRs. Since CRs are created in the `templates/` folder, they are treated by Helm like regular Kubernetes resource templates. CRs also typically do not require elevated permissions to the level of `cluster-admin`, so they can typically be installed by normal users.

Throughout this chapter, we have discussed using templates to render Kubernetes resources with Helm. In the next section, we will discuss how advanced Helm chart users can further process Kubernetes resources while running an installation.

Post rendering

When developing Helm charts, you should carefully consider each of the different values that need to be included in your chart. For example, if you know users may need to change the Service type within Service templates, you should expose a value to do so to keep your chart flexible. The same idea holds true for image names, resources, health checks, and other settings users would need to configure based on your use case.

Sometimes, however, users will still require additional flexibility that is not provided by a Helm chart. This is where post rendering comes into play. Post rendering is an advanced feature of Helm that allows users to perform further modifications to rendered chart templates when they install your chart. It is often seen as a last resort if they require modifications that your Helm chart does not allow.

Post rendering is applied by adding the `--post-renderer` flag to the `install`, `upgrade`, or `template` commands. Here is an example:

```
$ helm install <release-name> <path-to-chart> --post-renderer
<path-to-executable>
```

The `<path-to-executable>` parameter is an executable file that invokes the post-renderer. The executable could be anything from a Go program to a shell script invoking another tool, such as **Kustomize**. Kustomize is a tool used for patching YAML files, so it is often used for post rendering.

We won't dive deep into Kustomize because it is out of scope for this book. However, we have included an example of using Kustomize as a post-renderer in the Git repository at `chapter6/examples/post-renderer-example` that can be invoked as follows, assuming that the `kustomize` command-line tool is available on the local machine:

```
$ cd chapter6/examples/post-renderer-example/post-render
$ helm template nginx ../nginx --post-renderer ./hook.sh
```

The `hook.sh` file invokes Kustomize, which patches the deployment and service YAML resources with custom environment variables and the `NodePort` service type, as defined in the `kustomization.yaml` file.

In this section, we discussed post rendering. One note before we depart from this topic is that post rendering should not be considered part of normal Helm usage. As a chart developer, you should ensure that your chart is flexible enough for users to leverage your chart as-is out of the box. As a chart user, you should try to avoid using post renders unless absolutely necessary. This is because you need to remember to use the `--post-renderer` flag on each Helm upgrade, or the patch will be inadvertently omitted. Post-renderers also require additional effort from the user to maintain, as there may be tooling or other prerequisites needed.

Throughout this chapter, we have covered each of the key components of Helm templates. Next, we will tie this all in by returning to our Guestbook chart. We will make small updates to the scaffolded `values.yaml` file and the `deployment.yaml` template, and we will deploy our Guestbook Helm chart.

Updating and deploying the Guestbook chart

In order to successfully deploy our Guestbook application, we need to add values to configure the following details:

- Configure the Redis service names and disable Redis authentication
- Create environment variables for defining the names of the Redis leader and follower

We will begin by first handling Redis values.

Updating Redis values

In *Chapter 5, Helm Dependency Management*, we created a Redis dependency for creating a backend. Now, we will add a couple of values to our `values.yaml` file to complete the configuration.

The values that we need to add are in the Git repository at `https://github.com/PacktPublishing/Managing-Kubernetes-Resources-using-Helm/blob/main/chapter6/guestbook/values.yaml#L5-L8` and are shown in the following snippet:

```
redis:
  fullnameOverride: redis
  auth:
    enabled: false
```

The `redis.fullnameOverride` value is used to ensure that deployed Redis instances are prefixed with `redis`. This will help ensure the Guestbook application is talking to consistently named instances.

Setting the `redis.auth.enabled` value to `false` will disable Redis authentication. This is necessary because the Guestbook frontend is not configured to authenticate with Redis.

That's all the changes needed for Redis. Let's update the Guestbook values and templates next.

Updating Guestbook's deployment template and values.yaml file

The `helm create` command we used in *Chapter 4, Scaffolding a New Helm Chart*, did an excellent job of giving us almost all of the templating features we need for this application, but there is one gap that we need to fill in order to deploy Guestbook. We need to be able to set environment variables in the Guestbook deployment in order to tell the frontend how to connect to Redis.

If we observe the Guestbook source code at https://github.com/GoogleCloudPlatform/kubernetes-engine-samples/blob/main/guestbook/php-redis/guestbook.php, we can see three different environment variables that need to be set, as follows:

- GET_HOSTS_FROM: Informs Guestbook whether or not it should retrieve the Redis hostnames from the environment. We will set this to env so that hostnames are retrieved from the two environment variables defined next.
- REDIS_LEADER_SERVICE_HOST: Provides the hostname of the Redis leader. Because the Redis dependency we are using specifies the leader as redis-master, we will set this value to redis-master.
- REDIS_FOLLOWER_SERVICE_HOST: Provides the hostname of the Redis follower. The Redis dependency we are using specifies the follower as redis-replicas, so we will set this value to redis-replicas.

Since the scaffolded deployment.yaml template did not allow for environment variables to be created, we need to write this logic into the template ourselves. We can do this by adding the lines located at https://github.com/PacktPublishing/Managing-Kubernetes-Resources-using-Helm/blob/main/chapter6/guestbook/templates/deployment.yaml#L50-L51, which are also shown here:

```
env:
  {{- toYaml .Values.env | nindent 12 }}
```

Here, we added a new env object. Underneath, we are using the toYaml function to format the env value (which we will add shortly) as a YAML object. Then, we are using a pipeline and the nindent function to form a new line and indent by 12 spaces.

Next, we need to add the env object with the associated content to our values.yaml file. An example of this is located at https://github.com/PacktPublishing/Managing-Kubernetes-Resources-using-Helm/blob/main/chapter6/guestbook/values.yaml#L10-L16 and is also displayed here:

```
env:
  - name: GET_HOSTS_FROM
    value: env
  - name: REDIS_LEADER_SERVICE_HOST
    value: redis-master
  - name: REDIS_FOLLOWER_SERVICE_HOST
    value: redis-replicas
```

With the Guestbook chart's values and template updated, let's move on to the next section.

Deploying the Guestbook chart

Now, it's time to deploy a fully functional Guestbook instance with our Helm chart! First, start your minikube environment and create a new namespace for this chapter, as shown here. If you already started and created the `chapter6` name at the beginning of this chapter, you can skip the next two commands:

```
$ minikube start
$ kubectl create namespace chapter6
```

Then, use the `helm install` command to deploy the Guestbook instance, as illustrated here. You should also watch the pods in the namespace for the Redis pods to become ready:

```
$ helm install guestbook chapter6/guestbook -n chapter6
$ kubectl get pods -n chapter6 -w
```

Once the Redis instances are ready, hit *Ctrl+C* to stop watching resources and then use the `kubectl port-forward` command to expose your Guestbook frontend to localhost on port `8080`:

```
$ kubectl port-forward svc/guestbook 8080:80 -n chapter6
```

Once the Guestbook service is exposed, you can navigate to the `http://localhost:8080` **Uniform Resource Locator** (**URL**) in your browser. The Guestbook frontend should appear. Try entering a message, such as **Hello world!**, and a message should appear under the blue **Submit** button, as illustrated here:

Guestbook

Messages

Submit

Hello world!

Figure 6.2 – The Guestbook frontend after the Hello world! message has been submitted

If you are able to load the page in a browser and enter a message, then congratulations! You have successfully built and deployed your first Helm chart! However, as with any software product, you can always continue to make improvements. We will enhance this chart in the next chapter by adding upgrade and rollback hooks for performing backup and restore of the Redis database.

For now, when you are done working, feel free to clean up your environment and stop your minikube instance, as follows:

```
$ kubectl delete ns chapter6
$ minikube stop
```

This brings us to the end of the section.

Summary

Templates represent the core of Helm's functionality. They allow you to create a variety of different Kubernetes resource configurations by enabling dynamic YAML generation. Helm's template engine, based on Go templates, contains several built-in objects upon which chart developers can build charts, such as the `.Values` and `.Release` objects. Templates also provide many different functions to provide robust formatting and manipulation, along with control structures for enabling conditional logic and loops. Besides rendering Kubernetes resources, templates can also be used to abstract boilerplate by using named templates and library charts.

By incorporating the capabilities provided by templates, we were able to make small modifications to the Guestbook chart at the end of the chapter by enhancing the content of the values and the `deployment.yaml` chart template, which resulted in the ability to deploy the Guestbook application successfully. In the next chapter, we will continue to explore templates and enhance our Helm chart by learning about and leveraging lifecycle hooks.

Further reading

To learn more about the basics behind creating Helm charts, consult the *Chart Template Developer's Guide* page on the Helm documentation at `https://helm.sh/docs/chart_template_guide/`.

Questions

See if you can answer the following questions:

1. Which Helm templating construct can you take advantage of to generate repeating YAML portions?
2. What is the purpose of the `with` action?
3. What are the different built-in objects in Helm templates?
4. How does a Kubernetes resource template differ from a named template?
5. How does an application chart differ from a library chart?
6. What can a chart developer do to perform input validation?
7. What are some examples of different functions commonly used in Helm templates?
8. What is the difference between a template variable and a value?

7
Helm Lifecycle Hooks

A Helm release undergoes several different phases during its lifetime. The first phase, **install**, occurs when the Helm chart is first installed. The second phase, **upgrade**, occurs when the Helm release is updated by either updating values or the Helm chart itself. At a later point, a Helm user may need to execute the **rollback** phase, which reverts the Helm release to an earlier state. Finally, if a user needs to delete the Helm release and its associated resources from the Kubernetes cluster, users must execute the **uninstall** phase.

Each phase is powerful on its own, but to provide additional capabilities around the release lifecycle, Helm features a **hooks** mechanism that allows custom actions to be undertaken at different points within a release cycle. For example, you may use hooks to do the following:

- Perform operations on a database, such as back up after upgrading or restoring a chart from a previous snapshot during a rollback.
- Fetch secrets from a secrets management engine after installing a chart.
- Clean up external assets after uninstalling a chart.

In this chapter, we will explore Helm hooks and understand how they can be used to enhance the capabilities of a Helm chart. Then, we will implement hooks in our Guestbook Helm chart to back up and restore the Redis database when the Helm release is upgraded and rolled back.

In this chapter, we will cover the following topics:

- The basics of a Helm hook
- Hook life cycle
- Hook cleanup
- Writing hooks in the Guestbook Helm chart
- Cleaning up

Technical requirements

For this chapter, you will need the following tools:

- minikube
- kubectl
- Helm
- Git

We will use minikube to explore several examples throughout this chapter, so feel free to start your minikube environment using the following command:

```
$ minikube start
```

Once minikube has started, create a new namespace for this chapter:

```
$ kubectl create namespace chapter7
```

If you have not already cloned the example `git` repository in previous chapters, clone the repository by running the following command:

```
$ git clone https://github.com/PacktPublishing/Managing-Kubernetes-Resources-using-Helm.git
```

Next, let's understand the basics of a Helm hook and explore an example of running one.

The basics of a Helm hook

A hook executes as a one-time action at a designated point in time during the life span of a release. A hook is implemented as a Kubernetes resource and, more specifically, within a container. While the majority of workloads within Kubernetes are designed to be long-living processes, such as an application serving API requests, hooks are made up of a single task or set of tasks that return 0 to indicate success or non-0 to indicate a failure.

The options that are typically used in a Kubernetes environment for creating short-lived tasks are a bare **pod** or a **job**. A bare pod is a pod that runs until completion and then terminates but will not be rescheduled if the underlying node fails. A bare pod differentiates from a standard pod by toggling the `restartPolicy` property. By default, this field is configured as `Always`, meaning that the pod will be restarted if it completes (either due to success or failure). Even though there are use cases for running bare pods, it is preferred to run lifecycle hooks as jobs, which has advantages over bare pods, including that you can reschedule the hook if the node fails or becomes unavailable.

Since hooks are simply defined as Kubernetes resources, they are created like other Helm templates and are placed in the `templates/` folder. However, hooks are different in that they are always annotated with the `helm.sh/hook` annotation. Hooks use this annotation to ensure that they are not rendered in the same fashion as the rest of the resources during standard processing. Instead, they are rendered and applied based on the value specified within the `helm.sh/hook` annotation, which determines when it should be executed within Kubernetes as part of the Helm release lifecycle.

The following is an example of a hook. This example can also be found in this book's GitHub repository at `chapter7/examples/hook-example/templates/hooks/job.yaml`:

```yaml
apiVersion: batch/v1
kind: Job
metadata:
  name: {{ .Release.Name }}-hook
  annotations:
    "helm.sh/hook": post-install
spec:
  template:
    metadata:
      name: {{ .Release.Name }}-hook
    spec:
      restartPolicy: Never
      containers:
      - name: {{ .Release.Name }}-hook
        command: ["/bin/sh", "-c"]
        args:
          - echo "Hook executed at $(date)"
        image: alpine
```

This trivial example prints out the current date and time after the chart is installed. A use case for this type of hook is to integrate with an auditing system that tracks when applications are installed in a Kubernetes environment. Note that although the hook is saved under the `template/hooks/` folder, it could have also been saved directly under `templates/`. The additional `hooks/` subdirectory was created only to separate application-specific templates from hook templates.

To demonstrate the behavior of Helm hooks, let's see this hook in action by installing the Helm chart located within `chapter7/examples/hook-example`:

1. First, install the `hook-example` Helm chart:

   ```
   $ helm install my-app chapter7/examples/hook-example -n
   chapter7
   ```

Note that this command may hang for longer than the Helm commands that have been invoked in the past. This is because Helm is waiting for the hook to be created and completed before returning.

Next, view the pods in the namespace. You will see two pods. The first is the application, while the second is the hook:

```
$ kubectl get pods -n chapter7
NAME                                      READY   STATUS
my-app-hook-example-6747bfbb6-dd9xz       1/1     Running
my-app-hook-p8rrd                         0/1     Completed
```

2. The pod with a status of `Completed` is the hook. Let's check the pod logs to view the output produced by the hook:

```
$ kubectl logs jobs/my-app-hook -n chapter7
Hook executed at Mon Jan 17 21:40:38 UTC 2022
```

As you can see, the hook logged the time just after the Helm chart was installed.

3. Uninstall the release and check the remaining pods. You will see that the hook remains in the namespace:

```
$ helm uninstall my-app -n chapter7
$ kubectl get pods -n chapter7
NAME                  READY   STATUS
my-app-hook-p8rrd     0/1     Completed
```

Once hooks have been created and executed, they become unmanaged. (This happens unless the `helm.sh/hook-delete-policy` annotation is applied. We will cover this later in this chapter in the *Advanced hook concepts* section.) As a result, we are responsible for cleaning up the hook ourselves. Let's do this now by deleting the job:

```
$ kubectl delete job my-app-hook -n chapter7
```

At this point, all the resources associated with the installation of the chart have been cleaned up.

Since hooks may contain long-running tasks, the release may time out. By default, Helm sets a timeout value of 5 minutes to complete all the steps related to a release. The timeout related to a release can also be controlled using the `--timeout` flag when performing a `helm install` or `helm upgrade` when an alternate value is desired. Modifying this value may be needed if a hook is long-running and may extend past the default timeout value.

Now that we have a basic understanding of Helm hooks, let's take a look at the different hook life cycle options.

Helm hook life cycle

As you saw regarding the job hook in the previous section, the point at which the job was executed was based on the value of the `helm.sh/hook` annotation. Since `post-install` was specified, the job was executed once all the associated resources were created as part of the release. The `post-install` option represents one of the points during the life span of a Helm chart where a hook can be executed.

The following table describes the available options for the `helm.sh/hook` annotation. A description of each hook can be found in the official Helm documentation, which can be found at https://helm.sh/docs/topics/charts_hooks/#the-available-hooks:

Annotation Value	Description
`pre-install`	Executes after templates are rendered but before any resources are created in Kubernetes.
`post-install`	Executes after all resources are created in Kubernetes.
`pre-delete`	Executes due to a deletion request before any resources are deleted from Kubernetes.
`post-delete`	Executes due to a deletion request after all the release's resources have been deleted.
`pre-upgrade`	Executes due to an upgrade request after templates are rendered but before any resources are updated.
`post-upgrade`	Executes due to an upgrade after all the resources have been upgraded.
`pre-rollback`	Executes due to a rollback request after templates are rendered but before any resources are rolled back.
`post-rollback`	Executes due to a rollback request after all resources have been modified.
`test`	Executes when the `helm test` subcommand is invoked. This will be discussed in more detail in *Chapter 9, Testing Helm Charts*.

Sometimes, you may have multiple resources with the same `helm.sh/hook` setting. For example, you may have a ConfigMap resource and a job resource both marked as hooks to run in the same phase, such as `pre-upgrade`. In this case, you can define the order in which these resources are created by using the `helm.sh/weight` annotation. This annotation is used to assign weighted values to each of the hook resources that are marked to execute in the same phase. Weights are sorted in ascending order, so the resource marked with the lowest weight is executed first. If weights are not applied but the Helm chart contains multiple hooks that execute in the same phase, then Helm infers the order by sorting the templates by resource kind and name in alphabetical order.

The following example illustrates setting the annotation value for a hook's weight to 0:

```
annotations:
  "helm.sh/hook": pre-upgrade
  "helm.sh/weight": "0"
```

This hook will be executed during the chart upgrade process and after the necessary resources have been rendered, but before them being applied to the Kubernetes cluster.

Apart from being able to position hooks in a single lifecycle phase, we can use the `helm.sh/hook` annotation to specify multiple phases. This can be done by specifying a comma-separated list of lifecycle phases. The following example defines a hook that should be installed both before and after a chart has been installed:

```
annotations:
  "helm.sh/hook": pre-install,post-install
```

In this example, where both the `pre-install` and `post-install` options are selected, the `helm install` command would be executed as follows:

1. The user initiates the installation of a Helm chart (by running, for example, `helm install wordpress bitnami/wordpress`).
2. Any CRDs in the `crds/` folder, if present, are installed in the Kubernetes environment.
3. The chart templates are verified and the resources are rendered.
4. The `pre-install` hooks are ordered by weight, then rendered and applied to the Kubernetes environment.
5. Helm waits until the hook resources have been created and, for pods and jobs, are reported to have been `Completed` or in an `Error` state.
6. The template resources are rendered and applied to the Kubernetes environment.
7. The `post-install` hooks are ordered by weight and then executed.
8. Helm waits until the `post-install` hooks have finished running.
9. The results of the `helm install` command are returned.

In this section, we reviewed the options for running hooks within different lifecycle phases. Next, we will discuss the cleanup process for hook-related resources.

Helm hook cleanup

In the *Helm hook basics* section, we noted that Helm hooks, by default, are not removed with the rest of the chart's resources when the `helm uninstall` command is invoked. Instead, we must clean up the resources manually. Luckily, several strategies can be employed to automatically remove hooks during a release's life cycle. These options include configuring a deletion policy and setting a **time to live** (TTL) on a job.

The `helm.sh/hook-delete-policy` annotation is used to set a deletion policy on hook resources. This annotation determines when Helm should remove the resources from Kubernetes. The following table highlights the available options. You can find descriptions for these in the Helm documentation at `https://helm.sh/docs/topics/charts_hooks/#hook-deletion-policies`:

Annotation Value	Description
`before-hook-creation`	Deletes the previous resources before the hook is launched (this is the default)
`hook-succeeded`	Deletes the resources after the hook is successfully executed
`hook-failed`	Deletes the resources if the hook failed during execution

If the `helm.sh/hook-delete-policy` annotation is not provided, then the `before-hook-creation` policy is applied by default. This means that if any existing hook resources are deleted (if they are present), they are recreated when the hook is executed. This is useful, especially for jobs, as conflicts can occur if jobs are recreated with the same name. By making use of the `before-hook-create` annotation, we can avoid this situation.

There are also situations where the other types of hook cleanup policies could be used. For example, you may want to apply the `hook-succeeded` value, which cleans up the hook if it is successfully executed, to avoid retaining excess resources. However, if an error does occur during the execution of the hook, the resources will remain to help with any troubleshooting to determine the cause of the error. The `hook-failed` cleanup type, as you can probably guess, removes the associated hook resources from the hook upon failure. This can be a useful option if you don't wish to retain the assets associated with a hook, regardless of whether it completes successfully or fails. Similar to the `helm.sh/hook` annotation, multiple deletion policies can be applied by setting the `helm.sh/hook-delete-policy` annotation with a comma-separated string:

```
annotations:
  "helm.sh/hook-delete-policy": before-hook-creation,hook-succeeded
```

The Helm delete policy represents the most encompassing way to clean up after hooks, but you can also leverage a job's `ttlSecondsAfterFinished` configuration to define a TTL in which jobs should be retained before they are automatically deleted. This will limit the amount of time that the job is retained in the namespace after it is completed. The following code shows an example of using the `ttlSecondsAfterFinished` job setting:

```
apiVersion: batch/v1
kind: Job
metadata:
  name: {{ .Release.Name }}-hook
  annotations:
    "helm.sh/hook": post-install
spec:
  ttlSecondsAfterFinished: 60
  <omitted>
```

In this example, the job will be removed 60 seconds after it completes or fails.

In this section, we discussed ways to automatically clean up resources and how regular chart resources (that is, resources that are not associated with hooks) are automatically removed when `helm uninstall` is invoked. There may be some situations, however, when you want specific chart resources to follow the behavior of hooks and remain installed in the cluster, even when the `helm uninstall` command is invoked. A common use case for this is when your chart has created persistent storage via a standalone `PersistentVolumeClaim` resource (as opposed to a `PersistentVolumeClaim` resource managed by a `StatefulSet` object). You may want this storage to be retained beyond the release's normal life cycle. You can enable this behavior by applying the `helm.sh/resource-policy` annotation to the resource, as shown in the following snippet:

```
annotations:
  "helm.sh/resource-policy": keep
```

Note that when using this annotation on non-hook resources, naming conflicts may occur if the chart is reinstalled.

So far, we have covered Helm hooks and the various options that are associated with them. Now, let's look at the power that hooks bring by writing a hook in our Guestbook Helm chart.

Writing hooks in the Guestbook Helm chart

As you may recall, the Guestbook Helm chart uses a Redis database to persist messages created by the user. Using Helm hooks, we can create a process that performs simple backup and restore processes of the Redis database at various points of the chart's life cycle. Let's take a look at the two hooks that we will create in this section:

- The first hook will occur in the `pre-upgrade` lifecycle phase. This phase takes place immediately after the `helm-upgrade` command is run, but before any Kubernetes resources have been modified. This hook will be used to take a data snapshot of the Redis database before the upgrade is performed, ensuring that the database is backed up in case any errors occur during the upgrade.
- The second hook will occur in the pre-rollback lifecycle phase. This phase takes place immediately after the `helm-rollback` command is run, but before any Kubernetes resources are reverted. This hook will restore the Redis database to a previously taken snapshot and ensure that the Kubernetes resources are reverted so that they match the configuration at the point in time when the snapshot was taken.

By the end of this section, you will be more familiar with lifecycle hooks and some of the powerful capabilities that can be performed with them. Be sure to keep in mind that the hooks that will be created in this section are simple and are designed for demonstration purposes only. It is not advised to use these hooks as-is in applications that may use Redis.

Let's begin by creating the `pre-upgrade` hook.

Creating the pre-upgrade hook to take a data snapshot

In Redis, data snapshots are contained inside a file called `dump.rdb`. We can back this file up by creating a hook that creates a new PVC in the Kubernetes namespace to store database backup contents. The hook can then create a `Job` resource that copies the `dump.rdb` file to the newly created `PersistentVolumeClaim`.

While the `helm create` command generates some powerful resource templates that allow the initial `guestbook` chart to be created quickly, it does not scaffold out any hooks that can be used for this task. As a result, you can create the pre-upgrade hook from scratch by following these steps:

1. First, you should create a new folder that will contain the hook templates. While this is not a technical requirement, it does help you organize the structure of your chart so that your hook templates are separate from the regular chart templates. It also allows you to group the hook templates by function (backup versus restore).

    Create a new folder called `templates/backup` in your `guestbook` Helm chart, as follows:

    ```
    $ mkdir -p guestbook/templates/backup
    ```

2. Next, you should create the two template files required to perform the backup. The first template that's required is a `PersistentVolumeClaim` template since this will be used to contain the backup `dump.rdb` file. The second template will be a job template that will be used to perform the copy.

   Create two empty template files to serve as placeholders, as follows:

   ```
   $ touch guestbook/templates/backup/persistentvolumeclaim.yaml
   $ touch guestbook/templates/backup/job.yaml
   ```

   You can double-check your work by referencing this book's GitHub repository. The file structure should reflect the example at https://github.com/PacktPublishing/Managing-Kubernetes-Resources-using-Helm/tree/main/chapter7/guestbook/templates/backup.

3. Now, let's fill in the contents of the `persistentvolumeclaim.yaml` template. Since the template's content is relatively lengthy, we'll copy each template from the GitHub repository and then take a deep dive into how they were created.

4. Copy the contents of the file shown in the following screenshot to your `backup/persistentvolumeclaim.yaml` file. You can find this file at https://github.com/PacktPublishing/Managing-Kubernetes-Resources-using-Helm/blob/main/chapter7/guestbook/templates/backup/persistentvolumeclaim.yaml:

```
 1  {{- if .Values.redis.master.persistence.enabled }}
 2  apiVersion: v1
 3  kind: PersistentVolumeClaim
 4  metadata:
 5    name: {{ include "guestbook.fullname" . }}-{{ .Values.redis.fullnameOverride }}-backup-{{ sub .Release.Revision 1 }}
 6    labels:
 7      {{- include "guestbook.labels" . | nindent 4 }}
 8    annotations:
 9      "helm.sh/hook": pre-upgrade
10      "helm.sh/hook-weight": "0"
11  spec:
12    accessModes:
13      - ReadWriteOnce
14    resources:
15      requests:
16        storage: {{ .Values.redis.master.persistence.size }}
17  {{- end }}
```

Figure 7.1 – The backup/persistentvolumeclaim.yaml template

- Lines 1 and 17 of the `backup/persistentvolumeclaim.yaml` file consist of an `if` action. Since this action encapsulates the whole file, it indicates that this resource will only be included if the `redis.master.persistence.enabled` value is set to `true`. This value defaults to `true` in the Redis chart and can be observed using the `helm show values` command.

- Line 5 determines the name of the new backup PVC (`PersistentVolumeClaim`). This name is based on the release name, Redis name, and the revision number from which the backup was taken. Notice the usage of the `sub` function, which aids in calculating the revision number. This is used to subtract 1 from the revision number since the `helm upgrade` command increments this value before the templates are rendered.

- Line 9 creates an annotation to declare this resource as a `pre-upgrade` hook. Finally, line 10 creates a `helm.sh/hook-weight` annotation to determine the order in which this resource should be created compared to other pre-upgrade hooks. Weights are run in ascending order, so this resource will be created before other pre-upgrade resources.

5. Now that the `persistentvolumeclaim.yaml` file has been created, we must create the final pre-upgrade template – that is, `job.yaml`. Copy the following contents to your previously created `backup/job.yaml` file. This can also be copied from this book's GitHub repository at https://github.com/PacktPublishing/Managing-Kubernetes-Resources-using-Helm/blob/main/chapter7/guestbook/templates/backup/job.yaml:

```yaml
{{- if .Values.redis.master.persistence.enabled }}
apiVersion: batch/v1
kind: Job
metadata:
  name: {{ include "guestbook.fullname" . }}-{{ .Values.redis.fullnameOverride }}-backup-{{ sub .Release.Revision 1 }}
  labels:
    {{- include "guestbook.labels" . | nindent 4 }}
  annotations:
    "helm.sh/hook": pre-upgrade
    "helm.sh/hook-weight": "1"
    "helm.sh/hook-delete-policy": before-hook-creation,hook-succeeded
spec:
  template:
    spec:
      containers:
        - name: backup
          image: redis:alpine3.15
          command: ["/bin/sh", "-c"]
          args:
            - |-
              redis-cli -h {{ .Values.redis.fullnameOverride }}-master save
              cp /data/dump.rdb /backup/dump.rdb
          volumeMounts:
            - name: redis-data
              mountPath: /data
            - name: backup
              mountPath: /backup
      restartPolicy: Never
      volumes:
        - name: redis-data
          persistentVolumeClaim:
            claimName: redis-data-{{ .Values.redis.fullnameOverride }}-master-0
        - name: backup
          persistentVolumeClaim:
            claimName: {{ include "guestbook.fullname" . }}-{{ .Values.redis.fullnameOverride }}-backup-{{ sub .Release.Revision 1 }}
{{- end }}
```

Figure 7.2 – The backup/job.yaml template

- Once again, line 9 defines this template as a pre-upgrade hook, while line 10 sets the hook weight to 1, indicating that this resource will be created after the `persistentvolumeclaim.yaml` template.
- Line 11 sets the `helm.sh/hook-delete-policy` annotation to specify when this job should be deleted. Here, we have applied two different policies. The first is `before-hook-creation`, which indicates it will be removed during subsequent `helm upgrade` commands if the job already exists in the namespace, allowing a fresh job to be created in its place. The second policy is `hook-succeeded`, which deletes the job if it finishes successfully. Another policy we could have added is `hook-failed`, which would delete the job if it failed. However, given that we want to keep failures around for the sake of troubleshooting, we haven't implemented this policy.
- Lines 19 through 22 contain the commands for backing up the Redis database. First, `redis-cli` is used to save the current state. Then, the `dump.rdb` file is copied from the master to the backup PVC created in the `backup/persistentvolumeclaim.yaml` template.
- Finally, lines 29 through 35 define the volumes that reference the master and backup PVCs.

In this section, we created two `pre-upgrade` hooks – one to create a backup PVC and another to copy the Redis `dump.rdb` file to the PVC. In the next section, we will create the `pre-rollback` hooks for restoring Redis to a previously taken backup. Afterward, we will deploy the `guestbook` chart to see these hooks in action.

Creating the pre-rollback hook to restore the database

Whereas the `pre-upgrade` hook was written to copy the `dump.rdb` file from the Redis master PVC to the backup PVC, a `pre-rollback` hook can be written to do the opposite – that is, restore the database to a previous snapshot.

This hook can be implemented by copying the `dump.rdb` file from the backup PVC to the master Redis instance. Then, a rollout of Redis must be performed to create new Redis replica pods. When the replicas reconnect to the master, they will load the backup `dump.rdb` file for the Guestbook frontend to read.

Follow these steps to create the `pre-rollback` hook:

1. Create the `templates/restore` folder, which will be used to contain the `pre-rollback` hook:

   ```
   $ mkdir guestbook/templates/restore
   ```

2. Next, scaffold the templates that are required for this hook. We need to create a `serviceaccount.yaml` template and a `rolebinding.yaml` template to create a **ServiceAccount** with permission to redeploy the Redis replicas. Then, we need a `job.yaml` template to perform the restore task:

```
$ touch guestbook/templates/restore/serviceaccount.yaml
$ touch guestbook/templates/restore/rolebinding.yaml
$ touch guestbook/templates/restore/job.yaml
```

You can check that you have created the correct structure by referencing this book's GitHub repository at https://github.com/PacktPublishing/Managing-Kubernetes-Resources-using-Helm/tree/main/chapter7/guestbook/templates/restore.

3. Now, let's create the first `pre-rollback` hook, `serviceaccount.yaml`. Copy the contents shown in the following screenshot into `restore/serviceaccount.yaml`. This code can also be found within this book's GitHub repository at https://github.com/PacktPublishing/Managing-Kubernetes-Resources-using-Helm/blob/main/chapter7/guestbook/templates/restore/serviceaccount.yaml:

```
1  apiVersion: v1
2  kind: ServiceAccount
3  metadata:
4    name: {{ include "guestbook.fullname" . }}-rollout
5    labels:
6      {{- include "guestbook.labels" . | nindent 4 }}
7    annotations:
8      "helm.sh/hook": pre-rollback
9      "helm.sh/hook-delete-policy": before-hook-creation,hook-succeeded
10     "helm.sh/hook-weight": "0"
```

Figure 7.3 – The restore/serviceaccount.yaml template

Line 8 defines this template as a `pre-rollback` hook. Since the hook's weight is 0 (on line 10), this will be created before the other pre-rollback templates.

4. The previous template created a ServiceAccount that we will use later in the job, but now, we need to give the ServiceAccount permission to roll out new Redis replica pods when it communicates with the Kubernetes API. To keep it simple for this example, we will give the ServiceAccount `edit` permission in the `chapter7` namespace.

Copy the contents shown in the following screenshot into the `restore/rolebinding.yaml` template. This code can also be found in this book's GitHub repository at https://github.com/PacktPublishing/Managing-Kubernetes-Resources-using-Helm/blob/main/chapter7/guestbook/templates/restore/rolebinding.yaml:

```
1  apiVersion: rbac.authorization.k8s.io/v1
2  kind: RoleBinding
3  metadata:
4    name: {{ include "guestbook.fullname" . }}-rollout
5    labels:
6      {{- include "guestbook.labels" . | nindent 4 }}
7    annotations:
8      "helm.sh/hook": pre-rollback
9      "helm.sh/hook-delete-policy": before-hook-creation,hook-succeeded
10     "helm.sh/hook-weight": "1"
11 roleRef:
12   apiGroup: rbac.authorization.k8s.io
13   kind: ClusterRole
14   name: edit
15 subjects:
16 - apiGroup: ""
17   kind: ServiceAccount
18   name: {{ include "guestbook.fullname" . }}-rollout
19   namespace: {{ .Release.Namespace }}
```

Figure 7.4 – The restore/rolebinding.yaml template

Lines 11 through 14 reference the `edit` ClusterRole that we want to grant, while lines 15 through 19 target our ServiceAccount in the namespace we are going to release to (which will be the `chapter7` namespace).

5. Finally, we need to add content to the `job.yaml` file. Copy the following content to your `restore/job.yaml` template. This content can also be found at https://github.com/PacktPublishing/Managing-Kubernetes-Resources-using-Helm/blob/main/chapter7/guestbook/templates/restore/job.yaml:

Writing hooks in the Guestbook Helm chart

```yaml
{{- if .Values.redis.master.persistence.enabled }}
apiVersion: batch/v1
kind: Job
metadata:
  name: {{ include "guestbook.fullname" . }}-{{ .Values.redis.fullnameOverride }}-restore-{{ .Release.Revision }}
  labels:
    {{- include "guestbook.labels" . | nindent 4 }}
  annotations:
    "helm.sh/hook": pre-rollback
    "helm.sh/hook-delete-policy": before-hook-creation,hook-succeeded
    "helm.sh/hook-weight": "2"
spec:
  template:
    spec:
      serviceAccountName: {{ include "guestbook.fullname" . }}-rollout
      initContainers:
        ## This will reload the master's database with the backup dump.rdb file
        - name: restore-master-state
          image: redis:alpine3.15
          command: ["/bin/sh", "-c"]
          args:
            - |-
              cp /backup/dump.rdb /data/dump.rdb
              redis-cli -h {{ .Values.redis.fullnameOverride }}-master debug reload nosave
          volumeMounts:
            - name: redis-data
              mountPath: /data
            - name: backup
              mountPath: /backup
      containers:
        ## This will roll out new Replica pods
        - name: rollout-new-replicas
          image: bitnami/kubectl
          command: ["/bin/sh", "-c"]
          args:
            - |-
              kubectl rollout restart statefulset {{ .Values.redis.fullnameOverride }}-replicas
      restartPolicy: Never
      volumes:
        - name: redis-data
          persistentVolumeClaim:
            claimName: redis-data-{{ .Values.redis.fullnameOverride }}-master-0
        - name: backup
          persistentVolumeClaim:
            claimName: {{ include "guestbook.fullname" . }}-{{ .Values.redis.fullnameOverride }}-backup-{{ .Release.Revision }}
{{- end }}
```

Figure 7.5 – The restore/job.yaml hook

This `job.yaml` template is where the core pre-rollback logic takes place. Lines 18 through 29 define an `initContainer` that copies the backup `dump.rdb` file to the Redis master and performs a reload, reverting the state of the master, as represented in the backup `dump.rdb` file. An `initContainer` is a container that runs until completion before any of the containers listed under the `containers` section are run. We created this first to ensure that the master is reverted before we move on to the next step.

Lines 30 through 37 represent the next step of the rollback. Here, we restart the Redis replica's `StatefulSet`. When the replicas reconnect to the master, they will serve the data represented by the backup `dump.rdb` file.

With the `pre-upgrade` and `pre-rollback` hooks created, let's see them in action within the minikube environment.

Executing the life cycle hooks

To run the lifecycle hooks you created, you must install your chart by running the `helm install` command:

```
$ helm install guestbook chapter7/guestbook -n chapter7
--dependency-update
```

When each pod reports the `1/1 Ready` state, access your Guestbook application by running a `port-forward` command, as follows:

```
$ kubectl port-forward svc/guestbook 8080:80 -n chapter7
```

Next, access the Guestbook frontend at `http://localhost:8080`, write a message, and click **Submit**. An example message can be seen in the following screenshot:

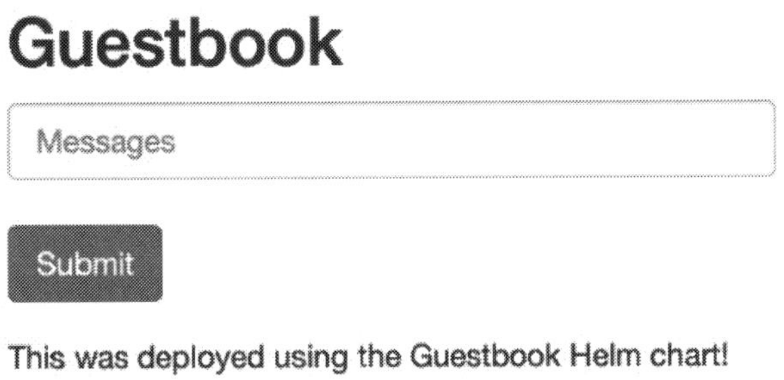

Guestbook

| Messages |

Submit

This was deployed using the Guestbook Helm chart!

Figure 7.6 – Entering a message in the Guestbook frontend

Once a message has been entered, run the `helm upgrade` command to trigger the `pre-upgrade` hook. The `helm upgrade` command will hang briefly until the backup has finished:

```
$ helm upgrade guestbook guestbook -n chapter7
```

When the command returns, you should find a new PVC that was created that contains the backup. The PVC is called `guestbook-redis-backup-1`:

```
$ kubectl get pvc -n chapter7
NAME                          STATUS
redis-data-redis-master-0     Bound
redis-redis-backup-1          Bound
```

Now that a backup has been completed, let's add another message. We plan to roll back after this message is entered. The following screenshot shows an example of the `guestbook` application after both messages have been added:

Guestbook

Messages

Submit

This was deployed using the Guestbook Helm chart!
This message should disappear after the rollback

Figure 7.7 – A second message entered in the Guestbook frontend

Now, let's run the `helm rollback` command to revert to the first revision. This command will hang briefly until the `helm rollback` command returns:

```
$ helm rollback guestbook 1 -n chapter7
```

When this command finishes, the Redis replicas should roll out. This rollout can be observed with the following command:

```
$ kubectl get pods -n chapter7 -w
```

Once the new replicas have been rolled out, refresh your Guestbook frontend in your browser. You will see the message you added after the upgrade disappears, as shown in the following screenshot:

Guestbook

Messages

Submit

This was deployed using the Guestbook Helm chart!

Figure 7.8 – The Guestbook frontend after the pre-rollback phase

Hopefully, this example provided you with a greater understanding of Helm hooks. We want to emphasize again that this was just a simple example and is not a production-ready solution.

Note that while this chapter focused on developing and running lifecycle hooks, hooks can be skipped by adding the `--no-hooks` flag to the `helm install`, `helm upgrade`, `helm rollback`, and `helm delete` commands. Adding this flag will cause Helm to skip the hooks associated with the lifecycle phase that was executed.

Let's wrap things up by cleaning up the minikube environment.

Cleaning up

First, delete the `chapter7` namespace to delete the `guestbook` release and associated PVCs:

```
$ kubectl delete ns chapter7
```

Next, stop the minikube environment:

```
$ minikube stop
```

With that, everything has been cleaned up.

Summary

Lifecycle hooks open the door to additional capabilities by allowing chart developers to install resources at different lifecycle phases. Hooks commonly include job resources to execute the actions that take place within a hook, but they also often include other resources, such as ServiceAccounts, policies including `RoleBindings`, and `PersistentVolumeClaims`. At the end of this chapter, we added lifecycle hooks to our Guestbook chart and ran through a backup and restore of the Redis database.

In the next chapter, we will discuss publishing a Helm chart to a chart repository.

Further reading

To learn more about lifecycle hooks, visit the Helm documentation at `https://helm.sh/docs/topics/charts_hooks/`.

Questions

Answer the following questions to test your knowledge of this chapter:

1. What are the nine different types of lifecycle hooks?
2. What annotation is used to define a hook?
3. What annotation is used to define the order in which a hook should be created?
4. What can a chart developer add to ensure that hooks are always deleted upon success?
5. How can a Helm user skip lifecycle hooks?
6. What Kubernetes resource is most often used to execute a lifecycle hook?

8
Publishing to a Helm Chart Repository

Helm could not be regarded as the package manager for **Kubernetes** without the concept of a **Helm chart repository**. Repositories are used to publish Helm charts to the community. In this chapter, we will understand different methods of creating a Helm chart repository. Later, we will get hands-on practice with different repository implementations by publishing our Guestbook Helm chart to an HTTP-based repository and an OCI registry.

In this chapter, we will cover the following topics:

- Understanding Helm chart repositories
- Publishing to an HTTP repository
- Publishing to an OCI registry

Technical requirements

For this chapter, you will need a GitHub account. If you already have a GitHub account, you can log in at `https://github.com/login`. Otherwise, you can create a new account at `https://github.com/join`.

You should also clone the Packt Git repository locally:

```
$ git clone https://github.com/PacktPublishing/Managing-
Kubernetes-Resources-using-Helm.git
```

To begin, let's understand the basics of a Helm chart repository.

Understanding Helm chart repositories

Helm chart repositories are used for publishing Helm charts and making them available to a wide community of Helm users. This is conceptually similar to the repositories that are used in Linux package management, such as RPM or Debian repositories, in which packages are installed using tools such as `dnf` or `apt-get`. Public Helm chart repositories can be found at Artifact Hub (https://artifacthub.io).

A Helm chart repository is created using one of two high-level implementations:

- An HTTP server
- An OCI registry

Using an HTTP server is the most common implementation for publishing charts since it has been in supported the longest. To create a Helm chart repository using an HTTP server, you can use tools such as **Apache httpd**, **NGINX, Amazon S3**, and **GitHub Pages**. **ChartMuseum** (https://github.com/helm/chartmuseum) is another popular option as it provides an API for more advanced operations. In the *Publishing to an HTTP repository* section, we will use GitHub Pages to create our repository.

A repository that's been created using an HTTP server must consist of the following components:

- Helm charts, packaged as `.tgz` archives
- An `index.yaml` file, containing metadata about the charts contained in the repository

Basic chart repositories require maintainers to generate `index.yaml` files using the `helm repo index` command, which we will explore later, but more advanced solutions such as ChartMuseum can automatically generate the `index.yaml` file when new charts are uploaded to the repository.

Besides HTTP, the other type of repository a Helm chart maintainer can distribute charts to is an **Open Container Initiative** (**OCI**) registry. OCI is an open governance structure for creating open standards for container runtimes and formats. Artifacts is an OCI initiative that allows you to store and serve additional content, such as Helm charts, within container registries aside from container images. Since images and their registries are already a fundamental construct in both Kubernetes and Helm, the ability to leverage the same registry to store both container images and Helm charts reduces the amount of effort needed by Helm maintainers to publish charts. We will explore publishing Helm charts using OCI registries in greater detail in the *Publishing to an OCI registry* section.

In the next section, we'll publish our Guestbook Helm chart to GitHub Pages. Here, you will get an understanding of how a basic Helm chart repository is created and interacted with.

Publishing to an HTTP repository

GitHub Pages is a feature within GitHub that allows you to serve static content from a repository. In this section, we'll create a new GitHub repository with Pages enabled to publish our Guestbook Helm chart.

To follow the example in this section, you must have a GitHub account. Directions for creating a GitHub account or logging into an existing one were provided in the *Technical requirements* section.

Once you are logged into GitHub, continue to the next section to create your repository.

Creating a GitHub Pages repository

Follow these steps to create a GitHub Pages repository:

1. Go to `https://github.com/new` and access the **Create a new repository** page.
2. Provide a name for your chart repository. We suggest `Chart-Repository-Example`.
3. Select the checkbox next to **Initialize this repository with a README**. This is required because GitHub does not allow you to create a static site if it does not contain any content. You can leave the rest of the settings at their default values. Note that to leverage GitHub Pages, you must leave the privacy setting set to **Public** unless you have a paid GitHub Pro account.

Your **Create a new repository** page should now look as follows:

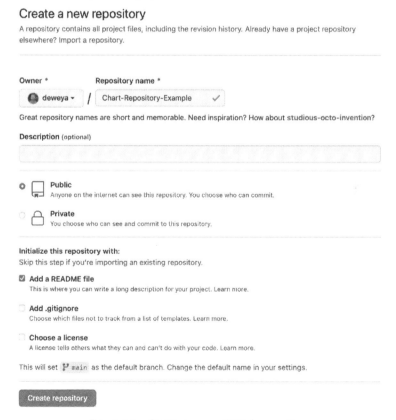

Figure 8.1 – Creating a new GitHub repository

4. Click the **Create repository** button to create your repository.

   Although your repository has been created, it is not ready to serve Helm charts until GitHub Pages is enabled.

5. Click the **Settings** tab within your repository to access your repository settings. From there, select the **Pages** tab from the left-hand column. Then, under **Source**, select the **main** option from the drop-down list. Finally, click the **Save** button. This will instruct GitHub to create a static site that serves the contents of your main branch.

   At this point, your screen should look similar to the following:

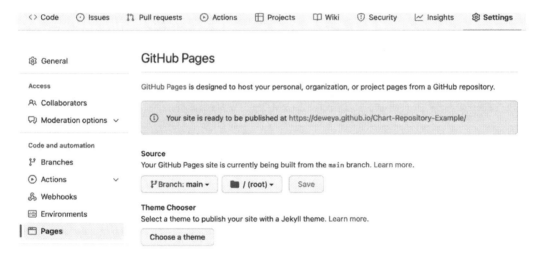

Figure 8.2 – Finding GitHub Pages settings

Now that you have configured your GitHub repository, you should clone it to your local machine so that you can add the Guestbook Helm chart to it later. Follow these steps to clone your repository:

1. Navigate to the root of your repository by selecting the **Code** tab at the top of the page.
2. Select the green **Clone or download** button. This will reveal the URI to your GitHub repository (note that this is not the same as the URL for the static site). You can use the following screenshot as a reference to find your repository URI:

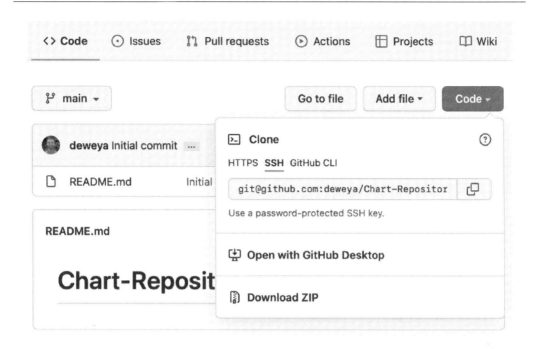

Figure 8.3 – Locating the git URI

3. Once you have acquired your repository's URI, clone the repository to your local machine. You may want to ensure you are in your home directory first before you clone to ensure you do not accidentally clone to an existing git repo:

```
$ cd ~
$ git clone <repository URI>
```

Now that you have cloned the repository, you can publish your Guestbook chart.

Publishing the Guestbook chart

Publishing a Helm chart to an HTTP repository consists of a three-step process:

1. Packaging the Helm chart as a `.tgz` archive
2. Generating an `index.yaml` file
3. Uploading the `.tgz` archive and the `index.yaml` file to the server

Helm provides several different commands to make the publishing process a simple task. We'll walk through these commands in this section.

First, you can use the `helm package` command to package your chart into a `.tgz` archive. We'll use the Guestbook chart located in the Packt Git repository at `chapter8/guestbook` as part of this example:

```
$ helm dependency update chapter8/guestbook
$ helm package guestbook chapter8/guestbook
```

If these commands execute successfully, a file called `guestbook-0.1.0.tgz` will be created.

Note that we executed the `helm dependency update` command before running `helm package`. This is because the Guestbook chart must have the dependencies downloaded first to be included in the archive. To simplify this, we could have combined the previous two commands into a single step by providing an additional flag to the `helm package` command:

```
$ helm package chapter8/guestbook --dependency-update
```

This would ensure that the dependencies are included in the final package.

Once your chart has been packaged, the resulting `.tgz` file should be copied to your local GitHub Pages repository clone. This can be done by using the `cp` command:

```
$ cp guestbook-0.1.0.tgz <GitHub Pages repository clone>
```

When this file is copied, you can use the `helm repo index` command to generate the `index.yaml` file. This command takes the location of your chart repository clone as an argument. Run the following command to generate your `index.yaml` file:

```
$ helm repo index <GitHub Pages repository clone>
```

The command will succeed quietly, but you will see the new `index.yaml` file inside your GitHub Pages clone. The contents of this file provide the Guestbook chart metadata and will look as follows:

```
apiVersion: v1
entries:
  guestbook:
  - apiVersion: v2
    appVersion: v5
    created: "2022-02-20T04:13:36.052015-05:00"
    dependencies:
    - condition: redis.enabled
      name: redis
```

```
      repository: https://raw.githubusercontent.com/bitnami/
charts/archive-full-index/bitnami

    version: 15.5.x
    description: An application used for keeping a running
record of guests
    digest: 983dee22d05be37fb73cf6a06fa5a2b2c320c1678ad6a8
df3d198a403f467343
    name: guestbook
    type: application
    urls:
    - guestbook-0.1.0.tgz
    version: 0.1.0
generated: "2022-02-20T04:13:36.045492-05:00"
```

If additional charts were added to this repository, their metadata would be listed in this file as well.

Your Helm chart repository should now contain the `.tgz` archive and the `index.yaml` file, with the contents listed similar to the output from the following command:

```
$ ls <GitHub Pages repository clone>
README.md guestbook-0.1.0.tgz index.yaml
```

To finish the publishing process, you should commit and push these files to GitHub using the following commands:

```
$ cd <GitHub Pages repository clone>
$ git add --all
$ git commit -m "publishing the guestbook helm chart"
$ git push origin main
```

Once you have pushed to the remote repository, your Guestbook Helm chart will be served from the GitHub Pages static site. We can verify this is working properly by adding our repository and performing a search.

First, find your GitHub Pages site URL. This URL was displayed in the **Settings** tab and takes the form of `https://<github username>.github.io/Chart-Repository-Example/`. Once you have identified the URL, use it to add the chart repository:

```
$ helm repo add example <GitHub Pages Site URL>
```

This command will allow Helm to interact with your repository. You can verify that your chart was published successfully by searching for the Guestbook chart against your locally configured repos. This can be done by running the following command:

```
$ helm search repo guestbook
```

You should find the example Guestbook chart that was returned in the search output.

Congratulations! You have published the Guestbook chart to your Helm chart repository. Note that while we have published our chart to an unauthenticated repository in this chapter, we will explore authentication and security in detail in *Chapter 12, Helm Security Considerations*.

In the next section, we will explore OCI registry support and publish our Guestbook chart to a container registry.

Publishing to an OCI registry

Publishing a Helm chart to an OCI registry follows a similar workflow to the one you would follow when working with a standard container image. Commands such as `docker login`, `docker pull`, and `docker push` have analogous commands in Helm. These commands and their descriptions can be seen in the following table:

Command	Description
`helm registry login`	Log in to a registry
`helm registry logout`	Log out of a registry
`helm push`	Push a packaged chart to a registry
`helm pull`	Pull a chart from a registry

Table 8.1 – Helm commands for OCI management

Note that full support for OCI-based charts became available in version 3.8.0. Before this version, it was included as an experimental feature and required an environment variable to be present to activate the feature. If you are using a version older than 3.8.0, the `HELM_EXPERIMENTAL_OCI=1` environment variable must be set, as shown here:

```
$ export HELM_EXPERIMENTAL_OCI=1
```

The `helm pull` command is just one example where OCI-based charts can be used interchangeably with charts sourced from different locations (such as an HTTP repository or a local filesystem). Other Helm commands that can be used in this manner include the following:

- `helm show`
- `helm template`

- `helm install`
- `helm upgrade`

OCI-based charts can be differentiated from other sources by specifying the OCI protocol (`oci://`) as part of a chart's location. For example, a chart sourced from a registry at `localhost:5000/helm-charts/mychart` is referenced in Helm as `oci://localhost:5000/helm-charts/mychart`.

It is also important to note that while OCI artifacts can be served within the same registry alongside container images, not every registry fully supports the OCI artifact specification, so it cannot store OCI-based helm charts. Consult the documentation of the registry distribution beforehand.

To demonstrate how to interact with OCI-based helm charts, we can use the Guestbook chart and store it in an OCI registry. First, we must determine the registry where the chart should be stored. Since we are not only using GitHub to store the raw source code for our charts as it also acts as our Helm repository, the Container Registry provided as part of the GitHub packages offering can act as an OCI registry for helm charts. OCI artifacts are fully supported by the container registry, which is one less concern that we need to worry about.

To publish content to the container registry, a **Personal Account Token** (**PAT**) must be created. Follow these steps to create a PAT with the necessary permissions to push and pull images:

1. Once logged into GitHub, at the top right corner of the page, select your profile picture and click **Settings** from the dropdown.
2. Click **Developer Settings** and select **Personal Account Token**.
3. Click the **Generate New Token** button to initiate the token creation process.
4. Enter a unique name for the token, such as `Learn Helm`.
5. Select the date the token will expire.
6. Select the scopes (permissions) that will be granted to the token. The following scopes are required for managing content within the container registry:
   - `read:packages`
   - `write:packages`
   - `delete:packages`
7. Click the **Generate Token** button to create the token.

Be sure to copy the generated token as it cannot be retrieved once you've navigated away from the page.

Before interacting with the container registry, it is important to note how content is organized within the registry. While these details are specific to the GitHub service, these concepts can be applied to any container registry. Content is stored in the `ghcr.io/<OWNER>/<ARTIFACT>` format. OWNER, in this situation, represents the name of a user account or GitHub organization.

The primary reason why these details are so important is that Helm imposes a strict naming convention that is applied to OCI-based charts. Unlike publishing other artifacts to a container registry, where the repository name and tag can be specified, the repository name and tag are determined automatically based on the chart's name and semantic version, as defined in the Chart.yaml file. For example, a chart named mychart with version 0.1.0 would be stored in the GitHub container registry for a user named jdoe at ghcr.io/jdoe/mychart:0.1.0.

Now that we understand how charts are organized within OCI registries, let's push the chart we created previously to the GitHub registry. The first step is to log in to the registry using the PAT that we created previously using the helm registry login command.

The helm registry login command takes the following form:

```
$ helm registry login <registry>
```

To log in to the GitHub registry, execute the following command:

```
$ helm registry login ghcr.io
```

Enter your GitHub username and the PAT as the password when prompted. A **Login Succeeded** response will be returned upon successful authentication. --username, along with either the --password or --password-stdin flag, can be used to perform non-interactive authentication.

Now that we are logged in to the remote registry, we can push the previously created Helm chart to the remote registry using the helm push command. helm push requires a location of an already packaged chart to be provided, along with the destination registry, as shown here:

```
$ helm push <location_of_tgz_helm_package> <registry/reference>
```

Signed charts are also supported, so long as the provenance (.prov) file is located in the same directory as the packaged chart. No additional configuration or flags to the helm push command are needed. Provenance and chart signing will be discussed in greater detail in *Chapter 12, Helm Security Considerations*.

Push the packaged Guestbook chart to GitHub's container registry:

```
$ helm push guestbook-0.1.0.tgz oci://ghcr.io/<OWNER>
Pushed: ghcr.io/<OWNER>/guestbook:<version>
Digest: sha256:<SHA>
```

Once the chart has been pushed, it can be viewed within GitHub via the **Packages** tab of your user profile. From any page within GitHub, select your profile picture at the top-right corner of the page and select **Your Profile**. The **Packages** tab can be found at the top of the page.

After clicking on the **Packages** tab, the chart that you pushed previously should be visible, as shown in the following screenshot:

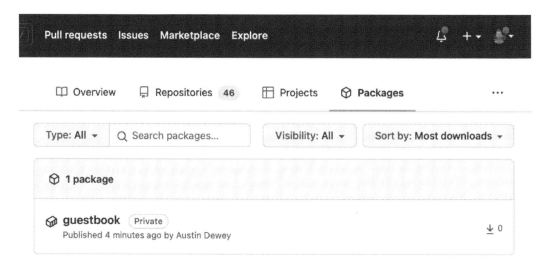

Figure 8.4 – The Packages tab in GitHub

By default, newly created packages are private and cannot be accessed by others. This configuration can be changed by selecting the package and, from the **Details** page, selecting **Package Settings** on the far right. Select **Change Visibility** in the **Danger Zone** section and select **Public**.

Alternatively, individual users or teams can be specified instead of changing the visibility if you wish to restrict access to the helm chart.

Pulling the OCI Guestbook chart

Pulling Helm charts from OCI registries is just as easy as publishing them and the `helm pull` command can be used to do this. The options found in the `helm pull` command are the same for OCI charts as they are for charts either located within chart repositories or located on the filesystem. Of the various options available, the `--version` flag allows the user to specify the chart to be received. Otherwise, the most recent version per SemVer convention is selected.

Pull the previously published chart from the GitHub container registry, as shown here:

```
$ helm pull oci://ghcr.io/<OWNER>/guestbook --version 0.1.0
```

The most recent version of the chart will be retrieved from the registry and the packaged chart (`.tgz`) will be stored locally.

Summary

After doing some hard work on developing a Helm chart, nothing beats the feeling of finally publishing your Helm chart to a repository for the world to see! In this chapter, we learned about HTTP and OCI Helm chart repositories. HTTP repositories allow you to publish your charts to simple web servers, while OCI registries allow you to publish your Helm charts alongside your container images. To practice, we published the Guestbook Helm chart to GitHub Pages (an HTTP server) and GitHub's container registry (an OCI registry).

In the next chapter, we will learn about the tooling and strategies behind testing Helm charts.

Further reading

To learn more about Helm chart repositories, visit the *Chart Repository Guide* section of the Helm documentation: `https://helm.sh/docs/topics/chart_repository/#helm`.

To learn more about OCI support, visit the documentation's *Registries* section: `https://helm.sh/docs/topics/registries/`.

Questions

Answer the following questions to test your knowledge of this chapter:

1. What are three different tools you can use to create an HTTP repository?
2. What command can you run to ensure that dependencies are always included in the `.tgz` archive?
3. What files are required when publishing to an HTTP server?
4. How is the process of publishing to an HTTP repository different from publishing to an OCI registry?
5. What Helm command is used to publish to an OCI registry?
6. What Helm command is used to download a Helm chart from an OCI registry?

9
Testing Helm Charts

Testing is a common task that engineers must perform during software development. Testing is performed to validate the functionality of a product, as well as to prevent regressions as a product evolves. Well-tested software is easier to maintain and allows developers to confidently provide new releases to end users.

A Helm chart should be tested properly to ensure that it delivers its features to the level of quality expected. In this chapter, we will discuss the ways that testing can be applied to Helm charts to verify the expected capabilities.

In this chapter, we will cover the following topics:

- Setting up your environment
- Verifying Helm templating
- Testing in a live cluster
- Improving chart tests with the Chart Testing tool
- Cleaning up

Technical requirements

For this chapter, you will need the following:

- `minikube`
- `kubectl`
- `helm`
- `git`
- `yamllint`
- `yamale`
- ct (chart-testing)

Additionally, you should clone the Packt GitHub repository locally: `$ git clone https://github.com/PacktPublishing/Managing-Kubernetes-Resources-using-Helm.git`.

In this chapter, we will use our `minikube` environment extensively throughout the scenarios. In the next section, you will set up the environment.

Setting up your environment

Run the following steps to set up your `minikube` environment:

1. Start `minikube` by running the `minikube start` command:

    ```
    $ minikube start
    ```

2. Then, create a new namespace called `chapter9`:

    ```
    $ kubectl create namespace chapter9
    ```

With your `minikube` environment ready, let's begin by discussing how Helm charts can be tested. We will begin the discussion by outlining the methods you can use to verify your Helm templates.

Verifying Helm templating

One of the primary purposes of Helm is to create **Kubernetes** resources. As a result, when developing and testing a Helm chart, you should ensure that your resources are being generated properly. This can be accomplished using a variety of methods. We will discuss these in the next section.

Validating template generation locally with helm template

The first way to validate the templating of your chart is to use the `helm template` command. We first introduced this command in *Chapter 6, Understanding Helm Templates*. In this chapter, we will describe using the `helm template` command to render a chart's templates locally.

The `helm template` command has the following syntax:

```
$ helm template [NAME] [CHART] [flags]
```

You can see this command in action by demonstrating it against the Helm chart located in `chapter9/guestbook` in the Packt repository:

```
$ helm template my-guestbook guestbook
```

The result of this command will display each of the Kubernetes resources that would be created if they were applied to the cluster, as shown here:

```
---
# Source: guestbook/charts/redis/templates/serviceaccount.yaml
apiVersion: v1
kind: ServiceAccount
automountServiceAccountToken: true
metadata:
  name: redis
  namespace: "default"
  labels:
    app.kubernetes.io/name: redis
    helm.sh/chart: redis-15.5.5
    app.kubernetes.io/instance: my-guestbook
    app.kubernetes.io/managed-by: Helm
---
# Source: guestbook/templates/serviceaccount.yaml
apiVersion: v1
kind: ServiceAccount
metadata:
  name: my-guestbook
  labels:
    helm.sh/chart: guestbook-0.1.0
    app.kubernetes.io/name: guestbook
```

Figure 9.1 – The helm template output

The preceding output displays the beginning portion of the `helm template` output. As you can see, a fully rendered `ServiceAccount` is shown, along with the beginning of another `ServiceAccount` that would be created with a release. Rendering these resources allows you to understand how the resources would be created if the release was installed against a Kubernetes cluster.

During chart development, you may want to use the `helm template` command regularly to validate that your Kubernetes resources are being generated properly.

Some common aspects of chart development that you may want to validate throughout are as follows:

- Parameterized fields are successfully replaced by default or overridden values
- Control structures such as `if`, `range`, and `with` successfully generate YAML based on the provided values.
- Resources contain proper spacing and indentation.
- Functions and pipelines are used correctly to properly format and manipulate YAML.
- Input validation mechanisms such as the `required` and `fail` functions or the `values.schema.json` file properly validate values based on user input.
- Dependencies have been declared properly and their resource definitions appear in the `helm template` output.

In the next section, we will discuss how server-side validation can be enabled when rendering your resources with `helm template`.

Adding server-side validation to chart rendering

While the `helm template` command is important to the chart development process and should be used frequently to verify your chart rendering, it does have a key limitation. The main purpose of the `helm template` command is to provide client-side rendering, meaning it does not communicate with the Kubernetes API server to provide resource validation. If you would like to ensure that your resources are valid after they have been generated, you can use the `--validate` flag to instruct `helm template` to communicate with the Kubernetes API server:

```
$ helm template my-release <chart_name> --validate
```

With the `--validate` flag specified, any generated template that does not produce a valid Kubernetes resource emits an error message. Imagine, for example, a deployment template was used with the incorrect `apiVersion`. What may appear to be valid locally would be incorrect when applying the `--validate` flag. Here's an example error message that Kubernetes could throw with invalid content that was triggered through the use of the `--validate` flag:

```
Error: unable to build kubernetes objects from release
manifest: unable to recognize "": no matches for kind
"Deployment" in version "v1"
```

While `helm template` does provide server-side validation capabilities with the `--validate` flag, it is not the only way to determine if your chart is generating valid Kubernetes resources. As an alternative approach, you can apply the `--dry-run` flag against the `install`, `upgrade`, `rollback`, and `uninstall` commands. Here is an example of using this flag with the `install` command:

```
$ helm install my-chart <chart_name> --dry-run
```

The `--dry-run` flag is primarily used by end users to perform a sanity check before running an installation. This helps ensure that values have been provided properly and that the installation will produce the desired results. It is a good *last line of defense* that can be used to verify that errors will not be thrown before you execute the associated command.

While it is necessary to verify that templates are generated the way you intend, it is also important to perform linting to ensure that Helm charts and generated resources follow best formatting practices. There are a couple of ways to accomplish this goal. Let's take a look.

Linting Helm charts and templates

Linting a Helm chart involves two high-level steps:

1. Ensuring that a Helm chart is valid
2. Ensuring that a Helm chart follows consistent formatting practices

To ensure that a Helm chart is valid, we can use the `helm lint` command, which has the following syntax:

```
$ helm lint <chart-name> [flags]
```

The `helm lint` command is used to validate the `Chart.yaml` file and ensure that the Helm chart does not contain any breaking issues. Note that this command does not validate rendered resources or perform YAML style linting.

You can run the `helm lint` command against the `guestbook` chart located in the Packt repository, as shown here:

```
$ helm lint chapter9/guestbook
==> Linting chapter9/guestbook
[INFO] Chart.yaml: icon is recommended
1 chart(s) linted, 0 chart(s) failed
```

The preceding output shows that the chart is valid, noted by the `0 chart(s) failed` message. The `[INFO]` message reported that the icon field in the `Chart.yaml` file is recommended, but not required. Other types of messages include `[WARNING]`, which indicates that the chart breaks conventions, and `[ERROR]`, which indicates that the chart will fail at installation.

Let's run through several examples to illustrate each potential outcome. Consider the chart in `chapter9/no-chart-yaml`, which contains the following file structure:

```
no-chart-yaml/
  templates/
  Values.yaml
```

As you can probably guess from the name, this chart is missing a `Chart.yaml` definition file. When we run `helm lint` over this chart, we get an error:

```
$ helm lint chapter9/no-chart-yaml
==> Linting chapter9/no-chart-yaml
Error unable to check Chart.yaml file in chart: stat chapter9/no-chart-yaml/Chart.yaml: no such file or directory
Error: 1 chart(s) linted, 1 chart(s) failed
```

This error indicates that Helm cannot find the Chart.yaml file, resulting in an invalid chart.

We can see different errors if we add an empty Chart.yaml file. Let's run `helm lint` on the chapter9/empty-chart-yaml chart:

```
$ helm lint chapter9/empty-chart-yaml
==> Linting chapter9/empty-chart-yaml
[ERROR] Chart.yaml: name is required
[ERROR] Chart.yaml: apiVersion is required. The value must be either "v1" or "v2"
[ERROR] Chart.yaml: version is required
[INFO] Chart.yaml: icon is recommended
[ERROR] templates/: validation: chart.metadata.name is required
[ERROR] : unable to load chart
validation: chart.metadata.name is required
Error: 1 chart(s) linted, 1 chart(s) failed
```

The output lists each of the required fields that are missing from the Chart.yaml file.

The linter will also check for the existence of other files, such as the values.yaml file and the templates directory. It also ensures that files under the templates directory have valid .yaml, .yml, .tpl, or .txt file extensions.

The `helm lint` command is great for checking whether your chart contains the appropriate contents, but it does not carry out exhaustive linting of your chart's YAML style. To perform this type of linting, you can use another tool called yamllint, which can be found at https://github.com/adrienverge/yamllint. This tool can be installed using the pip3 (or pip) package manager across a range of operating systems by using the following command:

```
$ pip3 install yamllint –user
```

It can also be installed with your system's package manager, as described in the yamllint quick-start instructions at https://yamllint.readthedocs.io/en/stable/quickstart.html.

To use yamllint on your chart's resources, you must use it in combination with the `helm template` command to feed the output of the rendered templates as input to yamllint. Let's run yamllint against the chapter9/guestbook Helm chart:

```
$ helm template my-guestbook chapter9/guestbook | yamllint -
```

A snippet of the result is shown here:

```
556:81      error   line too long (92 > 80 characters)  (line-length)
557:81      error   line too long (89 > 80 characters)  (line-length)
558:81      error   line too long (90 > 80 characters)  (line-length)
559:81      error   line too long (89 > 80 characters)  (line-length)
561:1       error   trailing spaces  (trailing-spaces)
567:1       error   trailing spaces  (trailing-spaces)
581:1       error   trailing spaces  (trailing-spaces)
644:23      error   trailing spaces  (trailing-spaces)
723:1       error   wrong indentation: expected 2 but found 0  (indentation)
```

Figure 9.2 – yamllint output

The line numbers provided to the left reflect the entirety of the `helm template` output, which can make it difficult to determine which line from the `yamllint` output corresponds with which line from your template files. You can simplify this by redirecting the `helm template` output to determine its line numbers:

```
$ cat -n <(helm template my-guestbook chapter9/guestbook)
```

The `yamllint` tool performs linting against many different rules, including the following:

- Indentation
- Line length
- Trailing spaces
- Empty lines
- Comment format

You can define your own rules by authoring them in one of the following files:

- `.yamllint`, `.yamllint.yaml`, or `.yamllint.yml` in the current working directory
- `$XDG_CONFIG_HOME/yamllint/config`
- `~/.config/yamllint/config`

An example `.yamllint.yaml` file can be found in `chapter9/yamllint-override`. Here, we have defined the following contents:

```
rules:
  indentation:
    indent-sequences: whatever
```

This sample creates one rule that instructs `yamllint` not to enforce any particular method of indentation.

A deep dive into configuring `yamllint` rules is beyond the scope of this chapter, but you can refer to the `yamllint` documentation on the topic of rules to learn more: `https://yamllint.readthedocs.io/en/stable/rules.html`.

In this section, we discussed how you can validate the local rendering of your Helm charts by using the `helm template`, `helm lint`, and `yamllint` commands. This, however, does not verify your chart's functionality or the application's ability to run properly. In the next section, we will address this topic by learning how to create tests in a live Kubernetes cluster.

Testing in a live cluster

Understanding how to perform tests in a live Kubernetes cluster is an essential part of developing and maintaining a Helm chart. Live testing helps ensure your chart is functioning as intended and can be used to help prevent regressions as new additions are introduced to your chart over time.

Testing can involve, but is not limited to, the following two different constructs:

- Readiness probes and the `helm install --wait` command
- Test hooks and the `helm test` command

A readiness probe is a type of health check in Kubernetes that, upon success, marks a pod as `Ready` and makes the pod eligible to receive ingress traffic. An example of a readiness probe is located at `chapter9/guestbook/templates/deployment.yaml`:

```
readinessProbe:
  httpGet:
    path: /
    port: http
```

This readiness probe will mark the pod as `Ready` when an HTTP `GET` request succeeds against the `/` path.

Readiness probes can be used alongside the `-wait` flag, which forces Helm to return successfully only when the probe passes. If the readiness probe times out, Helm will return exit code `1`, indicating that the installation was not successful. A timeout occurs 5 minutes after the installation begins, by default. This can be configured with the `--timeout` flag.

The following is an example of invoking `helm install` with the `--wait` flag:

```
$ helm install my-guestbook chapter9/guestbook --wait
```

Other commands that also support the `--wait` flag include `upgrade`, `rollback`, and `uninstall`. However, when used with `uninstall`, Helm waits for each resource to be deleted instead.

Besides readiness probes, testing in Helm can also be performed by using test hooks and the `helm test` command. Test hooks are pods that perform custom tests after the Helm chart is installed to confirm they execute successfully. They are defined under the `templates` directory and contain the `helm.sh/hook: test` annotation. When the `helm test` command is run, templates with the test annotation are created and execute their defined functions.

We can see an example test in `chapter9/guestbook/templates/tests/test-connection.yaml`:

```yaml
apiVersion: v1
kind: Pod
metadata:
  name: "{{ include "guestbook.fullname" . }}-test-connection"
  labels:
    {{- include "guestbook.labels" . | nindent 4 }}
  annotations:
    "helm.sh/hook": test
spec:
  containers:
    - name: wget
      image: busybox
      command: ['wget']
      args: ['{{ include "guestbook.fullname" . }}:{{ .Values.service.port }}']
  restartPolicy: Never
```

As we can see, this test attempts to make a call to the guestbook frontend.

Let's work on running this Helm test in our `minikube` environment.

Running the chart test

To run a chart's tests, the chart must be installed in a Kubernetes environment using the `helm install` command. Because the `guestbook` chart contains readiness probes for the frontend and Redis instances (provided by the Redis dependency), we can add the `--wait` flag to our `helm` command to block until all pods are ready. Run the following command to install the `guestbook` chart:

```
$ helm install guestbook chapter9/guestbook -n chapter9 --wait
```

Once the chart has been installed, you can use the `helm test` command to execute the test life cycle hook. The syntax for the `helm test` command is as follows:

```
helm test [RELEASE] [flags]
```

Run the `helm test` command against the `guestbook` release:

```
$ helm test guestbook -n chapter9
```

If your test is successful, you will see the following results in the output:

```
NAME: guestbook
LAST DEPLOYED: Sun Mar 13 17:18:51 2022
NAMESPACE: chapter9
STATUS: deployed
REVISION: 1
TEST SUITE:     guestbook-test-connection
Last Started:   Sun Mar 13 17:26:00 2022
Last Completed: Sun Mar 13 17:26:03 2022
Phase:          Succeeded
```

When running your tests, you can also use the `--logs` flag to display the logs from your test pods. Let's run the test again and inspect the logs by including the `--logs` flag:

```
$ helm test guestbook --logs -n chapter9
<skipped>
POD LOGS: guestbook-test-connection
Connecting to guestbook:80 (10.98.198.86:80)
saving to 'index.html'
index.html           100%
|********************************|   920  0:00:00 ETA
'index.html' saved
```

As evidenced by the logs from our test pod, our application is up and running! As a final step, you can delete your release with `helm uninstall`:

```
$ helm uninstall guestbook -n chapter9
```

In this section, we ran a test hook that served as a smoke test for our chart installation. In the next section, we will discuss how the testing process can be improved by leveraging a tool called **ct**.

Improving chart tests with the Chart Testing tool

The testing methods described in the previous section are sufficient enough to determine whether a Helm chart can be successfully installed. However, some key limitations are inherent to the standard Helm testing process and need to be discussed.

The first limitation to consider is the difficulty of testing different permutations that can occur within a chart's values. Because the `helm test` command does not provide the ability to modify a release's values beyond those set at the time of an installation or upgrade, the following workflow must be followed when running `helm test` against different values:

1. Install your chart with an initial set of values.
2. Run `helm test` against your release.
3. Delete your release.
4. Install the chart with a different set of values.
5. Repeat *Step 2* through *Step 4* until a significant amount of value possibilities have been tested.

Each of these manual steps poses the risk of errors.

In addition to testing different value permutations, you should also make sure regressions do not occur when making modifications to your charts. The best way to prevent regressions is to include the usage of `helm upgrade` in your testing workflow:

1. Install the previous chart version.
2. Upgrade your release to the newer chart version.
3. Delete the release.
4. Install the newer chart version.

This workflow should be repeated against each set of values to ensure that there are no regressions or unintended breaking changes.

These processes sound tedious but imagine the additional strain chart developers face when maintaining Helm chart **monorepos**, where multiple charts need to be tested and maintained at the same time. A repository is considered a monorepo when multiple different artifacts or modules are contained in the same repository. A monorepo design is the most common way for a chart developer or an organization to develop and maintain its charts.

A Helm chart monorepo could have the following file structure:

```
helm-charts/
  guestbook/
    Chart.yaml
```

```
    templates/
    README.md
    values.yaml
 redis/            # Contains the same file structure as
'guestbook'
 wordpress/        # Contains the same file structure as
'guestbook'
```

Helm charts in a well-maintained monorepo should adhere to proper **SemVer** versioning to denote the types of changes made between releases. SemVer versions follow a `MAJOR.MINOR.PATCH` version format. Use the following list as a guideline on how to increase a SemVer version:

- Increment the `MAJOR` version if you are making a breaking change to your chart. A breaking change is a change that is not backward compatible with the previous chart version.

- Increment the `MINOR` version if you are adding a feature but you are not making a breaking change. You should increment this version if the change you are making is backward compatible with the previous chart version.

- Increment the `PATCH` version if you are making a bug fix or addressing a security vulnerability that will not result in a breaking change. This version should be incremented if the change is backward-compatible with the previous chart version.

With the responsibilities of chart testing and versioning, it can become increasingly difficult for a Helm chart maintainer to ensure that charts are properly tested, and their versions are incremented, especially if maintaining a monorepo with multiple Helm charts. This challenge prompted the Helm community to create a tool called ct to provide structure and automation around the testing and maintenance of Helm charts. We will discuss this tool next.

Introducing the Chart Testing project

The Chart Testing project, which can be found at `https://github.com/helm/chart-testing`, is designed to be used against charts in a Git monorepo to perform automated linting, validation, and testing. This automated testing is achieved by using Git to detect when charts have changed against a specified branch. Charts that have changed should undergo testing, while charts that were unchanged do not need to be tested.

The project's **Command-Line Interface** (**CLI**), ct, provides four primary commands:

- `lint`: Lints and validates charts that have been modified
- `install`: Installs the chart in a running Kubernetes cluster and runs test hooks against charts that have been modified

- `lint-and-install`: Combines the `lint` and `install` commands
- `list-changed`: Lists charts that have been modified

The `lint-and-install` command is the primary function of ct. It performs linting, installs charts in your Kubernetes cluster, and runs any test hooks that are present. It also checks whether you have increased the charts' `version` fields in `Chart.yaml` for any chart that has been modified. This validation helps maintainers enforce proper versioning of their Helm charts.

The ct tool also lets you test Helm charts against multiple different values files. During the invocation of the `lint`, `install`, and `lint-and-install` commands, ct loops through each test `values` file and performs linting and testing based on the different permutations of values provided. Test `values` files for use by ct are written under a folder called `ci/` and end with the `values.yaml` format. The following is an example Helm chart structure that includes the `ci` folder:

```
guestbook/
  Chart.yaml
  ci/
    nodeport-service-values.yaml
    ingress-values.yaml
  templates/
  values.yaml
```

Each `values` file under `ci/` should be named appropriately to determine the function that the values are testing. For example, `nodeport-service-values.yaml` might be used to ensure that **NodePort** services are configured properly, and `ingress-values.yaml` would test Ingress.

The most common ct command you are likely to use is the `lint-and-install` command. When this command is running, a series of steps are executed:

1. Detect the charts that have been modified within the Git monorepo. Ensure that the charts' versions have been incremented.
2. For each chart that has been modified, lint the chart and each `values` file under the `ci/` folder.
3. For each chart that has been modified, install the chart in the Kubernetes cluster and wait for the readiness probes to pass. Once the probes have passed, run test hooks, if present. Repeat *Step 3* for each `values` file in the `ci/` folder.
4. Uninstall the Helm release.

As you can see, this command performs a variety of steps to ensure your charts are properly linted and tested. However, by default, the `lint-and-install` command does not check for backward compatibility. This feature can be enabled by adding the `--upgrade` flag.

When the `--upgrade` flag is provided, ct checks if the MAJOR version number of the chart's version has been incremented. If a breaking change is not expected, then ct deploys the previous chart version first and then upgrades to the new version. This helps ensure that regressions have not occurred. Then, ct installs the new version directly using a standard release. We recommend adding the `--upgrade` flag when using the `lint-and-install` command.

Let's continue by installing ct and its dependencies locally. Then, we will look at an example of how ct can be used.

Installing the Chart Testing tools

To use ct, you must have the following tools installed on your local machine:

- `helm`
- `git` (version 2.17.0 or later)
- `yamllint`
- `yamale`
- `kubectl`

Instructions for installing `helm` and `kubectl` were provided in *Chapter 2, Preparing a Kubernetes and Helm Environment*, while `yamllint` was installed earlier in this chapter. Now, we'll install `yamale`, which is a tool for validating YAML schemas. It is used by ct to validate the `Chart.yaml` file.

`yamale` can be installed with the `pip3` package manager, as shown here:

```
$ pip3 install yamale –user
```

You can also install Yamale manually by downloading an archive from https://github.com/23andMe/Yamale/archive/master.zip. Once downloaded, unzip the archive and run the `setup.py` script:

```
$ python3 setup.py install
```

Once you have the prerequisite tooling installed, you should download ct from the project's GitHub releases page at https://github.com/helm/chart-testing/releases. Each release contains an *Assets* section with a list of archives associated with each release.

Download the archive that corresponds with the platform type of your local machine. Version **v3.5.1** was the version that was used for this publication:

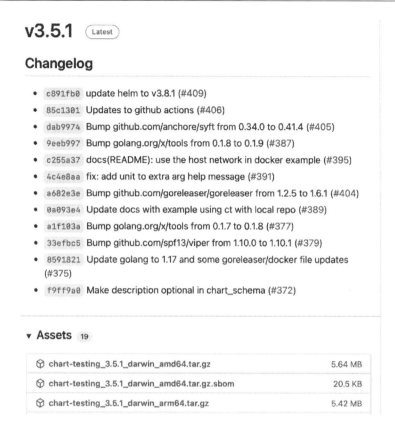

Figure 9.3 – The Helm releases page on GitHub

Unarchive the release once you have downloaded the appropriate archive from the GitHub releases page. Once unarchived, you will see the following contents:

```
LICENSE
README.md
etc/chart_schema.yaml
etc/lintconf.yaml
ct
```

The `LICENSE` and `README.md` files can be removed as they are not needed.

The `etc/chart_schema.yaml` and `etc/lintconf.yaml` files can be moved to either the `$HOME/.ct/` or `/etc/ct/` location on your local machine. These files provide `yamllint` and `yamale` rules for linting and schema validation. When moved to the suggested locations, they provide default rules for any invocation of ct, regardless of their location on the filesystem.

You should also move ct to a location that is included in your system's PATH variable. Moving ct as well as the files located under etc can be done with the following commands:

```
$ mkdir $HOME/.ct
$ mv $HOME/Downloads/etc/* $HOME/.ct/
$ mv $HOME/Downloads/ct /usr/local/bin/
```

Now that all of the required tools have been installed, let's clone the Packt repository – that is, if you did not clone it previously. We will interact with this repository to demonstrate the use of ct:

```
$ git clone https://github.com/PacktPublishing/Managing-Kubernetes-Resources-using-Helm.git
```

Once cloned, you will notice that this repository contains several ct-related files:

- `lintconf.yaml`: This is a copy of the same file that was included in the ct archive. When added to a repository, ct uses this local reference instead of the default file located at `$HOME/.ct/`.
- `chart_schema.yaml`: This is also a copy of the same file that was included in the ct archive. When added to a repository, ct uses this local reference instead of the default file located at `$HOME/.ct/`.
- `ct.yaml`: This file contains the configuration for ct.

The following are a couple of the configurations that are included in the `ct.yaml` file:

```
chart-dirs:
  - helm-charts/charts
chart-repos:
  - bitnami=https://raw.githubusercontent.com/bitnami/charts/archive-full-index/bitnami
```

The `chart-dirs` field indicates that the `helm-charts/charts` directory relative to `ct.yaml` is the root of the Helm chart monorepo. The `chart-repos` field provides a list of repositories that ct should add to download dependencies. A variety of other configurations can be added to this file to customize the execution of ct. The full list of available options can be reviewed in the Chart Testing documentation at `https://github.com/helm/chart-testing`.

Now, let's see ct in action by running the `lint-and-install` command.

Running the lint-and-install command

In the `helm-charts/charts` folder, which is the location of our Helm charts monorepo, we have two charts:

- **guestbook**: This is the `guestbook` chart that we wrote in *Part 2* of this book.
- **nginx**: This is a basic Helm chart that was created with `helm create` and is used to deploy an `nginx` reverse proxy.

The `guestbook` and `nginx` Helm charts are the charts that will be tested with ct. First, let's navigate to the top level of the Git repository:

```
$ cd Managing-Kubernetes-Resources-using-Helm
$ ls
LICENSE              chapter4           chapter6           chapter8
          chart_schema.yaml helm-charts
README.md            chapter5           chapter7           chapter9
          ct.yaml             lintconf.yaml
```

Since ct should run in the same folder as the `ct.yaml` file, we can simply run `ct lint-and-install` from the top level of the repository:

```
$ ct lint-and-install
```

After running this command, you should see the following message:

```
Linting and installing charts...
------------------------------------------------
No chart changes detected.
------------------------------------------------
All charts linted and installed successfully
```

Since none of the charts were modified, ct did not perform any testing on your charts. We should modify at least one chart in the `helm-charts/charts` directory to allow for testing to take place. Since normal development would likely involve feature branches, let's create a new Git branch where we will make modifications. Create a new branch called `chart-testing-example` by running the following command:

```
$ git checkout -b chart-testing-example
```

The modifications can be of any size and type, so for this example, we will simply modify the `nginx` chart's `Chart.yaml` file. Modify the description fields of the `helm-charts/charts/nginx/Chart.yaml` file so that they read as follows:

```
description: Deploys an NGINX instance to Kubernetes
```

Previously, this value was `A Helm chart for Kubernetes`. Verify that the `nginx` chart has been modified by running the `git status` command:

```
$ git status
```

You should see an output similar to the following:

```
On branch chart-testing-example
Changes not staged for commit:
  (use "git add <file>..." to update what will be committed)
  (use "git restore <file>..." to discard changes in working directory)
        modified:   helm-charts/charts/nginx/Chart.yaml

no changes added to commit (use "git add" and/or "git commit -a")
```

Figure 9.4 – Git status, displaying a change in Chart.yaml

Now, try to run the `lint-and-install` command again:

```
$ ct lint-and-install
```

This time, ct displays the charts from the monorepo that have changed:

```
Linting and installing charts...
------------------------------------------------------------
--
Charts to be processed:
------------------------------------------------------------
--
nginx => (version: "1.0.0", path: "helm-charts/charts/nginx")
------------------------------------------------------------
--
```

The process, however, fails later on because the `nginx` chart version was not modified:

```
Linting chart 'nginx => (version: "1.0.0", path: "helm-charts/charts/nginx")'
Checking chart 'nginx => (version: "1.0.0", path: "helm-charts/charts/nginx")' for a version bump...
Old chart version: 1.0.0
New chart version: 1.0.0
------------------------------------------------------------------------------------------------
 * nginx => (version: "1.0.0", path: "helm-charts/charts/nginx") > Chart version not ok. Needs a version bump!
------------------------------------------------------------------------------------------------
Error: Error linting and installing charts: Error processing charts
Error linting and installing charts: Error processing charts
```

Figure 9.5 – ct output when chart versions are not updated

This can be fixed by incrementing the version of the `nginx` chart. Since this change does not introduce new features, we will increment the PATCH version. Modify the `nginx` chart version to `1.0.1` in the `Chart.yaml` file:

```
version: 1.0.1
```

Once the version is updated, run the `lint-and-install` command again:

```
$ ct lint-and-install
```

Now that the chart version has been incremented, the `lint-and-install` command will follow the full testing workflow. You will see that the `nginx` chart has been linted and deployed to an automatically created namespace (though a specific namespace can be targeted by using the `--namespace` flag). Once the deployed pods are reported as ready, ct will automatically run the test hooks denoted by resources with the `helm.sh/hook test` annotation. ct will also print the logs of each test pod, as well as the namespace events.

You may notice that the `nginx` chart was deployed multiple times. This is because the `nginx` chart contains a `ci/` folder, located within the `helm-charts/charts/nginx/ci` directory. This folder contains two different values files, so the `nginx` Helm chart was installed two different times to test both sets of values. This can be observed throughout the output of `lint-and-install`:

```
Linting chart with values file 'nginx/ci/nodeport-values.
yaml'...
Linting chart with values file 'nginx/ci/ingress-values.
yaml'...
Installing chart with values file 'nginx/ci/nodeport-values.
yaml'...
Installing chart with values file 'nginx/ci/ingress-values.
yaml'...
```

While this process was useful for testing the functionality of updated charts, it did not validate whether upgrades to the newer version will be successful. To do this, we need to provide the `--upgrade` flag. Run `lint-and-install` again, but this time, let's add the `--upgrade` flag:

```
$ ct lint-and-install --upgrade
```

This time, an in-place upgrade will occur for each `values` file under the `ci/` directory. This can be seen in the following output:

```
Testing upgrades of chart 'nginx => (version: "1.0.1", path: "nginx")' relative to previous revision 'nginx => (version: "1.0.0", path: "ct_previous_revision216728160/nginx")'...
```

Recall that an in-place upgrade will only be tested if the `MAJOR` version between versions is the same. If the `--upgrade` flag was specified and the `MAJOR` version was changed, you would see a message similar to the following:

```
Skipping upgrade test of 'nginx => (version: "2.0.0", path: "helm-charts/charts/nginx")' because: 1 error occurred:
* 2.0.0 does not have same major version as 1.0.0
```

Now that you have an understanding of how to test your Helm charts robustly, we will conclude by cleaning up the `minikube` environment.

Cleaning up

If you have finished with the examples in this chapter, you can remove the `chapter9` namespace from your `minikube` cluster:

```
$ kubectl delete ns chapter9
```

Finally, shut down your `minikube` cluster by running `minikube stop`.

Summary

In this chapter, you learned about different methods you can apply to test your Helm charts. The most basic way to test a chart is to run the `helm template` command against a local chart directory and determine whether its resources were generated. You can also use the `helm lint` command to ensure that your chart follows the correct formatting for Helm resources, and you can use the `yamllint` command to lint the YAML style that's used in your chart.

Apart from local templating and linting, you can also perform live tests on a Kubernetes environment with the `helm test` command and the ct tool. In addition to performing basic chart testing capabilities, ct also provides features that make it easier to maintain Helm charts in a monorepo.

In the next chapter, you will learn how Helm can be used within a **continuous delivery (CD)** and GitOps setting.

Further reading

For additional information on the `helm template` and `helm lint` commands, please refer to the following resources:

- `helm template`: https://helm.sh/docs/helm/helm_template/
- `helm lint`: https://helm.sh/docs/helm/helm_lint/

The following pages from the Helm documentation discuss chart tests and the `helm test` command:

- Chart tests: https://helm.sh/docs/topics/chart_tests/
- The `helm test` command: https://helm.sh/docs/helm/helm_test/

Finally, see the Chart Testing GitHub repository for more information about the ct CLI: https://github.com/helm/chart-testing.

Questions

Answer the following questions to test your knowledge of this chapter:

1. What is the purpose of the `helm template` command? How does it differ from the `helm lint` command?
2. What tool can be leveraged to lint the YAML style of rendered Helm templates?
3. How is a chart test created? How is a chart test executed?
4. What is the difference between `helm test` and `ct lint-and-install`?
5. What is the purpose of the `ci/` folder when used with the ct tool?
6. How does the `--upgrade` flag change the behavior of the `ct lint-and-install` command?

Part 3: Advanced Deployment Patterns

The Helm **command-line interface** (**CLI**) is a robust toolkit, but efficiency can be further increased with automation. In *Part 3*, you will learn about incorporating Helm into industry-standard deployment methodologies. You will also take a deep dive into important security considerations throughout day-to-day Helm usage.

In this part, we will cover the following topics:

- *Chapter 10, Automating Helm with CD and GitOps*
- *Chapter 11, Using Helm with the Operator Framework*
- *Chapter 12, Helm Security Considerations*

10
Automating Helm with CD and GitOps

Throughout this book, we have demonstrated how to use different Helm commands to manage Kubernetes resources and applications. While these commands (namely `install`, `upgrade`, `rollback`, and `uninstall`) are effective in carrying out their respective tasks, we have been invoking them manually from the command line. Manual invocation can serve as a pain point when managing multiple different applications and can make it difficult for enterprises to scale. As a result, we should explore opportunities to automate our Helm deployments.

In this chapter, we will investigate concepts relating to **continuous delivery** (**CD**) and **GitOps**. These are methodologies that involve automatically invoking the Helm **command-line interface** (**CLI**) to perform automated chart installations based on the contents of a Git repository. By implementing the CD and GitOps concepts, you can further increase your efficiency with Helm.

In this chapter, we will cover the following topics:

- Understanding CI/CD and GitOps
- Setting up your environment
- Installing Argo CD
- Deploying a Helm chart from a Git repository
- Deploying a Helm chart from a remote Helm chart repository
- Deploying a Helm chart to multiple environments
- Cleaning up

Technical requirements

This chapter requires that you have the following technologies installed on your local machine:

- minikube
- Helm
- kubectl
- Git

In addition to these tools, you can find the Packt repository that contains the resources associated with the examples in this chapter on GitHub at `https://github.com/PacktPublishing/Managing-Kubernetes-Resources-using-Helm`. This repository will be referenced throughout this chapter.

Understanding CI/CD and GitOps

So far, we have addressed manually invoking the Helm CLI to install and manage Helm charts. While this is acceptable when getting started with Helm, as you look to manage a chart in a production-like environment, there are questions that you need to consider, including the following:

- How can I be sure that the best practices for Helm chart deployments are enforced?
- What are the implications for collaborators participating in the deployment process?

You may be familiar with the best practices and processes around deploying Helm charts; however, any new collaborators or team members may not have the same level of knowledge or expertise. Not to mention, you may become limited in the level of support that you can provide to others as your responsibilities among the number of applications you manage increases. Through the use of automation and repeatable processes, we can address these challenges.

While this chapter will focus primarily on CD and GitOps, we would be remiss if we were to avoid introducing **continuous integration** (**CI**), which is commonly paired with CD. We will discuss **continuous integration/continuous delivery** (**CI/CD**) and GitOps in the next section.

CI/CD

As enterprises sought to accelerate the software development life cycle over the years, the need for an automated development process arose, leading to the creation of CI. CI is enabled by using an orchestrator to automatically build and test application code. As new commits are pushed to a Git repository, the orchestrator automatically retrieves the source code and undergoes a predetermined set of steps to build the application (among other tasks, such as code quality scanning, vulnerability scanning, and so on). By performing automatic builds when new commits are added, regressions and breaking changes can be spotted early on in the software development life cycle. CI also helps address the challenges embodied by the phrase *it works on my machine* by providing a common build environment.

The ability to apply many of CI's concepts throughout the software development life cycle as an application moves toward production led to the creation of CD. CD is a set of defined steps provided to progress software through a release process. CD has gained acceptance and popularity among many organizations where proper change control is enforced, and approvals are required for the software to progress to the next stage. As many of the concepts around CI/CD are automated in a repeatable fashion, teams can look to fully eliminate the need for manual approval steps once they are confident that they have a reliable framework in place.

The process of implementing a fully automated build, test, deployment, and release process without human intervention is known as continuous deployment. While many software projects may never fully achieve continuous deployment, teams that can implement the concepts emphasized by CI/CD can produce real business value faster than less automated methods.

In the next section, we will introduce GitOps as a mechanism to improve how applications and their configuration are managed.

Taking CI/CD to the next level using GitOps

Kubernetes is a platform that embraces the use of declarative configurations. While applications can be managed using imperative `kubectl` commands, the preferred approach, which we covered in *Chapter 1*, *Understanding Kubernetes and Helm*, is to declaratively state the resources through the use of manifests. In the same way that an application traverses its way through a CI/CD pipeline, Kubernetes manifests can implement many of the same CI/CD patterns. Like application code, Kubernetes manifests should also be stored in a source code repository, such as Git, and can undergo the same type of build, test, and deployment practices.

The rise in popularity of managing the life cycle of Kubernetes applications and cluster configuration within Git repositories led to the concept of GitOps. First introduced by the software company *WeaveWorks* in 2017, GitOps has increased in popularity as a way to manage Kubernetes configurations. While GitOps is best known in the context of Kubernetes, its principles can be applied to any type of environment.

Similar to CI/CD, tools have been developed to manage the GitOps process. These include **Argo CD** from Intuit and **Flux** from WeaveWorks. However, you do not need to use a tool specifically designed for GitOps as any automation utility or CI/CD orchestrator can be used. The key differentiator between a traditional CI/CD tool and a tool designed for GitOps is a GitOps tool's ability to constantly observe the state of the target environment and apply desired configurations when the live state does not match the desired state, as defined in the manifests stored in Git. In the context of Kubernetes, these tools make use of the controller pattern, which is fundamental to Kubernetes itself.

Since Helm charts are ultimately rendered as Kubernetes resources, they, too, can be used to participate in the GitOps process. In this chapter, we will leverage Argo CD to deploy Helm chart resources to Kubernetes in a GitOps fashion. Note that this is not intended to be a comprehensive overview of Argo CD, but it will give you an idea of how it can be integrated with Helm to provide a GitOps approach toward Helm deployments.

Setting up your environment

In this chapter, we will create several namespaces to install Argo CD and deploy an example Helm chart across different namespaces.

Run the following commands to prepare your environment:

1. Start `minikube` by running the `minikube start` command:

   ```
   $ minikube start
   ```

2. Then, create a new namespace called `argo`, where we will later install Argo CD:

   ```
   $ kubectl create namespace argo
   ```

3. Next, create a namespace called `chapter10`, where we will deploy an example Helm chart from Argo CD:

   ```
   $ kubectl create namespace chapter10
   ```

4. Finally, create two namespaces called `chapter10-dev` and `chapter10-prod`. We will use these namespaces to demonstrate deploying a Helm chart across multiple environments using Argo CD:

   ```
   $ kubectl create namespace chapter10-dev
   $ kubectl create namespace chapter10-prod
   ```

With your `minikube` environment ready and your namespaces created, let's begin by deploying Argo CD. Then, we will walk through examples of using Argo CD to deploy an application to Kubernetes with Helm.

Installing Argo CD

Argo CD can be installed in Kubernetes by using a set of manifest files or by installing a Helm chart. Of course, we will choose to install Argo CD using the community-provided Helm chart.

The repository URL for the Argo CD Helm chart is `https://argoproj.github.io/argo-helm` (which can be found in Artifact Hub, a process described in *Chapter 3, Installing Your First App with Helm*).

Let's add this repository using the Helm CLI:

```
$ helm repo add argo https://argoproj.github.io/argo-helm
```

Once the repository has been added, you can install it. We have provided a `values` file you can use for the installation in the Packt repository at `https://github.com/PacktPublishing/Managing-Kubernetes-Resources-using-Helm/blob/main/chapter10/argo-values/values.yaml`. The provided `values` file disables Dex (an OpenID Connect provider), along with Argo's notification system, since we will not be using these components in this chapter.

Let's install Argo CD in the `argo` namespace by running the following command:

```
$ helm install argo argo/argo-cd --version 4.5.0 --values chapter10/argo-values/values.yaml -n argo
```

The Helm chart installs the following components in the `argo` namespace:

- **Argo CD Application Controller**, a controller that watches for `Application` custom resources. When an `Application` resource is created, Argo CD creates resources to the desired destination cluster and namespace.
- **Argo CD ApplicationSet Controller**, a controller that watches for `ApplicationSet` custom resources. `ApplicationSet` provides a convenient way to deploy multiple different yet related `Application` resources. We will work with ApplicationSets when we demonstrate how to deploy a Helm chart to multiple different environments or namespaces.
- **Redis**, which is used for caching backend data.
- **Argo CD Repo Server**, which provides a local instance of cloned Git repositories.
- **Argo CD Server**, which provides an API for interacting with Argo CD. This component also provides a frontend web interface.

Once each of the pods in the `argo` namespace reports the 1/1 ready state (shown by running `kubectl get pods -n argo`), we can access the Argo CD web UI. First, we need to get the admin password that was randomly generated during the Helm installation. We can do this by accessing a Kubernetes `secret` in the `argo` namespace:

```
$ kubectl get secret argocd-initial-admin-secret -n argo -o jsonpath='{.data.password}' | base64 -d
```

The username for accessing the web UI will be `admin`, and the password will be the string displayed after getting the password from the `argocd-initial-admin-secret`.

Finally, we can run `port-forward` to access the web UI. In a separate terminal, run the following `port-forward` command:

```
$ kubectl port-forward svc/argo-argocd-server 8443:443 -n argo
```

After running the `port-forward` command, navigate to `https://localhost:8443` in a web browser. Accept the self-signed certificate exception; you will be presented with the Argo CD login page:

Figure 10.1 – The Argo CD login page

For the username, enter `admin`, and for the password, provide the string that was displayed after getting the password from `argocd-initial-admin-secret`. After successfully logging in, you should see the following page titled **APPLICATIONS TILES**:

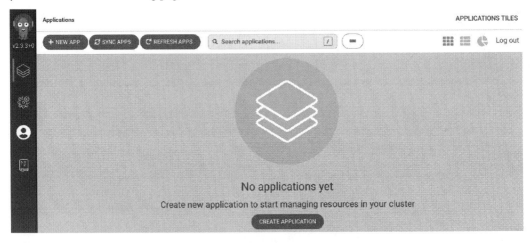

Figure 10.2 – The Argo CD APPLICATIONS TILES page

This page can be used to create new applications, which represent application deployments (or any set of Kubernetes resources). However, in the spirit of adhering to a more declarative configuration approach, we will make deployments in this chapter by applying `Application` YAML resources instead. With that said, this UI will populate with application tiles as we apply the `Application` resources directly using `kubectl`. Feel free to reference this UI throughout this chapter to see how they are visualized.

With Argo CD successfully deployed, let's continue by deploying a Helm chart from a Git repository.

Deploying a Helm chart from a Git repository

In true GitOps fashion, Argo CD can be used to deploy a Helm chart from a Git repository. The following diagram shows the flow involved in deploying a Helm chart from a Git repository using Argo CD:

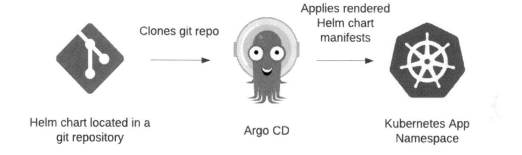

Figure 10.3 – Deploying a Helm chart from a Git repository

Here, you can see that Argo CD clones the Git repository containing the desired Helm chart. Then, Argo CD interprets the repository as one containing a Helm chart, since it notices the presence of the `Chart.yaml` file and surrounding Helm chart structure. From there, Argo CD proceeds by rendering the Helm chart manifests and applying them to the designated Kubernetes namespace.

Note that Argo CD *renders* the Helm chart templates and applies them as opposed to installing the Helm chart directly. This is because Argo CD only applies Kubernetes manifests, so it first runs a `helm template` internally to produce the full Kubernetes manifest from the provided Helm values. If you were to run the `helm list` command after deploying a chart using Argo CD, you would not see any releases listed. You would, however, be able to see the applied resources.

You may be curious about the implications that deploying rendered Kubernetes manifests has on application rollbacks since the `helm rollback` command cannot be used. With the GitOps ideology, you would ideally roll back by performing changes within your Git repository to revert such actions. Argo CD would then detect any new commits that have been created against the target branch and apply the desired changes. With that said, Argo CD does have a native rollback capability to roll back to a previous history ID. This enables users to roll back without reverting to their Git repository.

Let's begin to deploy a Helm chart from Git by observing the `Application` resource located in the Packt repository at `chapter10/local-chart/application.yaml` (https://github.com/PacktPublishing/Managing-Kubernetes-Resources-using-Helm/blob/main/chapter10/local-chart/application.yaml). We can break this resource down into separate components:

- First, we must define the resource's `kind` and provide the resource metadata:

    ```
    apiVersion: argoproj.io/v1alpha1
    kind: Application
    metadata:
      name: nginx
      namespace: argo
      finalizers:
        resources-finalizer.argocd.argoproj.io
    ```

    Notice the finalizer, `resources-finalizer.argocd.argoproj.io`. **Finalizers**, in Kubernetes, are used to trigger a pre-delete action on the managing controller. With this finalizer, we tell the application controller that if we delete this application resource, the controller should delete the rendered Kubernetes resources first. If we omit the finalizer, the application controller will simply remove the application resource without deleting the rendered Kubernetes resources.

- Next, we must define the application source. This is where we specify the Git repository URL and the path to the Helm chart:

    ```
    source:
      path: helm-charts/charts/nginx/
      repoURL: https://github.com/PacktPublishing/Managing-Kubernetes-Resources-using-Helm.git
      targetRevision: HEAD
      helm:
        values: |-
          resources:
            limits:
              cpu: 50m
              memory: 128Mi
            requests:
              cpu: 50m
              memory: 128Mi
    ```

As you can see from the configuration, Argo CD will clone the repository (`https://github.com/PacktPublishing/Managing-Kubernetes-Resources-using-Helm.git`) at the most recent commit (HEAD). Once cloned, it navigates to the `helm-charts/charts/nginx` path, which contains an Nginx Helm chart.

- Here, we also specified a set of Helm values, setting the resource limits and requests under the `helm.values` section. Values can also be provided by using the `helm.parameters` setting, like so:

```
source:
  helm:
    parameters:
      - name: resources.limits.cpu
        value: 50m
      - name: resources.limits.memory
        value: 128Mi
```

This would be similar to passing the --set flag on the command line.

Finally, values can also be provided using the `helm.valueFiles` setting. We will describe this use case in greater detail in the *Deploying a Helm chart to multiple environments* section.

- The final portion of the `Application` resource defines the destination and synchronization (sync) policy:

```
destination:
    server: https://kubernetes.default.svc
    namespace: chapter10
syncPolicy:
    automated:
      prune: true
      selfHeal: true
```

`destination` defines the Kubernetes server API of the target cluster and the namespace that resources should be deployed to. `syncPolicy` determines how the application should be synchronized. In this context, `sync` means to apply, or update, the resources in the cluster with those from the application source. Syncs can be done manually, but in this example, we have selected to automate it so that Nginx is deployed as soon as the application resource is created.

Under the `syncPolicy.automated` section, several additional configurations can be specified. The `prune` field is a Boolean that determines whether Kubernetes resources should be deleted if they are removed from the source. The `selfHeal` setting instructs Argo CD to ensure consistency between the desired state and the live state. If a resource is modified within the Kubernetes cluster, `selfHeal` will cause Argo CD to revert the modification so that it matches the source configuration.

Now that we understand the application resource for defining our Nginx application, we can install this `Application` resource by using the `kubectl apply` command:

```
$ kubectl apply -f chapter10/local-chart/application.yaml -n argo
```

The result creates the `Application` resource in the `argo` namespace, where Argo CD has visibility to application resources.

Upon creating the application resource, you can see the deployment status by running the following command:

```
$ kubectl get applications -n argo
NAME     SYNC STATUS    HEALTH STATUS
nginx    Synced         Healthy
```

`SYNC STATUS` shows whether or not the desired state has been synced with the live state, while `HEALTH STATUS` shows whether or not the rollout has been completed or if the pods are still starting up. It may take a moment for `SYNC STATUS` and `HEALTH STATUS` to reach these values as the `nginx` chart and the associated resources are installed in the cluster. We can see the status of the deployment using more traditional means – that is, by running the `kubectl get pods` command in the `chapter10` namespace:

```
$ kubectl get pods -n chapter10
NAME                      READY   STATUS    RESTARTS   AGE
nginx-7bf8646cff-qjv9h    1/1     Running   0          2m5s
```

With `Application` reporting as synchronized and healthy, you have successfully deployed a Helm chart from a Git repository using Argo CD! Let's delete the application resource (which will also remove the `nginx` pod from the `chapter10` namespace):

```
$ kubectl delete -f chapter10/remote-registry/application.yaml
```

Before we depart from this topic, it should be noted that, as expected in a GitOps model, changes to the `nginx` Helm chart in Git will automatically propagate to the Kubernetes environment. If you were to update the `nginx` chart and publish a new commit to the Git repository for the particular target branch, Argo CD would notice this change in the next polling interval and update the Kubernetes namespace with the desired state, as defined in the repository. For faster synchronization, webhooks can be configured on the Git repository to trigger an Argo CD sync in an event-driven fashion. Information on configuring webhooks is described in the Argo CD documentation at https://argo-cd.readthedocs.io/en/stable/operator-manual/webhook/.

Next, we will learn how to use Argo CD to deploy a Helm chart from a remote chart repository.

Deploying an application from a remote Helm chart repository

When installing Helm charts, users often interact with remote repositories. Similarly, we can use Argo CD to deploy an application from a specified Helm chart repository.

The following diagram shows the flow involved in deploying an application from a remote Helm chart repository with Argo CD:

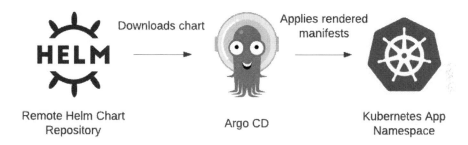

Figure 10.4 – Deploying an application from a remote Helm chart repository

First, Argo CD downloads the Helm chart configured in the `Application` resource. Then, it renders the Helm chart and applies the manifests to the destination cluster and namespace.

We have provided an example `Application` resource in the Packt repository at `chapter10/remote-registry/application.yaml` (https://github.com/PacktPublishing/Managing-Kubernetes-Resources-using-Helm/blob/main/chapter10/remote-registry/application.yaml). The resource is configured similarly to `Application` from the previous section, but we can observe one key difference in the `source` section:

```
source:
  chart: nginx
  targetRevision: 9.7.6
  repoURL: https://raw.githubusercontent.com/bitnami/charts/archive-full-index/bitnami
```

Here, instead of providing a Git repository, we provided the location of a remote Helm chart repository, as well as the chart's name and version. As you can see, this `Application` will instruct Argo CD to deploy version `9.7.6` of the `nginx` chart from the Bitnami chart repository.

The process of deploying a Helm chart from a chart repository is the same as deploying from a Git repository – simply apply the `Application` resource to the `argo` namespace. Feel free to walk through the same steps provided in the previous section to deploy the application to the `chapter10` namespace.

Where the process changes slightly is when we talk about deploying a Helm chart to multiple environments, a topic that we will cover in the next section.

Deploying a Helm chart to multiple environments

In the previous sections, we used Argo CD to deploy a Helm chart to a single environment (or namespace). However, when deploying applications in the enterprise, you will often expect to deploy across multiple different environments, achieving a process similar to what's shown in the following diagram:

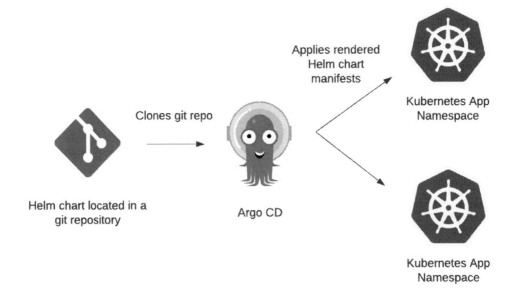

Figure 10.5 – Deploying to multiple namespaces

You may want to deploy charts to different environments (separate namespaces or even separate clusters) for a variety of reasons, including high availability or for deploying an application across multiple stages of a pipeline, such as dev, test, and prod. Luckily, we can achieve this in Argo CD using the `ApplicationSet` construct.

Imagine that we have two separate namespaces – one for dev and another for prod. We could create two separate `Application` resources, each targeting a separate namespace in the destination section:

- Dev would look as follows:

```
destination:
  server: https://kubernetes.default.svc
  namespace: dev
```

- Prod would be very similar, but we would specify `prod` in the `namespace` property:

```
destination:
  server: https://kubernetes.default.svc
  namespace: prod
```

Using two different `Application` resources – one for each environment – is a perfectly valid option for approaching this type of deployment. However, Argo CD introduced `ApplicationSet` as a method for wrapping multiple `Application` instances in a single resource, allowing you to define multiple destinations without managing multiple resource YAML files.

An example of an `ApplicationSet` is provided in the Packt repository at `chapter10/multiple-envs/applicationset.yaml` (`https://github.com/PacktPublishing/Managing-Kubernetes-Resources-using-Helm/blob/main/chapter10/multiple-envs/applicationset.yaml`). Let's break down the different sections of this resource:

- The first component of an `ApplicationSet` is the `generators` section, which generates parameters that are used later on to dynamically configure the application details, such as the source and destination. There are many different types of generators, which can be explored in greater detail in the Argo CD documentation at `https://argocd-applicationset.readthedocs.io/en/stable/Generators/`. In our example, we used the `list` generator, which allows a list of simple key-value pairs to be provided:

```
generators:
  - list:
      elements:
        - env: dev
        - env: prod
```

As you can see, two elements that define our different environments are specified – `dev` and `prod`. We will reference these environments throughout the rest of `ApplicationSet` to deploy the `nginx` chart to both stages of our deployment pipeline.

- Next, we must define the `Application` template. We start by providing a name that `ApplicationSet` will inject into the generated `Applications`:

  ```
  metadata:
    name: nginx-{{ env }}
  ```

  The `{{ env }}` syntax denotes a placeholder that will be replaced by the `env` elements described in the `generators` section. So, when we create `ApplicationSet`, we can expect two different applications to be created: – `nginx-dev` and `nginx-prod`.

- Now that we have specified the names of the applications that will be created, we can configure the sources. This will look similar to what we have seen in the previous sections:

  ```
  source:
    path: chapter10/multiple-envs/nginx
    repoURL: https://github.com/PacktPublishing/Managing-Kubernetes-Resources-using-Helm.git
    targetRevision: HEAD
    helm:
      releaseName: nginx
      valueFiles:
        - values/common-values.yaml
        - values/{{ env }}/values.yaml
  ```

  This source indicates that Argo CD will deploy the Helm chart located under `chapter10/multiple-envs/nginx` at `https://github.com/PacktPublishing/Managing-Kubernetes-Resources-using-Helm.git`. However, instead of deploying the same configuration in each environment, we will apply slightly different values based on the environment. This can be seen under the `helm.valueFiles` setting, which provides a list of values files to be applied (similar to using the `--values` flag on the command line). Regardless of the environment, we will always apply a common set of values defined in the `values/common-values.yaml` file, but depending on the environment, we will also apply either the `values/dev/values.yaml` file or the `values/prod/values.yaml` file.

  These values files can be seen within the `chapter10/multiple-envs/nginx/values` directory (`https://github.com/PacktPublishing/Managing-Kubernetes-Resources-using-Helm/tree/main/chapter10/multiple-envs/nginx/values`). Note that, since Argo CD has been configured to use the `chapter10/multiple-envs/nginx` chart path, the values files must be located underneath this path. It is also important to note that this method of applying values files is only applicable when deploying a Helm chart from Git. When deploying from a remote Helm chart repository, values can be provided using the `helm.values` or `helm.parameters` method, as described in the *Deploying a Helm chart from a Git repository* section.

- Finally, we must define the destinations that Argo CD should deploy the resources to:

```
destination:
  server: https://kubernetes.default.svc
  namespace: chapter10-{{ env }}
```

This will deploy the Helm chart to the `chapter10-dev` and `chapter10-prod` namespaces. In this example, we separated environments by namespace for simplicity, but you can also instruct Argo CD to deploy to separate clusters by parameterizing the `destination.server` section in a fashion similar to how we have parameterized the namespace.

Now that we know how `ApplicationSet` is created, let's apply it to our Kubernetes cluster to deploy our Helm chart across different environments. First, apply `ApplicationSet` located at `chapter10/multiple-envs/applicationset.yaml` (https://github.com/PacktPublishing/Managing-Kubernetes-Resources-using-Helm/blob/main/chapter10/multiple-envs/applicationset.yaml):

```
$ kubectl apply -f chapter10/multiple-envs/applicationset.yaml -n argo
```

Shortly, we should see two different applications appear in the `argo` namespace:

```
$ kubectl get applications -n argo
NAME          SYNC STATUS    HEALTH STATUS
nginx-dev     Synced         Healthy
nginx-prod    Synced         Healthy
```

We can also observe the deployment running in our different environments:

```
$ kubectl get pods -n chapter10-dev
NAME                        READY   STATUS    RESTARTS   AGE
nginx-6d948d7f48-kkr4j      1/1     Running   0          75s
$ kubectl get pods -n chapter10-prod
NAME                        READY   STATUS    RESTARTS   AGE
nginx-6d948d7f48-76p22      1/1     Running   0          107s
nginx-6d948d7f48-bf76x      1/1     Running   0          107s
nginx-6d948d7f48-rcq4z      1/1     Running   0          107s
```

You can observe three different `nginx` pods in `chapter10-prod` because the `values` file under `chapter10/multiple-envs/nginx/values/prod/values.yaml` specifies three replicas, while the `dev values` file only specifies one.

If you were able to observe similar output in your minikube environment to those shown previously, congratulations! You have successfully deployed a Helm chart to multiple environments in a GitOps fashion with Argo CD.

Let's conclude this chapter by cleaning up the environment.

Cleaning up

First, let's remove the namespaces from this chapter and the Argo installation:

```
$ kubectl delete namespace chapter10-prod
$ kubectl delete namespace chapter10-dev
$ kubectl delete namespace chapter10
$ helm uninstall argo -n argo
$ kubectl delete namespace argo
```

Then, you can stop the minikube cluster with the `minikube stop` command.

Summary

CD and GitOps provide scalable methods for further abstracting the capabilities that Helm provides, allowing deployments to be controlled by the contents of a Git repository or a remote chart repository. In this chapter, we introduced the concepts of CI/CD and GitOps and explored them using Argo CD as a solution to implementing these models in the context of Helm. Then, we learned how to install Argo CD and how to create the `Application` and `ApplicationSet` resources, which are primitives for enabling Argo CD deployments and synchronizing them with specified Helm charts and values. Finally, we learned how to deploy a Helm chart across multiple different environments.

In the next chapter, we will explore another abstraction – the Helm operator.

Questions

Answer the following questions to test your knowledge of this chapter:

1. What is the difference between CI and CD?
2. What is the relationship between CD and GitOps?
3. What is the difference between an Argo CD `Application` and `ApplicationSet`?
4. What is the Argo CD equivalent of passing the `--values` flag on the command line?
5. What is the Argo CD equivalent of passing the `--set` flag on the command line?
6. What is an `ApplicationSet` generator? Why are generators useful when deploying to multiple environments?

11
Using Helm with the Operator Framework

One of the advantages of using Helm is the ability to declaratively define an application's desired state. With Helm, the desired state is managed with templates and Helm values, which, when provided using the `install` or `upgrade` commands, apply the values to synchronize the live state in a Kubernetes cluster. In previous chapters, this was performed by invoking those commands manually. Most recently, in *Chapter 10, Automating Helm with CD and GitOps*, we used Argo CD as a method of state synchronization.

Another way changes can be synchronized to a Kubernetes cluster is to use a controller that checks periodically that the desired state matches the current configuration in the environment. If the state does not match, the application can automatically modify the environment to match the desired state. This controller is the foundation of applications and is referred to as a **Kubernetes operator**.

In this chapter, we will create a Helm-based operator that helps ensure that the desired state always matches the live state of the cluster. If it does not, the operator will execute the appropriate Helm commands to reconcile the state of the environment.

In this chapter, we will cover the following topics:

- Understanding Kubernetes operators
- Understanding the Guestbook operator control loop
- Using Helm to manage operators, **Custom Resource Definitions** (CRDs), and **Custom Resources** (CRs)
- Cleaning up

Technical requirements

For this chapter, you will need to have the following technologies installed on your local machine:

- minikube
- Helm
- kubectl

In addition to these tools, you should find the Packt repository containing resources associated with the examples on GitHub at `https://github.com/PacktPublishing/Managing-Kubernetes-Resources-using-Helm`. This repository will be referenced throughout this chapter.

Understanding Kubernetes operators

One of the fundamental principles of Kubernetes is that the current state of resources within the cluster matches the desired state, a process known as the **control loop**. The control loop is an ongoing, non-terminating pattern of monitoring the state of the cluster through the use of controllers. Kubernetes includes numerous controllers that are native to the platform, with examples ranging from admission controllers that intercept requests made to the API server to replication controllers that ensure the configuration of pod replicas.

As interest in Kubernetes began to grow, the combination of providing users with the ability to extend the capabilities of the platform, as well as a way to provide more intelligence around managing the life cycle of applications, led to the creation of a couple of important features to support Kubernetes development. First, the introduction of CRDs enabled users the ability to extend the default Kubernetes API in order to create and register new types of resources. Registering a new CRD creates a new resource path on the Kubernetes API server. For example, registering a new CRD for an object type called **Guestbook** provides the capabilities to interact with the Guestbook resource through the Kubernetes API server. When using the Kubernetes CLI, `kubectl get Guestbook` can now be used to view all Guestbook objects that are currently available. With this new capability realized, developers could now create controllers of their own to monitor these types of CRs and manage the lifecycle of applications through the use of CRDs.

Another major feature that helped to shape the developer experience in Kubernetes included advances in the types of applications deployed to Kubernetes. Instead of small and simple applications, more complex and stateful applications were being deployed more frequently. Typically, these types of advanced applications require a higher level of management and maintenance, such as *day 2* activities including backups, restorations, and upgrades. These tasks extend beyond the typical types of controllers that are found natively in Kubernetes, as deep knowledge related to the application being managed must be embedded within. This pattern of using a CR to manage applications and their components is known as the **Operator** pattern. First coined by the software company **CoreOS** in 2016, operators aim to capture the knowledge that a human operator would have for managing the lifecycle of an application. Operators are packaged as normal containerized applications, deployed within pods, that react on changes to the API against CRs.

Operators are commonly written using a framework called **kubebuilder**, which contains features that simplify the creation of CRs and the interaction with a Kubernetes environment. Several additional frameworks have since been created to further extend the capabilities to support operator development. One such popular toolkit is the **Operator Framework**, which provides end users with the ability to create operators using one of the following three technologies:

- **Go**
- **Ansible**
- **Helm**

Go-based operators leverage the Go programming language to implement control loop logic. Ansible-based operators leverage the Ansible CLI tool and Ansible playbooks to manage the state of resources. Ansible is a popular open source configuration management tool.

In this chapter, we will focus on Helm-based operators. Helm operators base their control loop logic on Helm charts and a subset of features provided by the Helm CLI. As a result, they represent an easy way for Helm users to implement their own operators.

With an understanding of operators, let's continue by creating our own operator using Helm.

Understanding the Guestbook operator control loop

In this chapter, we will write a Helm-based operator that will be used to install the Guestbook Helm chart. This chart can be found in the Packt repository at `https://github.com/PacktPublishing/Managing-Kubernetes-Resources-using-Helm/tree/main/helm-charts/charts/guestbook`.

The following diagram demonstrates how the Guestbook operator will function once it has been deployed:

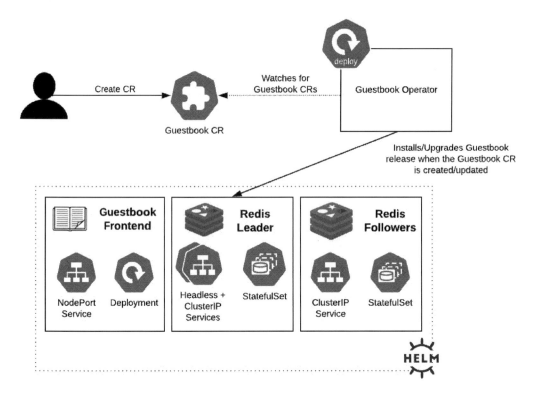

Figure 11.1 – The Guestbook operator control loop

The Guestbook operator constantly watches for the creation, deletion, or modification of Guestbook CRs. When a Guestbook CR is created, the operator will install the Guestbook Helm chart, and when the CR is modified, it upgrades the release accordingly so that the state of the cluster matches the desired intent as defined by the CR. Similarly, when the CR is deleted, the operator uninstalls the release.

With an understanding of how the operator's control loop will function, let's set up an environment where the operator can be built and deployed.

Preparing a local development environment

In order to create a Helm operator, you will need the following CLI tools at a minimum:

- `operator-sdk`
- A container management tool, such as `docker`, `podman`, or `buildah`

The `operator-sdk` CLI is a toolkit used to help develop Kubernetes operators. It contains inherent logic to simplify the operator development process. Under the hood, `operator-sdk` requires a container management tool that it can use to build the operator image. The supported container management tools are `docker`, `podman`, and `buildah`.

Installing the `operator-sdk` CLI is easy, as you can simply download a release from GitHub at https://github.com/operator-framework/operator-sdk/releases. However, the process used to install `docker`, `podman`, or `buildah` varies greatly depending on your operating system; not to mention, Windows users will not be able to use the `operator-sdk` toolkit natively.

Fortunately, the minikube **Virtual Machine** (**VM**) can be leveraged as a working environment for developers regardless of the host operating system since minikube is a Linux VM that also contains the Docker CLI. In this section, we will install the `operator-sdk` toolkit onto minikube and use the minikube VM as an environment to create the operator.

First, start the minikube VM:

```
$ minikube start
```

Once the VM has started, proceed by following these steps:

1. Access the VM by running the `minikube ssh` command:

    ```
    $ minikube ssh
    ```

2. Once inside the VM, you need to download the `operator-sdk` CLI. This can be accomplished using the `curl` command. Note that the `operator-sdk` version used during writing was version `v1.20.0`.

    To download this version of the `operator-sdk` CLI, run the following command:

    ```
    $ curl -o operator-sdk -L https://github.com/operator-framework/operator-sdk/releases/download/v1.20.0/operator-sdk_linux_amd64
    ```

3. Once downloaded, you will need to change the permission of the `operator-sdk` binary to be user-executable. Run the `chmod` command to make this modification:

    ```
    $ chmod u+x operator-sdk
    ```

4. Next, move the `operator-sdk` binary to a location managed by the `PATH` variable, such as `/usr/local/bin`. Because this operation requires root privileges, you will need to run the mv command using `sudo`:

    ```
    $ sudo mv operator-sdk /usr/local/bin
    ```

5. Finally, verify your `operator-sdk` installation by running the `operator-sdk version` command:

```
$ operator-sdk version
operator-sdk version: "v1.20.0", commit: "deb3531ae20a5805b7ee30b71f13792b80bd49b1", kubernetes version: "1.23", go version: "go1.17.9", GOOS: "linux", GOARCH: "amd64"
```

6. As an additional step, you should also clone the Packt repository in your minikube VM since we will need it later to build our Helm operator. Run the following commands to install `git` and clone the repository in your VM (notice that we will also install `make`, which is necessary for building our operator image later):

```
$ sudo apt update
$ sudo apt install git make
$ git clone https://github.com/PacktPublishing/Managing-Kubernetes-Resources-using-Helm.git
```

Now that you have a local development environment created in the minikube VM, let's begin writing the Guestbook operator. Note that an example of the operator code is located in the Packt repository at https://github.com/PacktPublishing/Managing-Kubernetes-Resources-using-Helm/tree/main/chapter11/guestbook-operator.

Scaffolding the operator file structure

Similar to Helm charts themselves, Helm operators built by the `operator-sdk` binary have a specific file structure that must be adhered to. The file structure is explained in the following table:

File/folder	Definition
`Dockerfile`	Used to build the operator image
`Makefile`	Provides a convenient set of targets for building the operator image and deploying it to Kubernetes
`PROJECT`	Provides `operator-sdk` metadata
`config/`	Contains Kubernetes resource manifests for CRDs, CRs, and the operator instance
`helm-charts/`	Contains the Helm charts that the operator is in charge of installing
`watches.yaml`	Defines the CRs that the operator is in charge of monitoring

Table 11.1 – The operator-sdk file structure

This file structure can be easily created using the `operator-sdk init` and `operator-sdk create api` commands. Let's walk through this process to create a `Guestbook` kind of a custom API version, `demo.example.com/v1alpha1`:

1. First, create a new folder for the operator and `cd` inside the newly created directory:

   ```
   $ mkdir guestbook-operator
   $ cd guestbook-operator
   ```

2. Next, use the `operator-sdk init` command to initialize the project:

   ```
   $ operator-sdk init --plugins helm --domain example.com
   ```

   Notice the usage of the `--plugins helm` parameter. This specifies that our project is a Helm operator and provides the necessary project scaffolding. The `-domain example.com` parameter specifies the Kubernetes API group that will be used for the CR. However, the command has not yet created the Guestbook CRD and control loop logic. This will be handled in the next step.

3. Run the `operator-sdk create api` command to create the Guestbook CRD and associated manifests:

   ```
   $ operator-sdk create api --group demo --version v1alpha1
   --kind Guestbook --helm-chart ../Managing-Kubernetes-
   Resources-using-Helm/helm-charts/charts/guestbook
   ```

You might see a warning about RBAC rules, but this can safely be ignored for this example. In practice, you should always ensure that the RBAC rules follow the principle of least privilege.

With the Guestbook operator successfully scaffolded, let's build the operator and push it to a container registry, where we will later pull the image for deployment.

Building the operator image

One of the files generated by `operator-sdk` was `Makefile`, which contains targets for building your operator image and pushing it to a container registry. However, before we can build our image, we need to have access to a container registry.

In *Chapter 8, Publishing to a Helm Chart Repository*, we used the GitHub container registry located at `ghcr.io` to publish images. We will use the same registry for publishing our Guestbook operator.

In order to publish to `ghcr.io`, you need to have first created a **Personal Access Token** (**PAT**). If you have already created one in *Chapter 8, Publishing to a Helm Chart Repository*, you do not need to create a new one (unless it has expired or you have misplaced the token).

However, if you do need to create a PAT, you can follow these steps:

1. Log into GitHub. Once you are logged in, from the upper-right corner of the page, select your profile picture and click on **Settings** from the drop-down menu.
2. Click on **Developer Settings** and select **Personal Account Token**.
3. Click on the **Generate New Token** button to initiate the token creation process.
4. Enter a unique name for the token, such as `Learn Helm`.
5. Select the date the token will expire. It is a recommended practice to specify an expiration date as it follows security best practices.
6. Select the scopes (permissions) granted to the token. The following scopes are required for managing content within the container registry:

    A. `read:packages`

    B. `write:packages`

    C. `delete:packages`

7. Click on the **Generate Token** button to create the token.

Be sure to copy the token before navigating away from the page. If you navigate away from the page before noting the content of the token, it can be regenerated at any time. However, the previously specified value will no longer be valid.

Once you have created your PAT and copied the access token, you can log into the `ghcr.io` registry from within your minikube VM by using the `docker login` command. For the `Username` prompt, provide your GitHub username, and for `Password`, paste the PAT token:

```
$ docker login ghcr.io
Username: <user>
Password: <Paste your PAT token here>
```

Once you have logged into the registry, you can continue by building and deploying your operator image. To do this, we can use the `make` utility to run different Makefile targets:

1. First, we need to define the image name. The Makefile defaults the image name to `controller:latest`. We can give a more descriptive name by setting the `IMG` environment variable:

    ```
    $ export IMG=ghcr.io/<GITHUB_USERNAME>/guestbook-operator:1.0.0
    ```

    Be sure to substitute your GitHub username when setting the `IMG` variable.

2. Next, we can begin the image build using the `docker-build` Makefile target:

   ```
   $ make docker-build
   ```

   If the build is successful, you will see the `Successfully tagged` message followed by the container image name and tag. Additionally, you can use the `docker images` command to verify the image was created:

   ```
   $ docker images
   REPOSITORY                                          TAG
   Ghcr.io/<GITHUB_USERNAME>/guestbook-
   operator                     1.0.0
   ```

3. Finally, we can push our image using the `docker-push` target:

   ```
   $ make docker-push
   . . .
   1.0.0: digest: sha256:1f73c8f37afea7c7f4eabaa741d5505880b
   5f1bda4de4fad15862acd7d16fb23 size: 1779
   ```

By default, your image will be private after you successfully push to `ghcr.io`. To avoid requiring the need for specifying a Kubernetes pull secret to access the image, we can update the image settings to make the image publicly available.

First, in GitHub, select your profile picture from the upper-right corner of the page, and choose **Your Profile**. On the next screen, select the **Packages** tab at the top of the page. After selecting the **Packages** tab, you should be able to see the `guestbook-operator` image (the guestbook image from *Chapter 8, Publishing to a Helm Chart Repository*, is visible in the screenshot, too):

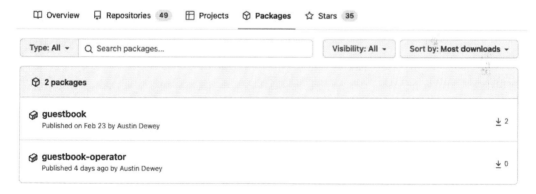

Figure 11.2 – The GitHub Packages page

Next, select the `guestbook-operator` package. On the far right of the screen, select **Package Settings**, then update the **Change Visibility** setting to **Public**.

If you were able to update your image's visibility to **Public**, then you have successfully pushed your image and can now access it without requiring credentials. Let's continue by deploying your operator to Kubernetes.

Deploying the Guestbook operator

Similar to building the operator, the deployment of our Guestbook operator can be performed using a set of Makefile targets. The Makefile generated by `operator-sdk` contains four targets related to the installation or removal of the operator:

- `install`: This installs CRDs onto the Kubernetes cluster. This target adds the Guestbook API to the cluster.
- `uninstall`: This uninstalls CRDs from the Kubernetes cluster. This target removes the Guestbook API from the cluster.
- `deploy`: This installs CRDs and deploys the Guestbook operator to the Kubernetes cluster. We'll use this target later for the deployment.
- `undeploy`: This undeploys (or removes) the CRDs and Guestbook operator instance from the Kubernetes cluster.

Under the hood, each target uses `kubectl` and a configuration management tool called **kustomize** to generate and apply manifests located under the `config` folder. Kustomize is a tool that, at a high level, uses `kustomization.yaml` files that specify the Kubernetes manifests that will be applied. Also, it adds patches and common configurations to each manifest, such as the target namespace and resource names.

The contents of the `config` folder contents are shown in the following table:

Folder	Definition
`config/crd/`	Contains the CRDs for extending the Kubernetes API. For our Guestbook operator, there is only one CRD.
`config/default/`	Contains a parent `kustomization.yaml` file for applying CRD, RBAC, and operator (also referred to as *manager*) resources.
`config/manager/`	Contains a deployment resource for creating the operator (or `manager`) instance.
`config/manifests/`	A superset of the `config/default/` folder. Here, `config/manifests` applies CRD, RBAC, and operator resources, but it also applies an example Guestbook CR and a *scorecard*, which is used for testing the operator.
`config/prometheus/`	Contains a Prometheus `ServiceMonitor` resource for tracking metrics. This is disabled by default but can be enabled in the `kustomization.yaml` file located under `config/default/`.

`config/rbac/`	Contains `Role`, `RoleBinding`, and `ServiceAccount` resources. These grant the operator permission to manage Guestbook resources. They also create Guestbook editor and viewer roles for users throughout the Kubernetes cluster.
`config/samples/`	Contains an example Guestbook manifest.
`config/scorecard/`	Contains manifests for testing the operator. They are unused by default.

Figure 11.4 – The contents of the config folder

When we run the `make deploy` command, Kustomize targets the `kustomization.yaml` file from `config/default/` to apply resources from the `config/crd/`, `config/manager/`, and `config/rbac/` directories. Then, when the operator is installed, we will apply the Guestbook CR, which is located at `config/samples/demo_v1alpha1_guestbook.yaml`. Let's take a look at a snippet from the `demo_v1alpha1_guestbook.yaml` file:

```yaml
apiVersion: demo.example.com/v1alpha1
kind: Guestbook
metadata:
  name: guestbook-sample
spec:
  # Default values copied from <project_dir>/helm-charts/guestbook/values.yaml
  affinity: {}
  autoscaling:
    enabled: false
    maxReplicas: 100
    minReplicas: 1
    targetCPUUtilizationPercentage: 80
  env:
  - name: GET_HOSTS_FROM
    value: env
  - name: REDIS_LEADER_SERVICE_HOST
    value: redis-master
  - name: REDIS_FOLLOWER_SERVICE_HOST
    value: redis-replicas
  fullnameOverride: ""
  image:
    pullPolicy: IfNotPresent
```

```
        repository: gcr.io/google_samples/gb-frontend
        tag: ""
```

Does the preceding YAML look familiar? Each of the entries under the `spec` stanza reference default values from the Guestbook chart's `values.yaml` file. This is how values are provided when using a Helm operator. Rather than providing a `values.yaml` file, users write values in the Guestbook CR. Then, when the resource is applied, the operator consumes the values and deploys the application accordingly.

With a basic understanding of the operator's `config/` folder and `Makefile` targets, let's deploy the Guestbook operator by following these steps:

1. In order to deploy the Guestbook operator, we need to be authenticated to the Kubernetes cluster. Because the minikube VM does not have `kubectl` installed, nor `kubeconfig`, which we can use for authentication, it will be simpler to deploy the operator from your host machine.

   Exit the minikube VM by running the following command:

   ```
   $ exit
   ```

2. The resources we created in the minikube VM are also located in the Packt repository under the `chapter11/guestbook-operator/` folder. You can clone this repository and navigate to the `guestbook-operator` folder by running the following commands:

   ```
   $ git clone https://github.com/PacktPublishing/Managing-Kubernetes-Resources-using-Helm.git
   $ cd Managing-Kubernetes-Resources-using-Helm/chapter11/guestbook-operator
   ```

   The files from the Packt repository are the same as the ones you created in the minikube VM with one exception. As you might recall from previous chapters, the Guestbook Helm chart contains hooks for backing up and restoring the Redis database. These hooks require the operator to have permission to manage the `Job` and `PersistentVolumeClaim` resources. Because the role generated by `operator-sdk` does not include these resources, we added them at the end of the role definition located at `chapter11/guestbook-operator/config/rbac/role.yaml`. Here are the permissions that we added:

   ```
     - apiGroups:
       - ""
       resources:
       - persistentvolumeclaims
       verbs:
       - create
       - delete
   ```

```
          - get
          - list
          - patch
          - update
          - watch
      - apiGroups:
          - batch
        resources:
          - jobs
        verbs:
          - create
          - delete
          - get
          - list
          - patch
          - update
          - watch
```

3. Next, we will use the `make` command to deploy the Guestbook CRD and operator to the Kubernetes cluster. Note that Windows users might need to install `make` first, which can be done by using the Chocolatey package manager:

   ```
   $ choco install make
   ```

   Proceed with the operator deployment by setting the `IMG` environment variable and running the following `make` command:

   ```
   $ export IMG=ghcr.io/<GITHUB_USERNAME>/guestbook-
   operator:1.0.0
   $ make deploy
   ```

4. The operator was installed in a namespace called `guestbook-operator-system`. Verify that the pod was deployed successfully in this namespace:

   ```
   $ kubectl get pods -n guestbook-operator-system
   NAME                                         READY    STATUS
   guestbook-operator-controller-manager...     2/2      Running
   ```

Now that the operator has been deployed, let's use it to install the Guestbook Helm chart.

Deploying the Guestbook application

When using Helm normally as a standalone CLI tool, you would install a Helm chart by running the `helm install` command. With a Helm operator, you can install a Helm chart by creating a CR.

First, create a new namespace for our deployment:

```
$ kubectl create namespace chapter11
```

Then, using the CR located in the Packt repository at `chapter11/guestbook-operator/config/samples/demo_v1alpha1_guestbook.yaml`, install the Guestbook Helm chart:

```
$ kubectl apply -f chapter11/guestbook-operator/config/samples/demo_v1alpha1_guestbook.yaml -n chapter11
```

Once the installation is complete, you'll see each pod in the ready state:

```
$ kubectl get pods -n chapter11
NAME                                READY   STATUS
guestbook-sample-76d48ccddb-dfrkr   1/1     Running
redis-master-0                      1/1     Running
redis-replicas-0                    1/1     Running
redis-replicas-1                    1/1     Running
redis-replicas-2                    1/1     Running
```

When you created the CR, the operator executed the `helm install` command against the Guestbook Helm chart. You can confirm the release was created by running `helm list`:

```
$ helm list -n chapter11
NAME               NAMESPACE    REVISION
guestbook-sample   chapter11    1
```

Upgrades are performed by reapplying the CR with a different set of values. A modified CR is located in the Packt repository at `chapter11/guestbook-operator/config/samples/upgrade-example.yaml`. In this file, the `replicaCount` value has been changed to 2, as opposed to 1 in the original CR.

Apply the updated CR by running the following command:

```
$ kubectl apply -f chapter11/guestbook-operator/config/samples/upgrade-example.yaml -n chapter11
```

This modification of the Guestbook CR causes the operator to trigger `helm upgrade` against the `guestbook-sample` release. As you might recall from *Chapter 7*, *Helm Lifecycle Hooks*, the

Guestbook chart contains an upgrade hook that initiates a Redis backup. If you watch the pods in the `chapter11` namespace after modifying the CR, you will see the backup job begin, and then you will shortly see two Guestbook pods appear. You will also notice that the revision number of the release increased to 2:

```
$ helm list -n chapter11
NAME                NAMESPACE   REVISION
guestbook-sample    chapter11   2
```

Although the revision number increased to 2, as of writing, one limitation of Helm operators is that you cannot initiate a rollback to a previous version as you can do when using the CLI. If you attempt to run `helm history` against the `guestbook-sample` release, you will notice that only the current revision is available in the release history:

```
$ helm history guestbook-sample -n chapter11
REVISION    UPDATED                     STATUS      CHART
2           Sun May 8 22:44:41 2022     deployed    guestbook-0.1.0
```

This is an important difference between using Helm regularly with the CLI and using Helm as an operator. Because the release history is not retained, Helm operators do not allow you to perform explicit rollbacks. However, `helm rollback` will be run implicitly in situations where upgrades fail. This would also trigger any rollback hooks that might be defined in the chart.

Although Helm operators do not retain the release history, one area where they excel is in synchronizing the desired and live states of an application. This is because the operator constantly watches the state of the Kubernetes environment and ensures that the application is always configured to match the CR. In other words, if one of the Guestbook application's resources has been modified, the operator will immediately revert the change to synchronize it with the configuration defined within the CR. You can see this in action by modifying one of the live resources. As an example, we will change the Guestbook deployment's replica count from 2 to 3 and watch the operator revert this change back to 2 immediately to resync the state to match the CR. Run the following `kubectl patch` command to change the replica count on the deployment from 2 to 3:

```
$ kubectl patch deployment guestbook-sample -p
'{"spec":{"replicas":3}}' -n chapter11
```

Normally, this would create an additional Guestbook pod replica. However, because the Guestbook CR currently defines only 2 replicas, the operator quickly changes the replica count back to 2 and terminates the additional pod that was created. If you actually wanted to increase the replica count to 3, you would need to update the `replicaCount` value on the CR. This process provides the advantage of ensuring the desired state matches the live state at all times.

Uninstalling releases created by the Helm operator is as simple as removing the CR. Delete the `guestbook-sample` CR to uninstall the release:

```
$ kubectl delete -f chapter11/guestbook-operator/config/
samples/demo_v1alpha1_guestbook.yaml -n chapter11
```

You can also remove the Guestbook operator and its resources since we will not need them in the next section. You can do this by running another `make` command:

```
$ make undeploy
```

In general, you should always make sure that you delete the CR first before deleting the operator. If you delete the operator before the CR, then the operator will not be able to automatically run `helm uninstall`, and you would have to run it manually from the command line.

Over the course of this chapter, you created a Helm operator and learned how to install a Helm chart using an operator-based approach. In the next section, we will continue our discussion on operators by investigating how they can be managed using Helm.

Using Helm to manage operators, CRDs, and CRs

In this chapter, we installed the Guestbook operator and CRD by using the `Makefile` instance generated by `operator-sdk`. Then, we installed a Guestbook CR using `kubectl apply`. While this is an acceptable way of creating these resources, we could also install the operator, CRD, and CR by using Helm charts to provide a more repeatable solution for installing and managing an operator.

Helm allows you to create CRDs by adding them to a directory called `crds/` in your Helm chart. Helm creates CRDs before any of the other resources defined under the `templates/` folder, making it simpler to install applications such as operators that depend on CRDs.

The following file structure depicts a Helm chart that could be used to install the Guestbook operator:

```
guestbook-operator/
  Chart.yaml
  crds/
    guestbooks_crd.yaml
  templates/
    deployment.yaml
    role_binding.yaml
    role.yaml
    service_account.yaml
  values.yaml
```

Upon installation, this Helm chart will first install the Guestbook CRD. If the CRD is already present in the cluster, it will skip the CRD creation and go straight into installing the templates. Note that while CRDs can be convenient to include in a Helm chart, there are a couple of limitations to be aware of. First, Helm does not allow CRDs to contain any Go templating, so CRDs do not benefit from parameterization as opposed to typical resources. Also, CRDs cannot be upgraded, rolled back, or deleted. Finally, including CRDs in your chart would require the user to have elevated cluster-level privileges within the Kubernetes cluster. Often, it is administrators who perform operator installations, so this is likely to be an acceptable approach.

The Helm chart that we described earlier could be used to install the Guestbook operator, but this is only half of the equation, as end users must still be able to create CRs that deploy the Guestbook application. To address this limitation, you could create a separate Helm chart that is used for templating a Guestbook CR. An example layout for this type of Helm chart is shown in the following file structure:

```
guestbook/
  Chart.yaml
  templates/
    Guestbook.yaml
  values.yaml
```

Unlike CRDs, CRs underneath the `templates/` folder benefit from Go templating and lifecycle management, as do all other resources. This methodology provides the most value when the CR contains complex fields or when other resources must be installed alongside the CR. You would also be able to manage the lifecycle of your CR with this method, and you would also be able to maintain a history of revisions.

However, users would need to be given permission to install Guestbook CRs, since this permission would not be included in Kubernetes by default. These permissions can be easily added by applying the `guestbook_editor_role.yaml` file under the operator's `config/rbac/` folder. Then, you can create a `RoleBinding` resource to assign the editor role to the appropriate users or groups.

Now that you have an understanding of how operators, CRDs, and CRs can be managed with Helm, let's close out the chapter by cleaning up the Kubernetes environment.

Cleaning up

First, delete the `chapter11` namespace:

```
$ kubectl delete namespace chapter11
```

Finally, run the `minikube stop` command to stop your minikube VM.

Summary

Operators are important for ensuring that the desired state always matches the live state. Such a feat allows users to more easily maintain a source of truth for resource configuration. Users can leverage a Helm operator to provide this type of resource reconciliation, and it is easy to get started because it uses Helm charts as its deployment mechanism. When a CR is created, the Helm operator installs the associated Helm chart to create a new release. Subsequent upgrades are performed when the CR is modified, and the release is uninstalled when the CR has been deleted.

To manage the operator, cluster administrators can create a separate Helm chart for creating the operator's resources and CRDs. Also, end users can create a separate Helm chart for creating CRs and other related resources.

In the next chapter, we will discuss best practices and topics around security within the Helm ecosystem.

Further reading

- To learn more about operators and their origins, check out the Kubernetes documentation at `https://kubernetes.io/docs/concepts/extend-kubernetes/operator/`.
- To discover other operators that have been developed throughout the community, check out *OperatorHub* at `https://operatorhub.io` or the *Operators* section of *ArtifactHub* at `https://artifacthub.io`.

Questions

1. What is an operator? How does an operator work at a high level?
2. What is the difference between installing a Helm chart with the Helm CLI versus a Helm operator?
3. What toolkit can you use to create Helm operators?
4. How does the `install`, `upgrade`, `rollback`, and `uninstall` hooks function with a Helm operator?
5. What is the purpose of the `crds/` folder in a Helm chart?

12
Helm Security Considerations

As you have likely come to realize throughout this book, Helm is a powerful tool that makes deploying applications on Kubernetes simple and efficient. With that said, we need to ensure that we do not lose sight of security best practices when leveraging Helm. Luckily, Helm provides several ways to incorporate good security practices into everyday usage in ways that are simple to achieve, from the moment the Helm CLI is downloaded to the moment a Helm chart is installed into a Kubernetes cluster.

In this chapter, we will cover the following topics:

- Data provenance and integrity
- Developing secure and stable Helm charts
- Configuring RBAC rules

Technical requirements

This chapter will make use of the following technologies:

- `minikube`
- `kubectl`
- `helm`
- `gpg` (GNU Privacy Guard)

You learned how to install and configure the `minikube`, `kubectl`, and `helm` **command-line interfaces** (**CLIs**) in *Chapter 2*, *Preparing a Kubernetes and Helm Environment*.

We will also leverage the guestbook chart from the Packt repository located at `https://github.com/PacktPublishing/Managing-Kubernetes-Resources-using-Helm` for an exercise later in this chapter. If you have not already cloned the repository, you can do so with the following command:

```
$ git clone https://github.com/PacktPublishing/Managing-Kubernetes-Resources-using-Helm.git
```

Let's begin by discussing data provenance and integrity.

Data provenance and integrity

When working with any kind of data, two often-overlooked questions should be considered:

- Does the data come from a reliable source?
- Does the data contain all of the contents that you expected it to?

The first question relates to the topic of **data provenance**. Data provenance is about determining the origin of data and determining where the data originated from.

The second question refers to the topic of **data integrity**. Data integrity is about determining whether the contents you received from a remote location represents what you expected to receive. It helps determine whether data was tampered with as it was sent across the wire.

Both data provenance and data integrity can be verified using a concept called **digital signatures**. An author can create a unique signature based on cryptography to sign data, and the consumer of that data can use cryptographic tools to verify the authenticity of that signature. If the authenticity is verified, then the consumer is assured that the data originates from the expected source and was not tampered with as it was transferred.

Authors can create a digital signature using a variety of tools. One such method is by using **Pretty Good Privacy** (**PGP**). PGP, in this context, refers to OpenPGP, which is a set of standards based on encryption. PGP focuses on establishing asymmetric encryption, which is based on the use of two different keys – private and public.

Private keys are meant to be kept secret, while public keys are designed to be shared. In PGP, the private key is used to encrypt data, while the public key is used by consumers to decrypt that data. The PGP key pair is often created using a tool called GPG, which is an open source tool that implements the OpenPGP standard.

To begin working with PGP, the first step is to create the key pair, which will generate a set of public and private keys. Once the PGP key pair has been created, the author can use GPG to sign the data. When data has been signed, GPG performs the following steps in the background:

1. A hash is calculated based on the contents of the data. The output is a fixed-length string called the **message digest**.
2. The message digest is encrypted using the author's private key. The output is the digital signature.

To verify the signature, consumers must use the author's public key to decrypt it. This verification can also be performed using GPG.

Digital signatures play a role in Helm in two ways:

- First, each Helm binary has an accompanying digital signature that's owned by one of the Helm maintainers. This signature can be used to verify the origin of the download, as well as its integrity.
- Second, Helm charts can also be digitally signed so that they benefit from the same form of verifications. Authors of Helm charts can sign the chart during packaging, and the chart users can verify the chart's authenticity by using the author's public key.

Now that you understand how data provenance and integrity come into play concerning digital signatures, in the next section, you will create a GPG key pair on your local machine that will be used to elaborate on the previously described concepts.

Creating a GPG key pair

To create a key pair, you must have GPG installed on your local machine. Use the following instructions as a guide to installing GPG on your respective machine. Note that this chapter is based on `gpg` version 2.3.6:

- For Windows, you can use the Chocolatey package manager:

    ```
    > choco install gnupg
    ```

    You can also download the installer for Windows from https://gpg4win.org/download.html.

- For macOS, you can use the Homebrew package manager by using the following command:

    ```
    $ brew install gpg
    ```

    You can also download the macOS-based installer from https://sourceforge.net/p/gpgosx/docu/Download/.

- For Debian-based Linux distributions, you can use the `apt` package manager:

    ```
    $ sudo apt install gnupg
    ```

- For RPM-based Linux distributions, you can use the `dnf` package manager:

    ```
    $ sudo dnf install gnupg
    ```

Once you have installed GPG, you can create your own GPG key pair, which we will use throughout our discussion on data provenance and integrity.

Follow these steps to configure your key pair:

1. First, we need to begin the generation process by running the gpg `--full-generate-key` command:

   ```
   $ gpg --full-generate-key
   ```

2. For the `Please select what kind of key you want` prompt, select `(1) RSA and RSA`:

   ```
   Please select what kind of key you want:
      (1) RSA and RSA
      (2) DSA and Elgamal
      (3) DSA (sign only)
      (4) RSA (sign only)
      (9) ECC (sign and encrypt) *default*
     (10) ECC (sign only)
     (14) Existing key from card
   Your selection? 1
   ```

   The reason we are using RSA instead of the default option (ECC) is that ECC is not supported by the crypto library used in Helm's source code.

3. Next, you will be prompted to enter the key size. For this example, we can simply select the default, so continue by pressing the *Enter* key:

   ```
   RSA keys may be between 1024 and 4096 bits long.
   What keysize do you want? (3072) <enter>
   Requested keysize is 3072 bits
   ```

4. After you enter your key size, you will be asked how long the key should be valid. Since this key will be used solely to run through the examples, we recommend setting a short expiration, such as 1 week (`1w`):

   ```
   Please specify how long the key should be valid.
            0 = key does not expire
         <n>  = key expires in n days
         <n>w = key expires in n weeks
         <n>m = key expires in n months
         <n>y = key expires in n years
   Key is valid for? (0) 1w
   Key expires at Sun May 22 12:26:09 2022 EDT
   Is this correct? (y/N) y
   ```

5. Now, you will be prompted for your name and email address. These will be used to identify you as the owner of the key pair and will be the name and email address displayed by those who receive your public key. You will also be prompted to provide a comment, which you can simply leave blank:

```
GnuPG needs to construct a user ID to identify your key.
Real name: John Doe
Email address: jdoe@example.com
Comment: <enter>
You selected this USER-ID:
    "John Doe <jdoe@example.com>"
```

6. Press the *O* key to continue.
7. Finally, you will be prompted to enter your private key passphrase. Providing a strong passphrase is essential for protecting your identity in the event your private key is stolen. This is because it must be provided each time you attempt to access your key.

To keep our example simple, we will create an empty string passphrase to avoid passphrase prompts. While this is acceptable in this demonstration, you should protect any private key you intend to use in a real-world situation with a strong passphrase.

To continue, simply press *Enter* to submit an empty passphrase. When prompted, select `<Yes, protection is not needed>`.

Once your GPG key pair has been created, you will see an output similar to the following:

```
pub    rsa3072 2022-05-15 [SC] [expires: 2022-05-22]
       D2557B1EDD57BBC41A5D4DA7161DADB1C5AC21B5
uid                      John Doe <jdoe@example.com>
sub    rsa3072 2022-05-15 [E] [expires: 2022-05-22]
```

The preceding output displays information about the public (`pub`) and private (`sub`) keys, as well as the fingerprint of the public key (the second line of the output). The fingerprint is a unique identifier that's used to identify you as the owner of that key. The third line, beginning with `uid`, displays the name and email address that you entered when generating the GPG key pair.

With your key pair now created, let's continue to the next section to learn how a Helm binary can be verified.

Verifying Helm downloads

As discussed in *Chapter 2, Preparing a Kubernetes and Helm Environment*, one of the ways Helm can be installed is by downloading an archive from GitHub. These archives can be installed from Helm's GitHub releases page (`https://github.com/helm/helm/releases`) by selecting one of the links shown in the following screenshot:

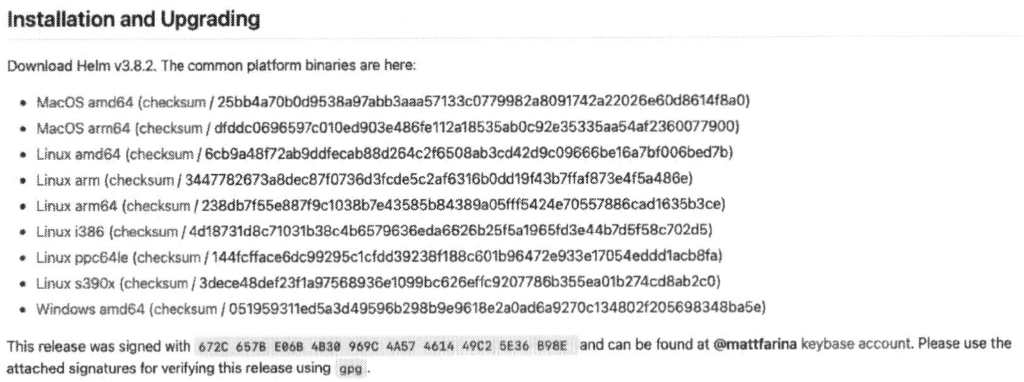

Helm Security Considerations

Installation and Upgrading

Download Helm v3.8.2. The common platform binaries are here:

- MacOS amd64 (checksum / 25bb4a70b0d9538a97abb3aaa57133c0779982a8091742a22026e60d8614f8a0)
- MacOS arm64 (checksum / dfddc0696597c010ed903e486fe112a18535ab0c92e35335aa54af2360077900)
- Linux amd64 (checksum / 6cb9a48f72ab9ddfecab88d264c2f6508ab3cd42d9c09666be16a7bf006bed7b)
- Linux arm (checksum / 3447782673a8dec87f0736d3fcde5c2af6316b0dd19f43b7ffaf873e4f5a486e)
- Linux arm64 (checksum / 238db7f55e887f9c1038b7e43585b84389a05fff5424e70557886cad1635b3ce)
- Linux i386 (checksum / 4d18731d8c71031b38c4b6579636eda6626b25f5a1965fd3e44b7d5f58c702d5)
- Linux ppc64le (checksum / 144fcfface6dc99295c1cfdd39238f188c601b96472e933e17054eddd1acb8fa)
- Linux s390x (checksum / 3dece48def23f1a97568936e1099bc626effc9207786b355ea01b274cd8ab2c0)
- Windows amd64 (checksum / 051959311ed5a3d49596b298b9e9618e2a0ad6a9270c134802f205698348ba5e)

This release was signed with `672C 657B E06B 4B30 969C 4A57 4614 49C2 5E36 B98E` and can be found at @mattfarina keybase account. Please use the attached signatures for verifying this release using `gpg`.

Figure 12.1 – The Installation and Upgrading section of Helm's GitHub releases page

At the bottom of the preceding screenshot, you will notice a paragraph explaining that the release was signed. Each Helm release is signed by a Helm maintainer and can be verified against the digital signature that corresponds to the downloaded release. Each of the signatures is located under the **Assets** section, as shown here:

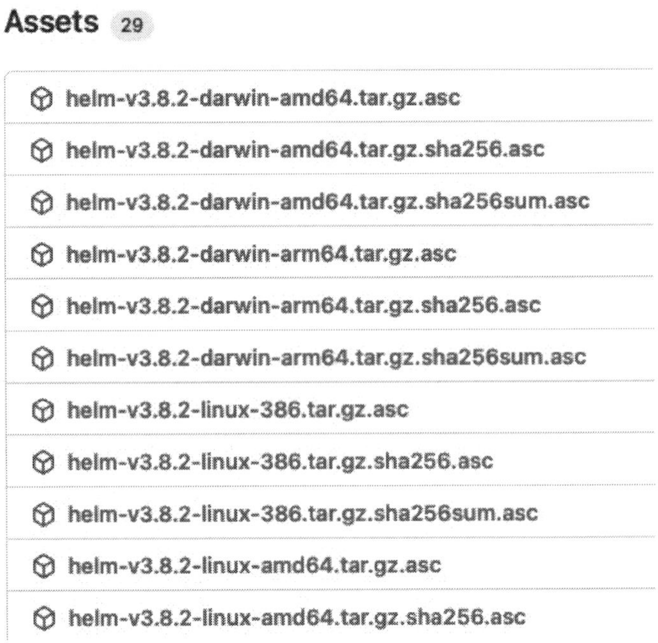

Assets 29

- helm-v3.8.2-darwin-amd64.tar.gz.asc
- helm-v3.8.2-darwin-amd64.tar.gz.sha256.asc
- helm-v3.8.2-darwin-amd64.tar.gz.sha256sum.asc
- helm-v3.8.2-darwin-arm64.tar.gz.asc
- helm-v3.8.2-darwin-arm64.tar.gz.sha256.asc
- helm-v3.8.2-darwin-arm64.tar.gz.sha256sum.asc
- helm-v3.8.2-linux-386.tar.gz.asc
- helm-v3.8.2-linux-386.tar.gz.sha256.asc
- helm-v3.8.2-linux-386.tar.gz.sha256sum.asc
- helm-v3.8.2-linux-amd64.tar.gz.asc
- helm-v3.8.2-linux-amd64.tar.gz.sha256.asc

Figure 12.2 – The Assets section of Helm's GitHub releases page

To verify the provenance and integrity of a Helm download, in addition to the binary itself, you should also download the corresponding `.asc` file. Note that `sha256` files are used to verify the integrity only. In this example, we will download the `.tar.gz.asc` file, which verifies both provenance and integrity.

Let's demonstrate how a Helm release can be verified. First, we should download a Helm archive, along with its corresponding `.asc` file:

1. Download a Helm archive that corresponds with your operating system. For this example, we will use version 3.8.2. If you are running an AMD64-based Linux system, the version for this distribution can be downloaded from the GitHub release page or by using the following `curl` command:

   ```
   $ curl -LO https://get.helm.sh/helm-v3.8.2-linux-amd64.tar.gz
   ```

2. Next, download the `.asc` file that corresponds with your operating system. When running an AMD64-based Linux system, `helm-v3.8.2-linux-amd64.tar.gz.asc` would be the resulting file that would be downloaded. You can download this file from the GitHub release page or by using the following `curl` command:

   ```
   $ curl -LO https://github.com/helm/helm/releases/download/v3.8.2/helm-v3.8.2-linux-amd64.tar.gz.asc
   ```

Once both files have been downloaded, you should see the two files located within the same directory on the command line:

```
$ ls -l
helm-v3.8.2-linux-amd64.tar.gz
helm-v3.8.2-linux-amd64.tar.gz.asc
```

The next step involves importing the Helm maintainer's public key to your local GPG keyring. This allows you to decrypt the digital signature contained in the `.asc` file to verify the provenance and integrity of your downloaded binary. GPG public keys are saved in public key servers such as `keyserver.ubuntu.com` and `pgp.mit.edu`. As such, we can use the `gpg --recv-key` command to download the maintainer's key from a public key server.

Let's import the maintainer's public key and continue with the verification process:

1. First, recall the maintainer's public key fingerprint from *Figure 12.1*:

   ```
   672C657BE06B4B30969C4A57461449C25E36B98E
   ```

2. Use the `gpg --recv-key` command to download and import the key into your local keychain:

```
$ gpg --recv-key 672C657BE06B4B30969C4A57461449C25E36B98E
gpg: key 461449C25E36B98E: public key "Matthew Farina
<matt@mattfarina.com>" imported
gpg: Total number processed: 1
gpg:                imported: 1
```

3. Now that the public key has been imported, you can verify the Helm release by using the `--verify` subcommand of GPG. This command has the `gpg --verify <signature> <data>` syntax:

```
$ gpg --verify helm-v3.8.2-linux-amd64.tar.gz.asc helm-v3.8.2-linux-amd64.tar.gz
```

This command decrypts the digital signature contained in the `.asc` file. If it is successful, it means that the Helm download (the file ending in `.tar.gz`) was signed by the person you expected (Matt Farina for this release) and that the download was not modified or altered in any way. A successful output looks similar to the following:

```
gpg: Signature made Wed Apr 13 14:00:32 2022 EDT
gpg:                using RSA key 711F28D510E1E0BCBD5F6BFE9436E80BFBA46909
gpg: Good signature from "Matthew Farina <matt@mattfarina.com>" [unknown]
gpg: WARNING: This key is not certified with a trusted signature!
gpg:          There is no indication that the signature belongs to the owner.
Primary key fingerprint: 672C 657B E06B 4B30 969C  4A57 4614 49C2 5E36 B98E
     Subkey fingerprint: 711F 28D5 10E1 E0BC BD5F  6BFE 9436 E80B FBA4 6909
```

Upon further inspection of this output, you may notice the WARNING message, indicating that the key was not certified, which may lead you to question whether or not the verification was successful. In this case, the verification was indeed successful, but you have not certified the maintainer's key yet, so GPG returns this warning.

The `This key is not certified` message is normally not an issue, but if you would like to ensure this warning does not appear in the future, you can follow these steps to certify the maintainer's public key:

1. Check that the public key's fingerprint (also referred to as the primary key from the `gpg --verify` output) matches the fingerprint displayed on the Helm releases page. As you will recall from *Figure 12.1*, the fingerprint was displayed, as shown here:

   ```
   This release was signed with 672C 657B E06B 4B30 969C
   4A57 4614 49C2 5E36 B98E and can be found at @mattfarina
   keybase account.
   ```

2. Because the key we imported matches the fingerprint displayed on GitHub, we know that we can trust this key. Trust can be associated with this key by using the `gpg --sign-key` subcommand:

   ```
   $ gpg --sign-key 672C657BE06B4B30969C4A57461449C25E36B98E
   ```

   In the `Really sign?` prompt, enter `y`.

Now that you have signed the maintainer's public key, the key has been certified. The next time you perform a verification with this key, you should no longer see the warning message:

```
$ gpg --verify helm-v3.8.2-linux-amd64.tar.gz.asc helm-v3.8.2-
linux-amd64.tar.gz
gpg: assuming signed data in 'helm-v3.8.2-linux-amd64.tar.gz'
gpg: Signature made Wed Apr 13 14:00:32 2022 EDT
gpg:                using RSA key
711F28D510E1E0BCBD5F6BFE9436E80BFBA46909
gpg: Good signature from "Matthew Farina <matt@mattfarina.com>"
[full]
```

Digital signatures also play a role in signing and verifying Helm charts. We will explore this topic in the next section.

Signing and verifying Helm charts

Similar to how the Helm maintainers sign releases, you can sign your Helm charts so that users can verify its origin as well as confirm it contains the expected content. To sign a chart, you must have a GPG key pair present on your local workstation (we created a GPG key pair earlier in the *Creating a GPG key pair* section).

There is one important caveat to note before we start signing charts. If you are using GPG version 2 or greater, you must export your public and secret keyrings to a legacy format. Early versions of GPG stored keyrings in the `.gpg` file format, which is the format that Helm expects your keyring to be in (at the time of writing). Newer versions of GPG store keyrings in the `.kbx` file format, which is not compatible at the time of writing.

Luckily, we can export our keys in the `.gpg` format by following these steps:

1. First, find your GPG version by running the following command:

   ```
   $ gpg --version
   gpg (GnuPG) 2.3.6
   libgcrypt 1.10.1
   Copyright (C) 2021 Free Software Foundation, Inc.
   ```

2. If your GPG version is 2 or greater, export your public and secret keyrings using the `gpg --export` and `gpg --export-secret-keys` commands:

   ```
   $ gpg --export > ~/.gnupg/pubring.gpg
   $ gpg --export-secret-keys > ~/.gnupg/secring.gpg
   ```

Once your keyrings have been exported, you will be able to sign your charts using the `helm package` command. The `helm package` command provides three key flags that allow you to sign and package charts:

- `--sign`: This allows you to sign a chart using a PGP private key.
- `--key`: The name of the key to use when signing.
- `--keyring`: The location of the keyring containing the PGP private key.

Let's run the `helm package` command to sign the guestbook Helm chart from the Packt repository:

```
$ helm package --sign --key <key_name> --keyring ~/.gnupg/secring.gpg helm-charts/charts/guestbook
```

The `<key_name>` placeholder refers to either the email, name, or fingerprint associated with the desired key. These details can be found by using the `gpg --list-keys` command.

If the `helm package` command is successful, you will see the following files displayed in the current directory:

```
guestbook-0.1.0.tgz
guestbook-0.1.0.tgz.prov
```

The `guestbook-0.1.0.tgz` file is the archive that contains the Helm chart. This file is always created by `helm package`, whether you are signing the chart or not.

The `guestbook-0.1.0.tgz.prov` file is called a **provenance file**. The provenance file contains a provenance record, which contains the following:

- The chart metadata from the file
- The sha256 hash of the `guestbook-0.1.0.tgz` file
- The PGP digital signature

Helm chart consumers leverage provenance files to verify the data provenance and integrity of the chart that they have downloaded. So, chart developers should be sure to publish both the `.tgz` archive as well as the `.tgz.prov` provenance file to their Helm chart repository.

While you have successfully signed the guestbook chart and have created the `.tgz.prov` file, it is not quite enough for users to verify the chart, as they still need to access your public key to decrypt your signature. You can make this key available for users by publishing it to the PGP key servers with the `gpg --send-key` command:

```
$ gpg --send-key <key_name>
```

End users can then download and import this key by using the `gpg --recv-key` command:

```
$ gpg --recv-key <key_name>
```

Once a user has imported your public key (and exported it to the `~/.gnupg/pubring.gpg` keyring, as shown earlier in this section), they can verify your Helm chart by using the `helm verify` command, provided both the `.tgz` chart archive and `.tgz.prov` provenance file have been downloaded to the same directory:

```
$ helm verify --keyring ~/.gnupg/pubring.gpg guestbook-0.1.0.tgz
Signed by: John Doe <jdoe@example.com>
Using Key With Fingerprint:
D2557B1EDD57BBC41A5D4DA7161DADB1C5AC21B5
Chart Hash Verified:
sha256:c8089c7748bb0c8102894a8d70e641010b90abe9bb45962a53468eacfbaf6731
```

If verification is successful, you will see that the signer, the signer's public key, and the chart have been verified. Otherwise, an error will be returned. The verification could fail for a variety of reasons, including the following:

- The .tgz and .tgz.prov files are not in the same directory.
- The .tgz or .tgz.prov files are corrupt.
- The file hashes do not match, indicating a loss of integrity.
- The public key used to decrypt the signature does not match the private key originally used to encrypt it.

The `helm verify` command is designed to be run on locally downloaded charts, so users may find it better to leverage the `helm install --verify` command instead, which performs the verification and installation in a single command, assuming that the .tgz and .tgz.prov files can both be downloaded from a chart repository.

The following command describes how the `helm install --verify` command can be used:

```
$ helm install guestbook <chart_repo>/guestbook --verify
--keyring ~/.gnupg/pubring.gpg
```

By using the methodologies described in this section, chart developers and consumers can be assured that the content is sourced from a trusted origin and has been unaltered.

With an understanding of how data provenance and integrity play a role in Helm, let's continue discussing Helm security considerations by moving on to our next topic – security concerning Helm charts and Helm chart development.

Developing secure and stable Helm charts

While provenance and integrity play a major role in the security of Helm, they are not the only concerns you need to consider. During the development process, chart developers should ensure that they are adhering to best practices around security to prevent vulnerabilities from being introduced when a user installs their chart into a Kubernetes cluster. In this section, we will discuss many of the concerns surrounding security as it relates to Helm chart development and what you, as a developer, can do to write Helm charts with security as a priority.

We will begin by discussing the security around any container images that your Helm chart may reference.

Using secure images

Since the goal of Helm (and Kubernetes) is to deploy container images, the image itself presents several areas of consideration concerning security. To start, chart developers should be aware of the differences between image tags and image digests.

A tag is a human-readable reference to a given image and provides both developers and consumers with an easy way to reference an image. However, tags can present a security concern as there are no guarantees that the contents of a given tag will always remain the same. The image owner may choose to push an updated image using the same tag, which would result in a different underlying image being executed at runtime (even though the tag is the same). Performing these actions against the same tag introduces the possibility of regressions, which can cause unexpected adverse effects for end users. Instead of referencing an image by tag, images can also be referenced by digest. An image digest is a computed `SHA-256` value of an image that not only provides an immutable identifier to an exact image but also allows for the container runtime to verify the integrity of the image that is retrieved from a remote registry. This removes the risk of deploying an image that contains an accidental regression against a given tag and can also remove the risks of a man-in-the-middle attack, where the tag's contents are modified with malicious intent.

As an example, an image referenced as `quay.io/bitnami/redis:5.0.9` in a chart template can be referenced by a digest as `quay.io/bitnami/redis@sha256:70b816f2127afb5d4af7ec9d6e8636b2f0f973a3cd8dda7032f9dcffa38ba11f`. Notice that instead of specifying the name of a tag after the name of the image, the `SHA-256` digest is explicitly specified. This assures that the image content will not change over time, even if the tag changes, thus strengthening your security posture.

As time progresses, a tag or a digest may become unsafe for deployment, as vulnerabilities may eventually be found in the underlying packages or base components. There are many different ways to determine whether there are any vulnerabilities associated with a given image. One way is to leverage the native capabilities of the registry that the image belongs to. Many different image registry solutions contain capabilities around image vulnerability scanning that can help provide insight as to when an image is vulnerable.

The Quay container registry, for example, can automatically scan images at specified intervals to determine vulnerabilities that may be present within a given image. The Nexus and Artifactory container registries are also examples of container registries that have similar capabilities. Outside of native scanning capabilities provided by container registries, other tools can be leveraged, such as **Vuls** and **OpenSCAP**. When your image registry or standalone scanning tool reports that an image is vulnerable, you should immediately update your chart's image to a newer version, if available, to prevent vulnerabilities from being introduced to your users' Kubernetes clusters.

To help simplify the process of updating the container image, you can develop a regular cadence where image updates are checked. This helps prevent you from getting to a point where your target image contains vulnerabilities that make it unfit for deployment. Many teams and organizations also restrict the source of images to trusted registries to reduce the potential of running images that do contain vulnerabilities. This setting can be configured at the container runtime level or within policies applied to a Kubernetes cluster. The specific location and configurations vary based on the specific implementation(s).

Apart from image vulnerability scanning and content sourcing, you should also avoid deploying images that run as **root** or **privileged**. Running containers as the root user (UID 0) is dangerous, as the process would also have root access to the underlying host if it can break out of the container. Your application likely does not need the level of permission that root provides, so you should run the container as a non-root user instead to limit its available permissions.

While running a container as root is dangerous, due to the process isolation that containers provide, it does not quite grant all available Linux capabilities by default. As a result, some users, often mistakenly, will further escalate permissions by running containers as privileged. Running a container as privileged grants all capabilities to the container, allowing it to interact with the underlying host from within the container. If your application does require additional capabilities, rather than running the container as privileged, you can instead select the exact list of capabilities in `securityContext` of a pod that is desired. A list of capabilities can be found in the *CAPABILITIES(7)* page of the Linux manual pages (http://man7.org/linux/man-pages/man7/capabilities.7.html).

In addition to the container image that has been deployed, chart developers should focus on the resources that have been granted to an application to ensure the integrity of the Kubernetes cluster. We will dive into this topic in the next section.

Setting resource requests and limits

Pods consume resources from the host (node) that it is running within. Resources are defined in terms of **requests** (the minimum amount of resources to allocate) and **limits** (the maximum amount of resources the pod is allowed to use). Pods that do not define requests run the risk of being scheduled on nodes that cannot support their minimum resource requirements. Pods that do not define limits run the risk of exhausting a node's resources, resulting in pod eviction and resource contention with other workloads. Because of the issues that can occur when resource requests and limits are not set, chart developers should ensure that their charts define these resource constraints while allowing users to override them with Helm values as needed.

For example, as a chart developer, you may write your chart so that it includes the following default values for configuring resources:

```
resources:
  limits:
    cpu: "1"
    memory: 4Gi
  requests:
    cpu: 500m
    memory: 2Gi
```

Then, if the chart is installed without explicitly setting the application's resource requirements, the defaults would be applied to avoid under- or over-utilizing cluster resources.

Apart from resource requests and limits, a Kubernetes administrator can also create `LimitRange` and `ResourceQuota` objects to restrict the number of resources requested and consumed by applications within namespaces. The `LimitRange` and `ResourceQuota` objects are applied separately from Helm, usually as part of a namespace provisioning process.

`LimitRanges` are used to restrict the number of resources a container or pod is allowed to consume within a given namespace. They are also used to set the default resources for containers that don't already have resource limits defined. The following is an example of a `LimitRange` definition:

```
apiVersion: v1
kind: LimitRange
metadata:
  name: limits-per-container
spec:
  limits:
    - max:
        cpu: 4
        memory: 16Gi
      default:
        cpu: 500m
        memory: 2Gi
      defaultRequest:
        cpu: 50m
        memory: 128Mi
      type: Container
```

In the example, `LimitRange` sets the maximum amount of allowed container resources to 4 CPU cores and 16 Gi of memory. For containers whose resource limits are undefined, a limit of 500 millicores of CPU and 2 Gi of memory will automatically be applied. For containers whose resource requests are undefined, a request of 50 millicores of CPU and 128 Mi of memory will automatically be applied. `LimitRanges` can also be applied at the pod level by setting the `type` field to `Pod`. This setting ensures that the sum of resource utilization of all containers in the pod satisfies the specified limits.

In addition to setting limits against CPU and memory utilization, you can configure `LimitRange` to restrict storage consumption by setting the `type` field to `PersistentVolumeClaim`. The following is a `LimitRange` example used to restrict storage claims to 8 Gi or fewer:

```
apiVersion: v1
kind: LimitRange
metadata:
```

```
      name: limits-per-pvc
    spec:
      - max:
          storage: 8Gi
        type: PersistentVolumeClaim
```

While `LimitRange` objects are used to restrict resources at the `Container`, `Pod`, or `PersistentVolumeClaim` level, `ResourceQuotas` are used by cluster administrators to restrict resource utilization at the namespace level. They are used to define the maximum number of resources a namespace can utilize in addition to limiting the amount of Kubernetes objects that can be created, such as Secrets and ConfigMaps. The following is an example `ResourceQuota` definition:

```
apiVersion: v1
kind: ResourceQuota
metadata:
  name: pod-and-pvc-quota
spec:
  hard:
    limits.cpu: "32"
    limits.memory: 64Gi
    requests.cpu: "24"
    requests.memory: 48Gi
    requests.storage: 20Gi
```

This `ResourceQuota` would ensure that the sum of all CPU and memory requests and limits remain under the defined amounts. It also sets a limit on the storage for `PersistentVolumeClaims` that can be requested within the namespace.

By setting reasonable defaults for resource constraints in your Helm charts, along with the usage of `LimitRange` and `ResourceQuotas`, you can ensure that users of your Helm charts do not exhaust cluster resources. You can also help ensure that applications request the minimum amount of resources necessary for a proper operation.

With an understanding of resource requests and limits, let's move on to the next topic – handling secrets in Helm charts.

Handling secrets in Helm charts

Handling secrets is a common concern when working with Helm charts. Consider the WordPress application from *Chapter 3, Installing Your First App with Helm*, where you were required to provide a password to configure an admin user. This password was not provided by default in the `values`.

`yaml` file because this would have left the application vulnerable if you forgot to override the `password` value. Chart developers should be in the habit of not providing defaults for secret values, such as passwords, and should instead require users to provide an explicit value. This can easily be accomplished by leveraging the `required` function. Helm can also generate random strings using the `randAlphaNum` function.

> **Note**
>
> Note that the `randAlphaNum` function generates a new random string each time the chart is upgraded. For that reason, developers should design charts with the expectation that users will provide their own password or another secret key, with the `required` function serving as a gate to ensure that a value is provided.

When using native Kubernetes resources to store secret information, chart developers should ensure that these sensitive assets are saved in a Kubernetes Secret, not a ConfigMap. Secrets and ConfigMaps are similar, but Secrets are reserved for sensitive data. Because secret and non-secret data is stored in separate objects, cluster administrators can set RBAC policies accordingly to restrict access to secret data while allowing permission to data that is non-secret (RBAC will be described further later in the *Configuring RBAC rules* section).

Chart users should ensure that secret values such as credentials are provided securely. Values are most commonly provided using the `--values` flag, in which properties are configured within `values` files. This is an appropriate method when working with non-secret values, but you should use caution when using this approach with secrets. Users should be sure that `values` files that contain secrets are not checked into a Git repository or an otherwise public location where those secrets could be exposed. One way that users can avoid exposing secrets is by leveraging the `--set` flag to pass secrets inline from the command line. This reduces the risk of credentials being exposed, but users should be aware that this could reveal the credentials in the bash history.

Another way that users can avoid exposing secrets is by leveraging an encryption tool to encrypt `values` files that contain secrets. This approach would continue to allow users to apply the `--values` flag, along with enabling the `values` file to be stored in a remote location, such as a Git repository. Then, the `values` file can only be decrypted by users that have the appropriate decryption key and would remain encrypted for all other users, only allowing trusted entities to access the data. Users can simply leverage GPG to encrypt the `values` files, or they can leverage a purpose-built tool such as **Secrets OPerationS** (**SOPS**). SOPS (`https://github.com/mozilla/sops`) is a tool designed to encrypt the values of YAML or JSON files, but leave the keys unencrypted. The following code depicts a secret key/value pair from a SOPS-encrypted file:

```
password: ENC[AES256_
GCM,data:xhdUx7DVUG8bitGnqjGvPMygpw==,iv:3LR9KcttchCvZNpRKqE5L
cXRyWD1I00v2kEAIl1ttco=,tag:9HEwxhT9s1pxo9lg19wyNg==,type:str]
```

Notice how the `password` key is unencrypted but the value is encrypted. This allows you to easily see the types of values contained within the file without exposing their sensitive values.

There are other tools capable of encrypting `values` files that contain secrets. Some examples include **git-crypt** (`https://github.com/AGWA/git-crypt`) and **blackbox** (`https://github.com/StackExchange/blackbox`). Additionally, purpose-built secret management utilities, such as **HashiCorp Vault** or **CyberArk Conjur**, can be used to encrypt secrets in the form of key/value stores. Secrets can then be retrieved by authenticating against the secret management system and then be utilized within Helm by specifying their values with the `--set` flag.

Now that you understand how security plays a role in Helm chart development, let's discuss how **Role-Based Access Control** (**RBAC**) can be applied in Kubernetes to provide greater security to your users.

Configuring RBAC rules

The ability of an authenticated user in Kubernetes to perform actions is governed by a set of RBAC policies. As introduced in *Chapter 2, Preparing a Kubernetes and Helm Environment*, policies, known as roles, can be associated with users or service accounts, and Kubernetes includes several roles with any installation. RBAC has been enabled by default in Kubernetes since version `1.6`. When thinking about Kubernetes RBAC in the context of Helm usage, you need to consider two factors:

- The user installing the Helm chart
- The service account associated with the pod running the workload

In most cases, the individual responsible for installing a Helm chart is associated with a Kubernetes user. However, Helm charts can be installed through other means, such as by a Kubernetes operator with an associated service account.

By default, users and service accounts have minimal permissions in a Kubernetes cluster. Additional permissions are granted through the use of roles, which have been scoped to an individual namespace, or cluster roles, which grant access at a cluster level. These roles are then associated with a user or service account using either a role binding or a cluster role binding, depending on the type of policy being targeted. While Kubernetes has several included roles, the **Principle of Least Privilege** should be used wherever possible. The Principle of Least Privilege is a security concept that emphasizes that a user or application is granted only the minimum set of permissions that is needed to function. For example, imagine we wanted to add functionality to our application that allows for pod metadata to be queried. While Kubernetes contains a built-in role called **view** that provides the necessary permissions for reading pod manifests in a given namespace, it also grants access to other resources, such as ConfigMaps and Deployments. To minimize the level of access that is provided to an application, a custom policy, in the form of `Role` or `ClusterRole`, can be created that provides only the necessary permissions that the application needs. Since most typical users of a Kubernetes cluster do not have access to create resources at a cluster level, let's create a role that is applied to the namespace that the Helm chart is deployed in.

The `kubectl create role` command can be used to create a Kubernetes `Role`. Alternatively, the `Role` and `RoleBinding` resources could have been created using YAML definitions. A basic role contains two key elements:

- The type of action (verb) made against the Kubernetes API
- The list of Kubernetes resources to target

As an example, to demonstrate how RBAC can be configured in Kubernetes, let's configure a set of RBAC rules to allow an authenticated user to view Pods within a namespace:

1. First, be sure to start your minikube cluster and create a new namespace for this exercise:

   ```
   $ minikube start
   $ kubectl create namespace chapter12
   ```

2. Next, use the `kubectl` CLI to create a new role called `pod-viewer`:

   ```
   $ kubectl create role pod-viewer --resource=pods
   --verb=get,list -n chapter12
   ```

   With this new role created, it needs to be associated with a user or service account. Since we want to associate the role with an application running in Kubernetes, we will apply the role to a service account. To abide by the Principle of Least Privilege, it is recommended to create a unique service account for the application (otherwise, the default service account would be used). This is to ensure that no other workloads are deployed in the same namespace that would accidentally inherit the same permissions.

3. Create a new service account called `example` by running the following command:

   ```
   $ kubectl create sa example -n chapter12
   ```

4. Finally, create `RoleBinding` called `pod-viewers` and associate it with the `example` service account:

   ```
   $ kubectl create rolebinding pod-viewers --role=pod-
   viewer --serviceaccount=chapter12:example -n chapter12
   ```

With the role and role binding created, the `example` service account has the appropriate permissions to list and get pods. To verify this assumption, we can use the `kubectl auth can-i` command:

```
$ kubectl auth can-i list pods
--as=system:serviceaccount:chapter12:example -n chapter12
yes
```

The `--as` flag makes use of the user impersonation feature in Kubernetes to allow you to debug authorization policies.

To confirm that the service account cannot access a resource it should not be able to, such as listing Deployments, you can run the following command:

```
$ kubectl auth can-i list deployments
--as=system:serviceaccount:chapter12:example -n chapter12
no
```

As you can see from the output of `no` for listing Deployments and `yes` for listing pods, the expected policies are in place. This service account can now be referenced by a Helm chart. Alternatively, a Helm chart could be written to create the `ServiceAccount`, `Role`, and `RoleBinding` resources natively, assuming that a user installing the chart has the appropriate privileges required.

When used effectively, Kubernetes RBAC aids in providing Helm chart developers with the tools needed to enforce least-privilege access, protecting users and applications from potential errant or malicious actions.

To clean up from this exercise, you can delete your namespace with `kubectl delete ns chapter12` and stop your minikube cluster with `minikube stop`.

Next, let's discuss how to access secure Helm chart repositories.

Accessing secure chart repositories

Chart repositories allow you to discover Helm charts and install them on your Kubernetes cluster. Repositories were explored in *Chapter 8, Publishing to a Helm Chart Repository*. There, you learned how to serve charts using an HTTP server (demonstrated using GitHub Pages) and an OCI registry (demonstrated using GitHub's container registry, `ghcr.io`).

Most chart repositories are readily available and open for those who are interested. However, chart repositories and hosting services do provide additional security measures for interacting with content stored within a repository, including the following:

- Authentication
- **Transport Layer Security (TLS)**

HTTP(S)-based chart repositories support basic and certificate-based authentication. For basic authentication, a username and password can be provided when adding a repository using the `helm repo add` command through the use of the `--username` and `--password` flags. For example, if you wanted to access a repository that is protected via basic authentication, adding the repository would take the following form:

```
$ helm repo add <repo_name> <repo_url> --username <username>
--password <password>
```

Under certain circumstances, you may also need to use the `--pass-credentials` flag in addition to `--username` and `--password`. Recall that an `index.yaml` file contains indexing of all Helm charts within the chart repository. Within the `index.yaml` file is a property field named `urls` that refers to the location of the associated Helm chart. Typically, the `urls` field contains relative paths within the chart repository, but in some cases, a location at an entirely different domain can be specified. Without the `--pass-credentials` flag, Helm will not forward your username and password along to these domains, which is a security feature implemented in Helm 3.6.1 to prevent your information from being exposed. However, if you do need to pass your credentials to another domain to authenticate against those endpoints, you can provide the `--pass-credentials` flag when using the `helm repo add` command.

OCI registries also support basic authentication using the `helm registry login` command. The username is provided using the `--username` flag, but there are two ways to specify the password:

- `--password`: Provides the password as an argument. This could reveal the password in plaintext in the bash history.
- `--password-stdin`: Provides the password from `stdin`. This allows you to keep the password hidden from the bash history by redirecting it from `stdin`.

It is recommended to use the `--password-stdin` flag to keep the password concealed from the bash history. As such, you can perform basic authentication against an OCI registry using the following command:

```
$ cat <password_file> | helm registry login <registry_host>
--username <username> --password-stdin
```

While basic authentication is most commonly used, certificate-based authentication is another way of verifying a client's identity. Helm, at the time of writing, does not provide flags for OCI certificate-based authentication, but for traditional Helm repositories, the Helm `repo add` command provides the `--cert-file` and `--key-file` flags, which are used to specify your client certificate and key, respectively.

Enabling basic authentication and certificate authentication on the chart repository itself depends on the repository implementation that is used. For example, **ChartMuseum**, a popular chart repository solution, provides the `--basic-auth-user` and `--basic-auth-pass` flags, which can be used on startup to configure the basic auth username and password. It also provides the `--tls-ca-cert` flag to configure the **certificate authority** (**CA**) certificate for certificate authentication. Other chart repository implementations may provide similar or additional capabilities.

Even with authentication in place, the packets sent between your Helm client and your chart repository must be transmitted securely using TLS-based encryption. While this is a given for certificate-based authentication, which leverages TLS natively, repositories that use basic authentication can still benefit from encrypting network traffic. Configuring TLS on the chart repository depends on the repository implementation being used, but for ChartMuseum, the `--tls-cert` and `--tls-key` flags can be used to provide the certificate chain and key files. More general web servers, such as NGINX, typically require a configuration file that provides the location of the certificate and key files on the server. Offerings such as GitHub Pages already have TLS configured.

Each of the Helm repositories that we have used so far has used certificates signed by publicly available CAs that are stored in your web browser and underlying operating system. As a result, we did not need to go out of our way to trust their certificates. Many large organizations, however, have their own CAs that are used to produce the certificate for the chart repository. Since this certificate is likely not from a publicly available CA, the Helm CLI may not trust the certificate, resulting in the following error:

```
Error: looks like "<repo_url>" is not a valid chart repository
or cannot be reached: Get <repo_url>/index.yaml: x509:
certificate signed by unknown authority
```

To allow the Helm CLI to trust the chart repository's certificate, the CA certificate, or CA bundle containing the certificate chain, can be added to the operating system's trust store. Alternatively, for HTTPS chart repositories, the `--ca-file` flag can be added to the `helm repo add` command.

Finally, depending on how the chart repository is configured, additional metrics can be obtained to perform request-level auditing and logging to determine who has attempted to access the repository.

Through the use of authentication and TLS, additional capabilities can be realized for enhancing the security footprint of Helm repositories.

Summary

In this chapter, you learned about different topics around security that pertain to Helm usage. First, you learned how to prove the data provenance and integrity of Helm releases and Helm charts. Next, you learned about Helm chart security and how a chart developer can leverage security best practices to write a stable and secure Helm chart. Then, we focused on using RBAC to create an environment based on the Principle of Least Privilege, and we finished by talking about how chart repositories can be secured using authentication and TLS. Now, by employing each of these concepts, you are well equipped to create a secure Helm architecture and working environment.

Thank you for reading *Managing Kubernetes Resources Using Helm*! We hope that this book helps you be confident and efficient as you use Helm to work within the Kubernetes ecosystem.

Further reading

To learn more about the topics that were covered in this chapter, take a look at the following resources:

- To learn more about data provenance and integrity in the context of Helm charts, go to `https://helm.sh/docs/topics/provenance/`.
- To learn more about Kubernetes RBAC, check out the *Using RBAC Authorization* section from the Kubernetes documentation at `https://kubernetes.io/docs/reference/access-authn-authz/rbac/`.
- Check out the chart repository guide from the Helm documentation to learn more about chart repositories: `https://helm.sh/docs/topics/chart_repository/`.
- Finally, visit the *Registries* page from the Helm documentation to learn more about OCI support: `https://helm.sh/docs/topics/registries/`.

Questions

Answer the following questions to test your knowledge of this chapter:

1. What are data provenance and integrity? How are data provenance and data integrity different?
2. What commands can a user run to verify the data provenance and integrity of a Helm chart? Which files are required to make this process possible?
3. What considerations need to be taken into account to use and maintain secure container images?
4. Why is it important to leverage resource requests and limits in your Helm chart? What other Kubernetes resources can be used to configure requests and limits?
5. What is the Principle of Least Privilege? Which Kubernetes resources allow you to configure authorization and achieve the least privilege?
6. Which flags can you use to authenticate to an HTTP(S) repository?
7. Which flags can you use to authenticate to an OCI registry?

Index

Symbols

--set flag 65
--values flag 65

A

Amazon S3 184
Apache httpd 184
application
   deploying, from remote Helm chart
      repository with Agro CD 229, 230
ApplicationSet Controller, generators
   reference link 231
Argo CD
   about 221
   installing 222-225
   used, for deploying application from remote
      Helm chart repository 229, 230
Argo CD Application Controller 223
Argo CD, Git Webhook Configuration
   reference link 229
Argo CD Repo Server 223
Argo CD Server 223
Argo Helm Charts
   reference link 222

Artifact Hub
   about 47
   URL 184
automated life cycle hooks
   providing 20

B

backup/persistentvolumeclaim.
      yaml template 172, 173
bare pod 164
Bitnami repository
   adding 51, 52
Bitnami repository chart retention policy 50
blackbox
   reference link 272
boilerplate 15
browser
   WordPress charts, viewing in 49, 50
built-in objects
   about 125, 126
   .Capabilities object 130
   .Chart object 128, 129
   .Files object 131-133
   .Release object 127, 128
   .Template object 130

C

cache path 37
capabilities, Linux manual page
  reference link 268
certificate authority (CA) certificate 275
chart definition 53, 94
chart dependencies
  declaring 102, 103
  downloading 104-108
chart development
  features 197
ChartMuseum 275
  about 184
  reference link 184
chart rendering
  server-side validation, adding 198
chart repository 47
charts 17
chart test
  improving, with Chart Testing tool 205, 206
  running 203, 204
Chart Testing project
  about 206, 207
  reference link 206
Chart Testing tool
  installing 208-210
Chart.yaml file
  about 94, 95
  Bitnami/WordPress Chart.yaml file 98
  dependencies map 103, 104
  fields 95, 96
  metadata, on Artifact Hub 97
child charts 116
chroots 5
Cloud Native Computing
    Foundation (CNCF) 5
cluster-admin role 41

code reuse
  enabling, with library charts 154, 155
  enabling, with named templates 153, 154
command line
  WordPress charts, searching from 48, 49
Command-Line Interface (CLI) 206
conditional dependencies
  creating 108-112
configuration path 38
container orchestration 6, 7
containers 5
Content Management System (CMS) 46
continuous integration/continuous
    delivery (CI/CD) 220
control loop 238
CRDs
  creating 155, 156
  managing 252, 253
CRs
  managing 252, 253
CyberArk Conjur 272

D

data integrity 256
data path 38
data provenance 256
declarative resources
  configuring, dynamically 19
dependencies map
  in Chart.yaml 103, 104
dependency names
  altering 112-116
dependency values
  altering 112-116
development-operations (DevOps) 4

digital signatures
  about 256
  verifying 257
dump.rdb file 171

E

edit role 41
Electronic Numerical Integrator and
    Computer (ENIAC) 4
environment variables
  about 37
  HELM_CONFIG_HOME or
    XDG_CONFIG_HOME 37
  HELM_DATA_HOME or
    XDG_DATA_HOME 37
  HELM_DRIVER 38
  HELM_NAMESPACE 38
  KUBECONFIG 38

F

finalizers 226
Flux 221

G

git-crypt
  reference link 272
GitHub Pages 184
GitHub Pages repository
  cloning 186, 187
  creating 185, 186
GitOps
  about 220
  using 221
Git repository
  Helm chart, deploying from 225-228

glob pattern 132
Go 123
Go templates 123
GPG key pair
  creating 257-259
Guestbook 238
Guestbook application
  about 84
  deploying 250-252
Guestbook chart
  deploying 160, 161
  deployment template, updating 158, 159
  Redis values, updating 158
  values.yaml file, updating 158, 159
Guestbook Chart.yaml file
  updating 99
Guestbook Helm chart
  hook, writing 170, 171
  publishing, to HTTP repository 184-189
  publishing, to OCI registry 190-193
  scaffolding 88, 89
  updating 117, 118
Guestbook operator
  deploying 246-249
Guestbook operator control loop
  about 239, 240
  local development environment,
    preparing 240-242
  operator file structure, scaffolding 242, 243
  operator image, building 243-245

H

HashiCorp Vault 272
Helm
  about 15, 23
  benefits 18-20
  configuring 34

downloads, verifying 259-263
installing 33, 34
reference link 33
security considerations 255
setting up 33
Helm chart
  about 45
  chart repositories, accessing 274-276
  deploying, from Git repository 225-228
  deploying, to multiple
    environments 230-234
  linting 199, 200
  security 266
  signing 263-265
  verifying 264-266
Helm chart repository 183, 184
Helm configuration
  authentication 39-41
  authorization 41, 42
  environment variables 37, 38
  plugins, adding 36
  tab completion 38
  upstream repositories, adding 34-36
helm create command
  about 88
  files 89, 90
  Guestbook Helm chart, scaffolding 88, 89
Helm Diff 36
helm get all command 64
helm get notes command 63
helm get values command 63
Helm hook
  about 164, 165
  cleanup 169, 170
  Helm chart, installation 165, 166
  life cycle 167, 168
  life cycle, executing 178, 179
  reference link 167

helm install command 58
Helm Monitor 37
Helm plugins
  examples, upstream plugins 36
  reference link 36
helm rollback command 76
helm search hub command 48, 49
Helm Secrets 36
helm show readme command 54
helmsman 6
Helm template
  basics 122, 123
  control structures 140-145
  functions 133-139
  linting 201
  server-side validation, adding
    to chart rendering 198
  validating, with helm template
    command 196, 197
  values 124, 125
  variables 146-148
  verifying 196
Helm template validation
  about 148
  fail function 148-150
  required function 150, 151
  values.schema.json file 151, 152
Helm Unittest 37
high availability (HA) 6, 7
hook
  about 164
  pre-rollback life cycle phase 171
  pre-upgrade life cycle phase 171
  writing, in Guestbook Helm chart 171
hook deletion policies
  reference link 169
horizontal scaling 7

HTTP repository
    Guestbook Helm chart,
        publishing to 184-189
HTTP server
    using 184

J

jails 5
JavaScript Object Notation (JSON) 87, 88, 122
job 164

K

key-value pairs
    defining 85
kubebuilder 239
kubeconfig file
    clusters 39
    contexts 39
    users 39
kubectl
    about 9
    declarative configuration 11-13
    downloading, from link 32
    download link, for Linux 32
    download link, for macOS 32
    download link, for Windows 32
    imperative configuration 10, 11
    installing 30
    installing, via minikube 30
    installing, without minikube 31
    package manager, using 31, 32
    setting up 29
kubectl config view command 40

Kubernetes
    about 5, 221
    community 7
    container orchestration 6, 7
    high availability (HA) 7
    resources 8, 9
    scalability 7
Kubernetes application
    deploying 8
Kubernetes environment
    creating 54, 55
Kubernetes operators 238, 239
Kubernetes package manager 16-18
Kubernetes resources
    complexity, abstracting 18, 19
Kustomize 157, 246

L

library charts
    code reuse, enabling 154, 155
lint-and-install command
    executing 207, 211-214
live Kubernetes cluster
    tests, performing in 202, 203
live state synchronization
    simplifying 20
local Kubernetes environment
    minibuke usage, exploring 28, 29
    minikube, installing 24, 25
    preparing, with minibuke 24
    VirtualBox, configuring as
        default driver 27, 28
    VirtualBox, installing 26, 27
local state synchronization
    simplifying 20

M

maps 86
message digest 256
microservices 4, 5
minikube
  about 24
  installing 24, 25
  reference link, of releases page 25
  resource allocation, configuring 28
  usage, exploring 28, 29
minikube environment
  setting up 196, 222
monolithic 4
monorepo 205

N

named templates
  code reuse, enabling 153, 154
NGINX 92, 184
NodePort services 207

O

OCI Guestbook chart
  pulling 193
ongoing history of revisions
  maintaining 19
Open Container Initiative (OCI) registry
  about 184
  Guestbook Helm chart,
    publishing to 190-193
OpenSCAP 267
Operator Framework 239
Operator pattern 239
operators
  managing 252, 253

P

package managers 16, 17, 45
parent chart 102
persistentvolumeclaim.yaml template 174
Personal Access Token (PAT) 243
Personal Account Token (PAT)
  creating 191
PHP: Hypertext Preprocessor (PHP) 84
pipelines 136
plugins
  about 36
  adding, to Helm 36
post rendering 156, 157
pre-rollback hook
  creating, to restore database 174-177
Pretty Good Privacy (PGP) 256
pre-upgrade hook
  creating, to store data snapshot 171-174
Principle of Least Privilege 272
private keys 256
provenance file 265

R

RBAC rules
  configuring 272, 273
Redis 84, 223
release history 19
release notes
  generating 145, 146
remote Helm chart repository
  Agro CD, used for deploying
    application from 229, 230
repository 47
resource configuration
  challenges 13-15

resource management
  approaches 9
resources
  deploying, in intelligent order 20
restore/job.yaml template 177
restore/rolebinding.yaml template 176
restore/serviceaccount.yaml template 175
revision 74
revision history
  example 19
role-based access control (RBAC) 41
RPM Package Manager (RPM) 17

S

scaffolded Guestbook chart
  deploying 91-93
Secrets OPerationS (SOPS)
  about 271
  reference link 271
security, Helm charts
  developing 266
    resource limits, setting 268-270
    resource requests, setting 268-270
    secrets, handling 270, 271
    secure images, using 266-268
self-hosted WordPress instance 46
self-hosted WordPress.org 46
SemVer versioning 206
server-side validation
  adding, to chart rendering 198
service 7
set-cluster command 39
set-context command 40
set-credentials command 39
software applications 4
Source Code Management (SCM) 65
source of truth (SOT) 14

T

templates 19, 121
time to live (TTL) 169

V

values 19
vertical scaling 7
view role 41, 272
VirtualBox
  configuring, as default driver 27
  download link 27
  installing 26
  URL 26
virtual machine (VM) 5
Vuls 267

W

WordPress
  about 46
  accessing 66-70
WordPress chart
  finding 47
  information, displaying from
    command line 52-54
  installation, running 58, 59
  installing 55
  release, inspecting 60-65
  searching, from command line 48, 49
  values file, creating for configuration 55-58
  viewing, in browser 49, 50
WordPress.com
  about 46
  disadvantages, over self-hosted
    WordPress.org 46

WordPress history
  inspecting 74-76
WordPress.org 46
WordPress release
  Helm values, modifying 70, 71
  rollback, running 76, 77
  rolling back 74
  uninstalling 78
  upgrade, running 71, 72
  upgrading 70
  values, resetting during upgrade 73, 74
  values, reusing during upgrade 73, 74
World Wide Web (WWW) 4

X

XDG Base Directory Specification 37

Y

YAML Ain't Markup Language (YAML)
  about 85, 122
  JSON format 87, 88
  key-value pairs, defining 85, 86
  value types 86, 87

Packt.com

Subscribe to our online digital library for full access to over 7,000 books and videos, as well as industry leading tools to help you plan your personal development and advance your career. For more information, please visit our website.

Why subscribe?

- Spend less time learning and more time coding with practical eBooks and Videos from over 4,000 industry professionals
- Improve your learning with Skill Plans built especially for you
- Get a free eBook or video every month
- Fully searchable for easy access to vital information
- Copy and paste, print, and bookmark content

Did you know that Packt offers eBook versions of every book published, with PDF and ePub files available? You can upgrade to the eBook version at `packt.com` and as a print book customer, you are entitled to a discount on the eBook copy. Get in touch with us at `customercare@packtpub.com` for more details.

At `www.packt.com`, you can also read a collection of free technical articles, sign up for a range of free newsletters, and receive exclusive discounts and offers on Packt books and eBooks.

Other Books You May Enjoy

If you enjoyed this book, you may be interested in these other books by Packt:

End-to-End Automation with Kubernetes and Crossplane

Arun Ramakani

ISBN: 9781801811545

- Understand the context of Kubernetes-based infrastructure automation
- Get to grips with Crossplane concepts with the help of practical examples
- Extend Crossplane to build a modern infrastructure automation platform
- Use the right configuration management tools in the Kubernetes environment
- Explore patterns to unify application and infrastructure automation
- Discover top engineering practices for infrastructure platform as a product

The Kubernetes Bible

Nassim Kebbani, Piotr Tylenda, Russ McKendrick

ISBN: 9781838827694

- Manage containerized applications with Kubernetes
- Understand Kubernetes architecture and the responsibilities of each component
- Set up Kubernetes on Amazon Elastic Kubernetes Service, Google Kubernetes Engine, and Microsoft Azure Kubernetes Service
- Deploy cloud applications such as Prometheus and Elasticsearch using Helm charts
- Discover advanced techniques for Pod scheduling and auto-scaling the cluster
- Understand possible approaches to traffic routing in Kubernetes

Packt is searching for authors like you

If you're interested in becoming an author for Packt, please visit `authors.packtpub.com` and apply today. We have worked with thousands of developers and tech professionals, just like you, to help them share their insight with the global tech community. You can make a general application, apply for a specific hot topic that we are recruiting an author for, or submit your own idea.

Hi!

We're Austin and Andrew, the authors of *Managing Kubernetes Resources Using Helm, Second Edition*. We really hope you enjoyed reading this book and found it useful for increasing your productivity and efficiency in Helm and Kubernetes delivery.

It would really help us (and other potential readers!) if you could leave a review on Amazon sharing your thoughts on *Managing Kubernetes Resources Using Helm, Second Edition*.

Go to the link below or scan the QR code to leave your review:

`https://packt.link/r/1803242892`

Your review will help us to understand what's worked well in this book, and what could be improved upon for future editions, so it really is appreciated.

Best Wishes,

Andy Block

Austin Dewey

Made in United States
Troutdale, OR
07/02/2024